THIS IS NOT WHO WE ARE

CONFESSIONS OF AN ELECTION OFFICIAL

BY

DAVID MAEDA

Publishing Services provided by Paper Raven Books LLC
Printed in the United States of America
First Printing, 2023

For Mom, Dad, Jenny Engh, Al Brown, the very real Maria, and six cool cats (23 legs between them) I was lucky enough to live with.

-30-

"The best you can do is just do the decent thing. There's no payoff. The good people of the world are those who, in spite of there being no payoff, do the decent thing anyway. That's what being human is. That's the example of a human, being."

—Liz Phair
Horror Stories

In journalistic parlance, "-30-" means the end of the story. It likely came to be when newspaper reporters sent their stories back to the newsroom by telegraph and -30- indicated the story was complete, nothing more to come. You still see it used in press releases.

Why am I starting at the end? Because in writing this memoir, I couldn't help but think about the life I didn't live instead of the life reflected in these pages. The difference between the person I thought I'd become and the person I actually became is wider than Lake Superior. I graduated from Macalester College in St. Paul, Minnesota with a history major and journalism minor. I was certain I was going to be a newspaper reporter, but that wasn't what I did with the cards I was dealt. I did use my journalism background mid-career, taking a step away from where my career path was leading me, to write news stories for legislative publications from 1999-2003 at the State Capitol in St. Paul. The four sessions I covered the legislature unintentionally occurred during former professional wrestler Jesse Ventura's term as the Minnesota governor. For a couple of years, Minnesota was working its way through a political experiment of a tripartisan government. Governor Ventura was a member of the Reform Party that later became the Independence Party. The State Senate was controlled by the Democrats, while the State House was controlled by the Republicans. To say the least, it was an interesting time to work at the legislature.

A few years after I got my first government job, Kofi Annan, the Secretary General of the United Nations and a fellow Macalester College alumnus, gave the commencement speech at our alma mater. I was back on campus for the first time since graduation because I wanted to hear his speech. He talked about the importance of public service. His words assured me there was value and nobility in becoming a bureaucrat. Most of my career was as an elections administrator, a profession most people didn't pay any attention to until the 2020 election, when President Trump claimed the election was rigged, and many of his supporters went along for the ride despite the lack of evidence for his claim. The horrible events of January 6, 2021 ensued and led us into a darkness far beyond any of my lifetime.

The thin line between reality and what we see as true has never been more splintered. Thus, the importance of being our authentic selves has never been more important in this divide. Real, true, and authentic were once considered synonymous before the chaos we endured when a global pandemic changed our lives forever. Prior to the pandemic, I saw the last chapter of my career was to become more authentic in telling my story, hopefully in an inspiring and insightful way. This was part of my legacy. This notion was shattered when everything significantly changed in 2020. The division in our country was reaching a crisis level. Humans crave authentic discourse and connection, and yet most connections are like fast food, lacking in anything nutritious and worthwhile.

The idea of writing a memoir rattled in my head, starting in 2010 when I bought the first iPad. I bought the device hoping it would inspire some writing. Becoming a published author was just about the only thing on my bucket list. Bob Dylan's memoir, *Chronicles Vol. 1*, provided the model for my own memoir's structure. Dylan's book of five chapters featured different periods of his life, different recording sessions, and remarkable details of his life that may be somewhat fictional. How could Bob remember such small details? Were the alternate lyrics he shared in the chapter of his recording the album *Oh Mercy* real? Because they seem like Bob's lifelong career trick of sharing a joke the rest of us are not in on.

I stopped and started a lot, trying any new tech app or gadget to help motivate me to write. And then I met someone who sparked the muse inside of me, and I knew I had to figure out a way to get the memoir written. I didn't have any great insight to share. I hadn't lived a terribly exciting life, but there were fragments here and there that I sensed had a universal message, even if I wasn't clear what that was. The pandemic presented the opportunity to write and reflect.

A journalist is expected to answer six questions with the stories they write: who, what, where, when, why, and how. Those six questions also apply to the lives we lead. Most people seem to focus most on what, where, who, when, and how questions. What am I going to do tomorrow? Where am I going to do it? When is the next meeting? Who am I going to do it with? How am I going to afford a house? How am I going to get a job? How am I going to afford my wedding? For me, the why has always been what makes me feel so different. Why am I doing what I'm doing? Why don't others need to understand the why of life? Why don't others need to find the meaning of things as much as I do? Why can't I be more like them?

Being Japanese American has been a consistent part of the "why" answers. It immediately made me different from the people I grew up with. And race never felt more confusing than life since 2020.

Race is part of my story, but it isn't what my story is about. The growing demonization of immigrants, refugees, and asylum seekers diminishes us. People who are coming here to better their lives and their children's lives should be welcomed and admired. But the demonization comes from not understanding the connection of human beings being human, confusing legal status with the universal basic need to live our lives the best we can. Sharing my story hopefully humanizes me beyond my race and experiences.

One of my earliest memories was flying my first kite and accidentally letting it unspool and fly away. That's the perfect metaphor for my life. I'm now 58 years old, and it feels like life got away from me at some point. It doesn't seem that long ago when I was three-year-old David.

I once dated a Korean American adoptee, the Lovely Leah, who revealed what she lacked throughout her life was her mapmaker. We were in our early 20s when we dated, so I wasn't quite sure I understood the weight of her revelation. I do now. All along my life's journey, I tried to do what made sense to move forward. That often meant taking the easiest path, but sometimes it was worth putting up a fight, diving through the most difficult challenges in surviving, for what I believed was right. Maybe if I had a mapmaker, I could have lived a better life. But in writing about so many memories, I wouldn't change much about the life I've lived. The one exception being the lack of connection with others.

During my life, I've lacked true and authentic connections. I wrote my story hoping it can somehow connect with someone, somewhere, in a meaningful way. This story I share documents a flawed life, at the same time glorifying the one thing I learned. Being the best me has always been figuring out how to share my most authentic self.

My story is one you see gazing out the window of a descending airplane, one of thousands of mysterious lights from the ground, as you marvel about how we never know, rarely think about, the day-to-day, month-to-month, year-to-year goings-on of the individual worlds of the many people we see from a distance. Our individual 'big picture' view of the world we know is ultimately but a tiny sliver.

Part One:
Bean Counter

I didn't make it to my dentist in 2020. His office is around 20 miles from my house, and making that trek seemed daunting. I rarely travelled anywhere outside a couple mile radius from my house during the pandemic. And taking time away from work seemed like a luxury that I couldn't afford. When I finally made it in to see Dr. Cassidy in spring 2021, he remembered I had switched jobs and asked what my 'new' job was. "I'm the director of elections for the Secretary of State," I said.

Dr. Cassidy burst out laughing. "Well, that can't be any fun."

He was right, although I didn't get into and stay in election administration work looking to have fun. The work seemed critically important and rewarding. Guardian of democracy, steward of the republic, big backbone bopper of bureaucrats.

On December 14, 2020, I found myself standing at the chief clerk's lectern in the Minnesota House of Representatives chamber. The chamber is a glorious part of the State Capitol designed by Cass Gilbert, a building capped with a marble dome and featuring beaming, gleaming, and formidable marble pillars. There are elaborate paintings throughout the building, portraits of past governors, paintings that were old before they were ever created. I had a job years back covering legislative action for a legislative publication, and even though the job paid little, I felt fortunate to get to work every day in such a historic building. The chamber was built long before electronic microphones, so there is a spot where the majority leader stands where one can whisper and everyone in the chamber can hear the spoken words.

This was my first time participating in the electoral college. I was reading the President/Vice President vote totals from our state into the record. My mask made it difficult to speak. Secretary of State Steve Simon stood behind me in the Speaker of the House spot, and office staff sat next to me. Our state's 10 electors were socially distanced in front of me sitting at the wood desks usually occupied by elected representatives of our legislature. The electors' family members sat in the upstairs gallery along with a few members of the press. Even though the buildings were closed to the public, the Capitol and State Office Building hallways were lined with law enforcement in case protestors tried to interfere with the proceedings. I thought that was a bit over the top, not knowing what would occur less than a month later in our nation's capital.

I read 7,940 votes cast for Kanye West into the official record. His 2013 LP, *808 & Heartbreak*, retains a truly special place in my heart. It was released 14 years after my mom's death, and much of the LP is Kanye dealing with his own mom's death. The power of the song cycle and raw feelings hit me in the gut every time I listen to it. Kanye is now seen as a pariah seemingly having a very public mental breakdown. But his best music remains powerful and impressive. Announcing votes for Kanye's minor party campaign for president somehow seemed strangely symbolic for 2020. I once would have cherished the moment getting to read votes for Kanye West for president into our state's historic record. This should have been the pinnacle moment of my career, but given what all of us went through, it seemed as if we were all just emerging among the ruins of a nuclear bomb, traumatized by what we just endured, and unsure of what the world was going to be like going forward.

When I was appointed to be the director in 2019, I tried my best to get up to speed on our state of elections, the challenges in front of me, and how I could best lead my team and our local county, city, township, and school district election administrator partners. I had a 25-year career in elections, and if you had told the younger me that one day my biggest challenge as identified by our federal intelligence agencies would be battling foreign adversaries to secure the integrity of Minnesota election systems, I would have laughed you off the face of the earth. No way, that's a scene out of a terrible movie.

And yet here it was. Our federal government partners had clear intelligence information that in 2016, Russia had penetrated two state's voter registration systems and had tried to do so in most other states, including Minnesota. So the focus of most of my peers in other states was to find ways to further secure our systems. I hired a 'cyber navigator' who would be responsible for developing and implementing a cybersecurity program to address an issue I never would have thought would exist. When I first started in the profession, the things that kept me up at night were issues like running out of ballots or poll workers not showing up on Election Day. Fighting the Ruskies? Me? Seriously?

So how exactly does one become a state's director of elections? Was this something I dreamed of becoming? When I earned my bachelor's degree from Macalester College in St. Paul, Minnesota, with a history major and a journalism minor, was this something I desired, strived to be? Was it part of my thoughts and dreams? Um, no.

After graduating college, I was struggling mightily with what to do next. The plan had been getting a job as a newspaper reporter, but for the first time in my life, I was having difficulty doing any writing. Getting a job that required me to write didn't seem like a good idea.

AN ACCIDENTAL CAREER

A few summers after graduating college, I joined my roommate's softball team. Most of the team, like my roommate, were pharmacy students at the University of Minnesota. We were at a bar following a game grabbing beers after a hard-fought victory, or maybe it was a heartbreaking loss. Over time, those things don't seem to matter.

I was seated next to the best hitter on the team, Jay Esselman, who was curious about my story. Jay's softball swing was picture perfect. Direct to the ball, fat part of the bat striking the ball with precision and power. I have paid many dollars to watch professional hitters with worse swings. Jay wondered why someone with a degree from an internationally respected liberal arts college, Macalester, was schlepping records at a small independent record store like some John Cusack *High Fidelity* wannabe.

Jay clearly picked up that I was struggling. It was written all over my face and in my deliberate movements. Jay told me I had to go see his mother, the person who could help me get a job with the State of Minnesota. He wrote her number down on a napkin. Another sign of my struggles: I was getting a woman's phone number in a bar, only it was the mother of a softball teammate who I wasn't all that excited to see.

But I clearly needed to find a 'real' job, so I called Mrs. Esselman the next day. Her office was part of a workforce development office on a busy stretch of University Avenue in St. Paul, not far from the record store I worked at. University Avenue is home to the State Capitol but used to be the busiest street in the city. Car dealerships lined the avenue, and some of the fanciest bars and restaurants were the places to be back in the day. I'm certain it was an area F. Scott Fitzgerald spent many a late night/early morning partying away. Now it was old and tired buildings, some vacant, others about to be in one of the poorer neighborhoods of the city. The state's burgeoning Hmong population was slowly transitioning the area from what had been a prominently African American neighborhood.

When I met Mrs. Esselman, she looked familiar. It turned out she was a member of my mom's bridge-playing group, the cackling group of ladies that kept me up many nights during my childhood. Ladies playing bridge once a month, rotating from suburban house to suburban house, to blow off steam. I'm sure there was alcohol involved with the bridge-playing, although I knew my mom didn't drink.

Mrs. Esselman gave me a typing test. I did well, my words per minute above average, my errors minimal. I could thank my mom for that, having made me sacrifice a summer in junior high to take a typing class. Mrs. Esselman told me with my skills and education background, I could move quickly up the state government ladder. I don't remember her exact words, but I left with the message I needed to keep my head down, work hard, and keep my eyes open for further opportunities.

Within a few days, Mrs. Esselman arranged a temporary job with the Minnesota Department of Education. The job was filing teacher licenses captured on microfiche slides into a rolling filing cabinet that was bursting at its seams. My biggest challenge was inserting an updated slide into the alphabetically sorted files. The task was to move the files of slides into the next available slot to create more space to file. Essentially, I was trying to cram microfiche slides into empty space that didn't exist. A college degree well spent.

The department was run by a retired brigadier general, and clearly, there were some personnel issues. Staff openly mocked and criticized the staff person who was bumbling her way through her job duties. There was a mix of Minnesota Nice, trying to all get along while making snide comments behind this person's back, and open hostility. This made me remember my mom's one piece of advice after I graduated college. She told me every office has its internal politics, and I needed to learn how to maneuver my way through this. At the time, it seemed like such an ominous personal lesson, and I had no idea what it meant. Like always, it turned out Mom was right. People tend to want to be polite above authentic. Peaceful coexistence trumps rattling the status quo.

Mrs. Esselman also got me an interview for a permanent position with the Office of the Secretary of State. It was another entry-level position, a Clerk Typist 1 job in the business services division of the office. It was only my fifth job interview experience, two in college for temporary jobs, an internship with a newspaper, and the interview I did to get my record store job. I thought I did fairly well in the latest interview. It was conducted in a dark conference room in the State Office Building, a historic building without a lot of character other than its marble exterior and red metal roof. It was the sad afterthought building next to the State Capitol.

I didn't get the job. But I was told there was another opening in the agency in the records, renewal, and registration division of the office. So, I tried again. And this time I was offered the job. The job involved mailing rejection letters out to corporations and other businesses that did something wrong with an annual filing required to be filed with our office. Rejection. The job had my name written all over it.

Every Friday, I got a break from mailing the form letters. I gathered a pile of voter registration forms mailed in from voters across the state. I sorted them into a large bin with individual slots to mail to our 87 counties. I made it a game of sorts, forcing myself to memorize what cities were in what counties. On most of the forms, the voters did not complete the county information or had written in "USA." I also, being a huge David Letterman fan, tried flinging the cards, slightly larger than a postcard, into the appropriate slot in the bin like Dave did with his notecards on his late-night TV show.

The office asked anyone interested in helping out on Election Night to sign up to lend assistance. So I did. We had two locations, one in the State Office Building (lovingly dubbed by staff and others as the SOB) where Secretary of State Joan Growe's office was located along with the elections staff. Growe was one of the true pioneer elected officials in Minnesota. Before becoming Secretary of State, she was elected to the state House of Representatives during a time when being an elected woman was rare. I was in the other location that housed huge IBM mainframe computer servers and our IT staff. My job on Election Night was to drive the secretary between the two locations. I was the original Uber driver.

I always thought my time as a public servant would be short, despite Mrs. Esselman's words about moving up the state government ladder. I was just doing the work because it offered stability and a bigger paycheck than working at the record store. But my destiny had to be greater than being a bureaucrat. The next rung on the ladder presented itself to me out of the blue. Another state agency, the Department of Trade and Economic Development (DTED), had a supervisor position open, and I was encouraged to apply by someone in that department. I had begun looking at other opportunities after a staff meeting where the main topic was the definition of being 'in or out' on our office in-and-out board. Did a cigarette break count as being 'out?' If someone was going to take longer than the allotted 15-minute break, shouldn't they mark themselves on the in-and-out board as being out? It was excruciating hearing others air obvious previously established grievances in this hour-long meeting. Government at its truest and worst, the very office politics Mom warned me about.

I interviewed and was offered the job with DTED. By accepting, I doomed myself to a government career. Once you go up the ladder, you want to keep climbing; you don't want to go back the other way or jump off. The department was a conglomerate of merged state agencies: the trade office, community development, the public facilities authority, and the tourism office. One of the big projects I worked on was finding a way to merge all the different agency's databases into one. My contribution was coming up with a name for the new comprehensive database: DYLAN, short for Data You're Looking At Now.

My first election administration job came when I was hired as the Washington County Elections Supervisor. Washington County was one of seven counties in the Twin Cities metropolitan area. It was quickly transitioning from a mostly rural county to a suburban one. There were some struggles with longtime employees adapting to the change. There was a sense of loss going from personally knowing those bringing in their property tax payments to serving scores of new residents homesteading their suburban McMansions.

I was hired in July 1996, with our State Primary in September and a Presidential Election in November. Other than my flinging voter registration applications into a metal bin, I didn't have any elections experience. It was a crash course in learning the election statutes, the proverbial drinking from a firehose or learning how to ride a bike using a Harley Davidson. I made some rookie mistakes that fortunately didn't cost me too much. One of the cities in the county was Marine on St. Croix. On their sample ballot, I renamed the city "Marine on the St. Croix," upsetting a whole lot of voters and city officials.

Precision in elections is a necessity. And perception ranks a close second. People view our elections as sacred, a civic duty of all citizens. Elections administrators are at the foundation of our government, keepers of the ballot box, referees of our democracy. The patron saints of security, access, and fairness. Pompous but provable. One of the other early elections I had to administer was for a county commissioner vacancy. One of the candidates was my boss, the auditor treasurer. The other was the brother of the acting county attorney. The district essentially was within two cities: Woodbury, one of the fastest-growing suburbs in the state; and Afton, a small city bursting with personality mostly known for its skiing hills. My boss lived in Woodbury, and the acting county attorney's brother lived in Afton. The *Pioneer Press*, one of the two major Twin Cities newspaper dailies, had recently hired a new reporter to cover Washington County. Her name was Mary Divine, which suited her well. The special election was Divine's first major story, and she called me almost daily with questions. I tried my best to be open and upfront, but it was clear a lot of her questions were based on discussions with the acting county attorney's brother, who was questioning if the county could run a fair election, given our boss being one of the candidates.

My direct boss was the assistant auditor treasurer. She and I had some disagreements based on the perception of us somehow favoring one candidate over the other. She suggested we change some of our processes to address this perception. I thought by doing so we would open ourselves up to even more criticism. It felt like we should do things the way we had always done in the past. The election administrator creed is not caring who wins but hoping whoever does wins with a large enough margin to avoid the dreaded "R" word, recount.

We finally got to Election Day when I got yet another call from Mary Divine. She heard that some of the Afton precincts were running out of I Voted stickers, while the Woodbury precincts had plenty. The brother of the acting county attorney accused me of deliberately shorting Afton of the stickers so other members in that community wouldn't see their neighbors wearing the stickers, and thus wouldn't know there was an election going on that day. And the opposite being the case in Woodbury. My tired and weary response to the latest allegation was, "That's the most absurd thing I've ever heard."

Thankfully, Mary, who remains a friend to this day, didn't use the quote because it might have ended my career as an elections administrator right then. Election officials can't criticize candidates. It weakens confidence in the profession.

My next big project was upgrading the county's voting system. I was piggybacking this effort with the state's largest county, Hennepin, whose chief election official, Marge Christianson, was known as the matriarch of Minnesota elections. Marge had a keen sense of humor, slightly dry, always skeptical. A seemingly naturally leisurely woman with short curly dark hair, her attire was forever casual, the type of person who would have looked out of place and unnatural in fancy dress clothes. Marge was known for her love of a Bloody Mary or two. She was responsible for helping draft most of the election statutes. She was instrumental in moving our election equipment to the latest technology, optical scan voting, a decade before the debacle of punch card voting that was an issue in the 2000 Presidential Election in Florida. Remember pregnant and hanging chads that were going to determine our next president until the U.S. Supreme Court decided the winner?

Marge was in the process of purchasing the next generation of voting equipment for Hennepin County, so I thought I'd partner with her on the effort. Coming from a much smaller county, it seemed like vendors might not be as interested in providing the cost savings if I went solo, and cost consideration needed to be an element of the decision. I convened a committee of city officials within the county to help evaluate the vendors' proposals. The committee's choice ultimately differed from my own. They chose a more compact voting system, easier to store (which was their responsibility). I preferred the system that had the newest technological feature, one Marge thought was really important: modems that could transfer results from polling places back to the county nearly instantaneously after the polls had closed.

There was a growing struggle between getting election results to the media, candidates, and public as quickly as possible versus introducing a potential security risk. Could the modem results be intercepted and altered? The vendor I preferred set up a meeting to clarify all the security in place to prevent this. He explained the latest modem technology, cellular digital packet data, that was an encryption process verifying what was sent on one end and received on the other had not been altered. And results sent by modem were unofficial. The official results were printed out first by the ballot tabulators on a tape. Those results were the ones that were to be used by the counties' canvassing boards to certify the election.

The rift with my boss only got larger as the county staff struggled with the changing demographics of the people they were serving. A big announcement was made with the demotion of several longtime staff and the promotion of one, me. The promotion wasn't the one I was promised salary-wise, and I had not been told others were being demoted. So I did a "far too young in my career" thing: I resigned. And I let the county HR staff know I thought all of it was unethical. Some of my city colleagues contacted me asking if my resignation was for racial reasons. I got a call from a local TV station to find out what happened. I declined. This was my first lesson on how serious election administrator jobs were in the eyes of the media.

The county purchased the voting system that the majority of the cities preferred, though it wasn't the one I wanted. That vendor eventually became Diebold, a vendor who became a target of election integrity skeptics following the 2004 Presidential Election. The issue of security and accuracy of voting equipment would rear its ugly head again following the 2020 election.

THE DREADED "R" WORD

In the 2008 U.S. Senate race in Minnesota between former St. Paul Mayor Norm Coleman and former *Saturday Night Live* writer and performer Al Franken, Coleman won by only 215 votes out of more than three million votes cast. A margin so small required the dreaded R word, a statewide recount. I had taken the job as the Minnetonka City Clerk 11 months earlier.

Minnetonka was a suburb of Minneapolis, one of several cities located by Lake Minnetonka, made famous in a few scenes in Prince's movie *Purple Rain.* The city itself only contained 3 percent of the lake's shoreline. I took the job in a deliberate attempt at learning new duties outside of elections. I was still the chief election official in the city, but election administration was but one of the many city clerk duties.

Being the city's chief election official wasn't my most powerful duty. The city had a summer festival on the City Hall campus, and at the end of the night there was a fireworks display. I had the final sign off on the fireworks, given I was responsible as the city's risk manager 'expert.' The fire department did all the legwork to make sure the fireworks vendor had all the safety measures in place, but I signed off on their insurance coverage. I could have said, "No, we're not going to shoot off fireworks at Summerfest" as some type of power ploy. That power was in my hands.

Conducting the recount of our ballots was done in our city council chambers. Teams of three poll workers sat at multiple tables with observers representing the two campaigns at each table. The poll workers would look at each ballot to determine who the vote should go to. The observers could challenge the poll workers' decisions, and those particular ballots got set aside. Minnesota election law had a provision prohibiting a voter from placing an identifying mark on a ballot. This was a leftover provision from the days ballots were hand-counted and was meant to prohibit someone from paying another person to vote a certain way. To prove to the payer that the voter indeed voted as instructed, an identifying mark would be placed on the ballot. But with the use of voting equipment, most ballots were never visually viewed in the count unless a recount was required.

The campaigns quickly seized on this old law to challenge ballots that had lipstick smears, coffee stains, or where the voter marked the ballot in a weird way. The most famous examples were a voter who wrote in a vote for "Lizard People" and another voter who wrote in a vote for "Spaghetti Monster." Things escalated because the media reported the daily results of the recount, and the campaigns figured out if they challenged votes from the opposition, that meant the daily results would show the opponent got fewer votes and was running behind. I got frustrated by the frivolous challenges and at one point in the multiple-day recount pulled the campaign representatives aside and pled with them to stop.

"If this was your ballot with a coffee stain, would you really want it to be thrown out?" I asked. Some of the challenges stopped, but mostly, things continued the way they were going. The challenged ballots would ultimately be decided by the State Canvassing Board.

The recount finished with Franken ahead by 312 votes. Most of the change came as a result of review of absentee ballots that were originally rejected by poll workers but upon further review should have been accepted. In Minnetonka we had 14 absentee ballots that were added to the recount count, almost all for Franken. Coleman filed an election contest, meaning a panel of judges would determine who was the actual winner. I was one of several election administrators called upon to testify in the trial. I was the one who determined the 14 rejected ballots should be counted. I had studied them, examined them multiple times, and there was no doubt in my mind our poll workers had made clear mistakes in rejecting the ballots.

The trial was held in our State Supreme Court chambers. I was sworn in. I felt strangely calm. I had memorized the 14 ballots over and over and was confident I could answer any question about them. My city attorney advised me to only answer the question asked. It would be tempting to give more context to the overall administration of the election, but that could lead to going down rabbit holes.

Taking the stand, I didn't realize how nervous I actually was until I picked up the glass of water in front of me to try and address my dry mouth. I could barely hold it up to my lips because my hands were shaking so badly. During a recess, I spoke with the attorney for Franken who was the one who questioned me, and he said he was impressed by how well I prepared myself. I also spoke with Ben Ginsberg, an attorney for Coleman. Ginsberg was part of President George W. Bush's Florida 2000 recount team.

There had recently been a movie, *Recount*, dramatizing all the events leading to Bush's election. Ginsberg had been played in the movie by the actor Bob Balaban, who had a small reoccurring role in the TV series *Seinfeld* as an NBC executive that George Costanza offended by leering at his daughter's cleavage. I asked Ginsberg what he thought of Balaban's portrayal of him. He laughed and said he thought Balaban did OK.

When I got back to City Hall, the city attorney said I did a great job testifying.

I assumed the 2008 recount would be the most difficult election challenge I would be a part of in my career. A recount is like running a marathon, and you can see the finish line in sight, only to see them move it further down the road. You've paced yourself to make it to one specific day, and then the goalposts keep moving. The 2008 senate election wasn't finished until April of the following year. We were bombarded with records requests from multiple law firms and the media. It sucked the air out of my job for many months.

Since most elections end in a result far outside any reasonable margin for a recount, it's often easy to forget that every ballot cast has its own story. Maybe this ballot was cast by someone who recently became a citizen or a felon who had their right to vote restored. Maybe they're a first-time, 18-year-old voter. Maybe it's a single parent who is struggling to get by and yet takes time off to vote to cast a ballot. Every ballot has a story behind it. The coffee stains, lipstick smears, and write-in votes for "Lizard People" are proof positive that voting in an election is a civic responsibility but, more importantly, a way to voice an individual opinion in a sea of other voices. In the end, all we care about is who wins an election. The more important takeaway is everyone able to cast a vote has an equal say with every other voter. The end result may not be what I want, but by casting my ballot, I get the opportunity to express how I think my community can become a better place to live for all. Elections are an idealistic dream but one where we as individuals truly do matter on a molecular level.

LEGACY

In 2002, Congress passed the Help America Vote Act that required every state to have a statewide voter registration system and provided money to states to upgrade old voting equipment. Voter registration systems in much of the country were done at the county level, and the federal law attempted to make sure voter records were part of a statewide database. No problem in Minnesota, which had a statewide system since the late 1980s.

The law also required that every polling place in the country have a device that would allow all voters the ability to vote privately and independently, pushed hard by advocates of the disability communities. Many states used the funding to go to touchscreen technology to meet the last requirement. In Minnesota the paper ballot was key to our elections. If a voting machine faltered or wasn't programmed correctly, the paper ballot would always be there to come up with an accurate count of the votes.

In 2003, I was the Hennepin County Elections Supervisor, happily helping fill Marge's large shoes and margarita glass, and was contacted by several companies wanting to show me their solution for meeting this new accessibility requirement. Datacard, an international company based in Minnetonka, asked for a meeting.

The device they showed me look like it came straight from the 1950s. It had been used in some African countries, and a unique feature was the ballot contained pictures of candidates and party symbols because of the high illiteracy rate of the voters. The Datacard representatives told me they could modify the device to meet the HAVA requirements. I was skeptical, and they picked up on it. At the end of the meeting, they asked me if there were other areas in elections that needed technology improvements. I named electronic pollbooks.

I saw electronic pollbooks for the first time during my work in upgrading the Washington County voting equipment. Basically, it would use computers to check in voters rather than the existing antiquated process of printing rosters on reams of paper for every election. Unlike ballots, checking in voters seemed to me to not require paper, as it didn't impact the actual results. And there was administrative benefit. The data from the pollbooks was available electronically. There was no longer the need to try and decipher handwriting when processing the voter data after the election. I suggested to the Datacard representatives this was an area they should look into as they hit the elevator button to go down.

Four years later, now the Minnetonka city clerk, I got a call from someone working for Datacard. The company had just been awarded a contract to implement electronic pollbooks in another state, and they asked if I could supply some of our poll workers to take the training to use the technology. I was more than happy to and picked people with diverse skills. I thought it was best to pick people both who I knew would catch on quickly and others who might struggle with using the computer technology. I was thrilled that my suggestion to the company years back led them to actually developing an electronic pollbook solution.

When our poll workers got back from the training, they asked when I was going to purchase the electronic pollbooks because they all agreed it would help them do their duties better. I soon opened up discussions with Datacard about developing their product to use in Minnesota. We were one of the few states that allowed voters to register at their polling place on Election Day. This was the most complex thing our poll workers had to administer and thus led to the most mistakes. Documents establishing residency in the precinct and photo ID were needed to register on Election Day. And it was critical to verify the voter was in the right precinct to cast a ballot. All led to mistakes from poll workers across the state. Using computer technology to walk poll workers through the process seemed like a no-brainer. And never let it be said a no-brainer process wasn't best implemented by a no-brainer, straight-from-the-heart guy like me.

Datacard came back to me showing that their electronic pollbook could scan a Minnesota driver's license to populate a voter registration application and confirm the voter was voting in the right precinct. I knew this could really be a game changer in administering our elections. I reviewed our election statutes, and there was nothing prohibiting me from using the electronic pollbooks, as long as the Secretary of State approved.

So I started small. I reached out to the state for permission to conduct a small pilot project. We would use the electronic pollbooks in a couple of our polling places in combination with using the paper rosters. The idea was to see how much it would improve the voting experience. At the end, being able to provide electronic files could potentially eliminate data-entry errors of the data that took counties significant time to enter into the statewide voter registration system after every election.

The pilot was a success. Our poll workers loved that the technology walked them through processes and procedures, eliminating mistakes. And I decided to try an expanded pilot in the 2010 federal and state elections. I tried to secure as many spare laptops and printers that I could. I was able to secure enough to use in roughly two-thirds of our polling places. Again, the feedback from the poll workers was nothing but positive.

At the same time, our state lawmakers were debating implementing voter ID in our state, a contentious issue with political overtones.

Republicans saw it as a straightforward integrity measure. Democrats saw it as a barrier with those lacking the necessary IDs often being people of color, students, and the elderly. I saw electronic pollbooks as a possible solution to bridge this divide. If we could include the voter's picture ID from the connection between the voter registration system and our state's driver's license database, there would be a shift in the dynamic. Instead of government requiring voters to prove who they were in order to vote, the onus would be on government to prove the voter wasn't who they said they were. A politically conservative principal.

This led to one of Minnetonka's state senators, Terri Bonoff, a Democrat, reaching out to me. A little later on, the Secretary of State Mark Ritchie, another Democrat, and, ultimately, the third Democrat, Governor Mark Dayton, also contacted me to learn more about my idea. This solution appealed to all of them as creative and an acceptable form of voter ID. Unfortunately, the Secretary's election staff clearly didn't agree with the work required to implement electronic pollbooks in the state. It would require necessary changes to the statewide voter registration system that would take time away from their other work and resources. I felt this was shortsighted, and I was going to do all I could to make this game-changing improvement to our elections. I had a new mission.

I was incredibly fortunate to have the support of both my city manager, John Gunyou, and my boss, Geralyn Barone, the assistant city manager. Both trusted my elections administration background and experience. Gunyou loved our city leading in improving government processes in all things, a risk-taker willing to challenge the status quo.

There were some in state government pushing for more public/private partnerships. My work with Datacard fell perfectly in that category. Because they were based in Minnetonka, it was easy for them to come to City Hall or for me to go to their headquarters for frequent meetings. One of the unique aspects of elections is every state has its own laws and processes. I was working with Datacard to develop an electronic pollbook that would specifically comply with Minnesota election laws while allowing them the flexibility to meet other state's laws.

When other vendors learned of my interest in electronic pollbooks, they offered me the use of their product in our pilot projects. This would require a lot of upfront work to make their products comply with our state's laws. But it was worth it because I was getting to use the technology free and was quickly becoming knowledgeable about what did and did not work with most products on the market. None of them were naturally equipped to handle Election Day registration because very few states allowed that, but rather required voters to register weeks before an election. Horse-and-buggy laws.

The Secretary of State's office wasn't exactly helpful in this work. I needed a file from the statewide voter registration system to upload into the electronic pollbooks. The state wasn't willing to put in work to program the system to create such a file. I was able to get reports that included the data, but this required the vendors to do some work to make the data work within their pollbooks. I knew it was not ideal having to rely on a vendor to manipulate voter registration data.

I somehow learned that the Cheyenne County clerk in Wyoming, my mom's home state, was doing some similar work in her state that I was doing in Minnesota. She implemented some electronic pollbook pilot projects and tried getting her Secretary of State interested in the technology. I found out she was going to do a demo for the other counties in the state at one of their county conferences. She invited me, and I flew to Cheyenne.

Mom was born and raised on a farm in Lingle, Wyoming. One of the great many U.S. small towns whose population as of the 2020 census was 420. The hotel I stayed in was in downtown Cheyenne and was quite old. It was apparent that back in the day, it was the classiest hotel in Wyoming. Plush carpeting, ornate decorations. It felt a little worn out, but it wasn't lost on me that Mom went to college in Cheyenne, and she would have been amazed that one day her youngest child would stay in the hotel, one that, likely, given her race, she would have been denied had she had the money to try.

Back home, the legislature was becoming interested in the work I was doing. There were several early morning meetings with a working group comprised of key legislators and staff and Datacard programmers. Senator Bonoff asked me to join. The idea was to draft minimum requirements for an electronic pollbook to be used in the state. The draft bill would also require the Secretary of State's office to produce the files needed. I fought hard to make sure the electronic pollbooks didn't fall under the statutory definition of voting equipment, which it clearly wasn't, since it didn't involve counting votes. With rapid advancements in technology, I didn't want the electronic pollbooks to need to be certified by the Secretary of State's office like voting equipment did. I didn't want some unforeseen technological improvement to have to wait for a bureaucratic certification before it could be used.

The Deputy Secretary of State, who I had worked with the past several years on other legislation, found out about this working group, and she said she was "disappointed" in me that I hadn't notified the office of the work we were doing. I felt it was unfair to use that word. This wasn't my working group; I had been asked to serve on it, not run it. And the office hadn't exactly been helpful so far.

The bill created a task force to discuss implementing electronic pollbooks in Minnesota. It passed with strong bipartisan support. I was appointed to serve on the task force. The voter ID idea that got the legislature interested quickly was cast aside because our state's driver license database wasn't capable of providing the photos in a way that would tie them to the license holder's voter information. The task force eventually came up with recommendations to the legislature.

I won some fights, like not including pollbooks under the voting equipment definition, but lost others, namely including the whole county's voter information on each pollbook rather than just the specific precinct's. The state election director felt including county-wide data on each ePollbook would lead to poll workers accessing voter information they didn't need to do their job. In working with vendors, I learned it was easier to update an existing record rather than to create a new record.

The bill that passed the House differed from the bill that passed the Senate. Thus, a conference committee was required to iron out the differences. The Secretary of State's office and the counties supported the House version. The Senate version included provisions pushed by now Senator Mary Kiffmeyer, former Secretary of State, about creating paper signature receipts for the voter to sign rather than allowing them to sign electronically. And the total number of voters checking in had to be determined by counting the voter signature slips. The counties strongly disagreed, fearing it was a way for Kiffmeyer to change the process that was used to determine the number of voters signing the paper rosters.

It appeared things were falling apart. And it was equally clear long-time distrust between the counties and Senator Kiffmeyer was at the core of the disagreement. This was personal. Senator Bonoff took me into the hallway and asked if I would be okay with killing the bill. I told her it was fine despite my passion and chess-playing work throughout the process and belief in this important improvement to our election processes.

The conference committee finally worked through its differences, and the bill, specifically allowing ePollbooks in Minnesota, became law. By 2020, more than half of Minnesota counties used ePollbooks. As the director of elections, I heard from county staff saying they couldn't imagine administering elections without ePollbooks. Few of these officials knew the role I played in this particular improvement to our elections.

DEDICATED FAIRNESS OF AN ELECTION OFFICIAL

Three of our city's polling places were located in our Community Center's Community Room, a large gathering space. The Community Center was adjacent to City Hall, so it made observing actual voting easier for me as it was a mere walk down the hall and down two flights of steps. On election evening 2008, I got a call from a voter complaining that the election judge greeting people at the door and directing them to the proper polling place was wearing an Obama sweatshirt. I politely ended the call and ran as fast as my Mama Cass legs could take me to the Community Center. I saw a young woman sitting on a stool right by the front doors. She was wearing a red 'Bama' sweatshirt, honoring the University of Alabama Crimson Tide. I have little doubt she knew what she was doing; maybe it was just an act of simply wearing her favorite and most comfortable sweatshirt. Perception and the art of subliminal messaging.

Before any voting equipment can be used in Minnesota elections, it goes through a rigorous federal and state certification process. The federal certification is done by an accredited testing lab, who not only tests voting equipment, but also tests things like airplanes and nuclear power plant equipment. The testing labs put election equipment through things like extreme temperatures, both hot and cold, given the equipment could be stored in the extreme conditions.

One day, the shelf holding three of the voting tabulators we had in Minnetonka broke, and the voting equipment fell four feet to the ground. The casing around one of the tabulators cracked; the other two seemed undamaged. I decided if asked to explain, I would say we were so thorough in Minnetonka that we did a drop test to our voting equipment. That might have seemed somewhat funny when it happened, but if the same thing occurred during our current elections environment, it might have led to national news stories.

Like nearly every other election administrator I've ever met, I was constantly looking for ways to improve our processes. Sometimes, big changes and solutions like electronic pollbooks. Other times, simple solutions that could be missed by being too familiar with the status quo. I'd gained a reputation for looking for the latest technology to implement in elections. A lover of gadgets, I was one of the first to buy a Betamax on my block, and I bought the very first iPhone sight unseen.

I loved technology but knew not all things can be solved with a computer. I didn't want to be boxed into a corner of being the gadget guy blind to simpler solutions. In Minnesota, while we use optical scan tabulators to tally the votes, every voter in our state votes on a paper ballot. We always have the actual source document if needed, just like we did in 2008. One of the ongoing issues we had in Minnetonka was we provided huge American flags to fly outside our polling place entrances. State law requires a flag to be placed identifying the polling place. The problem was our flags were heavy and sometimes blew over if there were strong enough winds. It wasn't a good look to have voters arrive and see the American flag lying on the ground.

Our finance director's son was in the Eagle Scouts, and his troop was looking for projects to help them earn their merit badge. One of the troop members approached me with an idea: designing and building flag stands that would prevent our flags from tipping over. The end result was stands with stacked-up wood, the bottom level being the biggest, and progressing up, each level was a little smaller, a square pyramid. The stands were heavy and sturdy, but they worked. We never again heard about a flag lying on the ground. The city was only out the cost of the wood and paint. Plus, I helped a Scout earn his badge. Score another one for democracy and the American way.

Sometimes the smallest, seemingly simple improvements led to unintended consequences. Our stack of "VOTE HERE" signs was getting worn and torn after years of being outside every election. So I asked our web designer to design modern-looking signs that we could send to a vendor to create. The design included the phrase, "Democracy Starts Here." I liked what he came up with.

The first election we used them, though, we got calls throughout the day from voters complaining about the signs. "This isn't a democracy," we heard over and over. "It's a republic." Actually, it's both, but it was clear what the concern was. One party's voters thought we were favoring the other side. That hadn't occurred to me when I approved the signs, never crossed my mind. But it wasn't worth fighting about. Since the slogan appeared at the bottom of the sign, I asked staff to cut it off so we could still use the standard "VOTE HERE" that took up the majority of space anyway.

I learned over the years sometimes it's just better to stick with the tried and true. Throwing in new processes and materials in an election takes careful consideration because voters intensely scrutinize their entire experience, convinced each side is looking for the smallest advantage. We are a representative democracy. The best analogy I've heard about this is for a dog owner you might live with a boxer, or a Great Dane, or a poodle, but ultimately, none of those distinctions matter. You live with a dog.

Election administration is a very human-reliant process. There are the mistakes I made. There are the mistakes the staff I supervised made. And in Minnesota there are 87 counties, thousands of cities, townships, and school district administrators tasked with overseeing elections, not to count the 30,000 poll workers deployed in our statewide elections. Those 30,000 people are our neighbors and friends, people trying to do their duties in our democracy, many of them retired seniors. And God bless them.

The thing I missed most after becoming the State's Elections Director was working with the Minnetonka poll workers, so dedicated, so diligent in doing their duties. The reason I know our elections are fair and secure might sound counterintuitive. We rely on so many to do the right thing at every moment of the process. Because the responsibility is so widely dispersed, elections occurring at the most local level, it is nearly impossible for widespread fraud to occur. Way too many people would have to be in on the fix; someone would spill the beans. We may live among nefarious people, but nefarious people seldom are silent. People love to brag about how they cheated the system, beat the man, outwitted the powerful.

Call me naïve, but I've always believed at our core, humans are good, have good intentions as our default position. This belief got seriously challenged during the 2016 election cycle. In Minnesota voters can vote absentee starting 46 days prior to the election. They can do so by mail or they can do so at their government office in person. The beginning of the absentee process was always slow. We would get a few voters a day coming into City Hall the first week. We administered the voting out of a small conference room that had a service window out into the lobby. Across from the conference room was our legal department that also had a service window. We didn't always staff the window but left a doorbell that would ring in our office space alerting one of us to go help the voter. The legal department had an even more creative alert system. They left a wood gavel for a resident to bang on the wood circle platform to call staff to the window.

There were a line of voters at our AB window, and I was trying to help voters as quickly as I could. Preparing the materials for the voters takes time, so there is no way to speed up the process.

On this particular day, there were around 10 voters standing in line. The line stood in front of the legal department's window and angled down the hallway. After I got through helping the voters, the legal department staff noticed their gavel was gone. I told my colleagues my faith in humanity had just gone down the drain.

Our IT department had security videos monitoring the City Hall lobby and hallway. They looked at the video recording and found what looked like the person stealing the gavel. It wasn't definitive, since it was a middle-aged couple, and the man stood in front of the woman, partially blocking what looked like her putting the gavel into her purse. Looking at the clock time of the video, I was able to search the Statewide Voter Registration System to see what absentee voting record I created at that time. I actually recalled the voters involved because we had a pleasant chat about how much they loved 'Oriental' food. I felt glad they weren't upset about having to wait in line. We met with police officers and decided to send a squad to the couple's house. They denied stealing the gavel. The police officers dropped the matter. Later, I learned the husband was taken to the hospital that day suffering from chest pains.

NO EXCUSE

Prior to 2014, voting by absentee ballot in Minnesota required the voter to provide the reason they could not vote at the polling place on Election Day: they were going to be out of town; they were serving as an election judge at another precinct; they had an illness or disability making it difficult to vote at the polling place; or there was a religious observance that prevented them from voting on Election Day.

The legislature passed a law changing Minnesota to a no-excuse absentee ballot state, meaning any eligible voter could choose to vote by absentee ballot. This greatly increased the popularity of absentee voting. For election administrators, it meant more work.

To vote absentee, each voter had to submit an application. Then, the election administrator had to look up the voter's registration status in the Statewide Voter Registration System. An absentee record was created in the system so voters couldn't receive multiple ballots or vote absentee and then try to vote at the polling place on Election Day. There were labels with unique barcodes affixed to the absentee ballot envelope.

A packet of absentee materials was put together, including the proper precinct's ballot. This was the case whether mailing the ballot to the voter or if the voter chose to vote in person at City Hall.

After the voter submitted their voted ballot, a ballot board of two election judges of different political parties reviewed the information from the absentee application and the signature envelope the voter placed their voted ballot in. If the ballot board agreed the information matched, the ballot was accepted. If something didn't match, the ballot was rejected, and the voter was issued a replacement ballot.

In-person absentee voting became even more popular a few years later when the legislature allowed voters to insert their in-person absentee ballots directly into a tabulator rather than inside absentee envelopes during the seven days prior to the election. This led to a further spike in the number of voters voting before Election Day.

In 2016 and 2018, nearly 40 percent of the voters in Minnetonka voted before Election Day. During the seven days before the election, there were lines of people waiting two to three hours to vote at City Hall. I heard several voters saying they were voting early to avoid standing in line on Election Day. There was no polling place in the city that had two-to-three-hour lines on Election Day. We had voters waiting in line ordering pizza.

State law required in-person absentee voting the Saturday before the election. I had to open up City Hall and flip on the lights that usually were already on during the work week. There was a panel of switches for the lights throughout City Hall. There was a map next to the panel indicating what lights lit up different areas of City Hall. But it didn't seem to be accurate, as I would flip a switch, and the lights I expected to come on didn't. So I usually just flipped every switch, nervous I was turning on and off the different traffic lights throughout the city.

When COVID-19 shut down society, our office encouraged voters to absentee vote by mail. We didn't want anyone to have to choose between staying safe and exercising the right to vote. Little could I know the 2020 election would blow 2008 out the door. The therapist I was seeing online in 2020 saw the off-the-charts stress I was under. He continually questioned why I was putting myself through it. I could answer how I was surviving but never really came up with a good why. I'm a guardian of democracy. Our state needed me. Our country needed me.

John Podolinsky was a veteran who served in the South Pacific during World War II. He voted by absentee ballot every year during my time as the city clerk from his Minnetonka residence. The first year he absentee voted, he screwed up his ballot by not properly completing the necessary certificate, thus having his ballot rejected. He did this three or four times, and finally, he demanded to talk to me to walk him over the phone what he needed to do to complete his absentee ballot. John obviously had a colorful personality, not afraid to drop a few choice curse words and make jokes about his wife with a complete stranger trying to help him cast his vote.

Every year, he would call when he got his absentee ballot and have me walk him through what he needed to do. The calls took close to an hour because John loved to share stories from his life with me. Being a WW2 veteran, I didn't know if he knew I was Japanese American and don't know if that would have mattered in any way. The first few years when I heard he was on the line, I rolled my eyes. I had far too much work to do during the crunch time in the election cycle to spend an hour with a solitary voter. But after a few years, I began to look forward to my chats with Mr. Podolinsky.

During the stress of that crunch time, he was a reminder of why I was doing the work. I was helping a voter understand what was needed to cast a legal vote. I didn't know politically how he voted. I didn't care. After administering the 2018 election, it dawned on me I hadn't heard from John. I looked him up in the voter registration system, and sure enough, his registration was inactivated due to a death record received by the county.

I also remember a particularly busy day sitting in my spot in the City Council chambers monitoring the activity in our absentee voting polling place when a man approached me. I felt apprehension that he was going to share a concern about something he felt we weren't doing right. Instead he said, "You probably don't remember me." He told me how four years earlier, he approached me in the same spot, angry that we had rejected his college daughter's absentee ballot.

It was the Friday before the election, and she couldn't make it home to cast an in-person ballot. I told him one option was for him to pay for overnight mailing materials, and we could overnight her a replacement ballot. She should get it Saturday, and if she overnighted it back, we likely would have it to count by the Election Day deadline for absentee ballots. He left and a short while later came back with overnight materials. He told me that she was able to get her replacement ballot accepted and counted.

He said that was her first election, and had she not got the ballot counted, she might never have voted again. He thanked me for going above and beyond to help his daughter. I didn't have the heart to tell him I told him exactly what was allowable in our election laws. I wasn't doing anything special for this particular voter; I would have offered the same thing to any voter. Again, I have no idea of his daughter's political leanings, nor do I care. Yet this parent taking the time to share this story with me meant the world to me. This is why I chose the career I chose. This is why I do what I do.

You can look at my career under an objective lens and say it's been a success in that I was able to start at the bottom and climb to the top of my profession. You can't be a has-been if you are a never-was. The thing is I didn't plan things. I just tried to do my best given the situation I was in, whether it be filing microfiche of teachers' licenses or giving a deposition in a legal proceeding. My career wasn't about climbing the ladder; it was a trapeze act. I didn't go from A to B to C; my career was more like a stirred bowl of alphabet soup. I made some leaps of faith, sometimes with a net of knowing I could easily get another job if I failed, but sometimes, there was no net. I had everything to lose by sticking my neck out.

Others have praised my calm, cool leadership skills that focus on finding a solution to an issue rather than looking for who's to blame.

But underneath the calm were churning emotions. I stepped into leadership roles when I saw a void, and as I enter the swan song of my career, the September of my years, I'm energized that several of the next generation of election administrators consider me to be a mentor.

And everything I did, I did with one hand tied behind my back, a victim of a soul-sucking enemy, one of the many victims of gravity, the weight of the world pushing down harder and harder.

Part Two:
The Big Lie

They say depression is a chemical imbalance in the brain. It's a disease, not a lifestyle. Just like for other diseases, science has developed drugs to treat the symptoms. But depression isn't always just a chemical imbalance. Life is hard, and some of us just don't know how to process things that come our way. We use the term "broke" for those who don't have any money. But it's a term that applies to the way depression can ruin life.

Over the years, I've tried a variety of antidepressants. While some of them made me feel differently, none of them made me feel better. All of them made me feel like I was under the influence of a drug, something I don't like to feel at all. The drugs were like giving a starving man a piece of gum.

Sometimes the worst depression was triggered by life events: the disappointment and heartbreak from a romantic relationship; the death of my mom or my cats; or losing the hearing in one ear that was replaced by constant ringing as my brain apparently was trying to make up for the lack of sound by creating its own. Thanks, brain. But no matter if the pain was caused by a broken heart or broken brain or broken ear or broken spleen, it really doesn't matter. Depression has defined much of my life. The opposite of depression isn't happiness; it's not feeling anything at all or feeling everything all too much.

My dad died at the age of 92 from Alzheimer's. The disease robbed him of his personality and self that was a lifetime of hardworking kindness. I was always more similar to Mom than Dad, always shared more common interests, but as Dad slowly descended into a personal hell, it became our most common bond ever. His Alzheimer's and my depression shared a core common affliction. The diseases robbed us of who we thought we were, who we wanted to be.

When is the cure worse than the disease? When is prolonging a hopeful return to the status quo, without an actual guarantee that's even possible, worse than agreeing to a treatment that feels like spitting into an ocean with the hope the tide can be turned around?

Dr. Jordan, a middle-aged, redheaded man with round glasses and a beard, was the first psychiatrist to prescribe an antidepressant to me. He is among a long list of therapists I've spent many hours of my life with. As he was scribbling out the prescription, and finding out my love of music, he told me he was a fan of the singer Nina Simone. I had never heard of her but picked up one of her records a short time later. What an amazing voice. Her music would help me fight depression better than any drug I've ever taken.

We all are the authors of our own stories. We see the world through the lens of our own identity. We tell ourselves stories to understand the world we perceive. We make decisions, usually banal and unimportant but sometimes life-altering, based on our thoughts, feelings, and intuition.

We seemingly need to do this to move through day-to-day life. To be a functioning part of a peaceful society, we try and have a collective story that others agree with and newspapers report on. But I've always wondered if the color blue I see is the same as anyone else's perception of the same color. How do I know the blue I see is the blue you see? And does it matter because both of us agree that the color blue exists in both of our shared worlds? Or how do I know how I feel love is anywhere in the same ballpark as how anyone else feels love? Shared concepts of shared experiences do matter on an important level.

If I'm seeing something completely different from what you are seeing, if I'm feeling something different from what you are feeling, it leads to a lack of understanding each other. And that, sadly, has been a key theme of my life.

EGO DEATH

The worst part about dying was losing the meaning of my life in the process. Through my darkest moments, the thing that kept me going was I believed that I had a masterpiece inside of me waiting to be written that could change the world, or at the very least one other person. Just like the great writing I've read—F. Scott Fitzgerald's *Babylon Revisited*, J. D. Salinger's *Nine Stories*, Jon Jay Osborn's *The Associates*, Kathryn Schulz's *Lost and Found*, Liz Phair's *Horror Stories*, and Bob Dylan's *Chronicles*—had done for me.

Reading those stories changed me fundamentally to my core. And that's what I thought I was capable of doing for others. This would be my legacy, that all the depression had to mean something in the end. Delusional? Likely. Determined? Almost always. If I could write my masterpiece, it would not only make all the suffering mean something in the end, but it also might inspire others to persevere through all of life's struggles.

I had agreed to try the ketamine treatment only after my therapist assured me the treatment wouldn't be worse than the disease. I suffered that fate years back when I was hospitalized for my depression in St. Mary's Hospital in Rochester, Minnesota, part of our state's famous Mayo Clinic. I still have nightmares, and sometimes daymares, of that experience as certain things drum up memories of that two-week lockup.

I had a hard time falling asleep the night before I died. Then, in the wee hours of the morning, of July 30, 2021, my blonde cat Norma Jean woke me up by flinging herself against my chest. She missed pouncing on her littermate brother, Alias, a grey-and-black striped tabby who was sleeping quietly next to me. The next hour and a half was spent wondering if I should just get up and occasionally drifting back to sleep. I had a dream.

I was in a *St. Elsewhere* TV scene where the hospital's emergency room was being overrun by a violent gang. They weren't only after drugs; they were out for anarchy and annihilation. A doctor was holding some medicine in his hand, and one of the gang came with shears and cut off the doctor's hand. I woke up with a shudder. It didn't take me long to figure out the violence behind the dream. I just watched the testimony of the police officers who were brutalized during the January 6 attack on the U.S. Capitol and how the mob had come there with the intent to kill whatever got in their way. The officers' sobering testimony colored my whole week.

My therapist warned me that ketamine could lead me to some dark, dark places. I worried that it would lead me to somewhere violent, even though violence wasn't much a part of my actual life or past.

The pill was soft like licorice and tasted like a bitter cough drop. I remained quite conscious. I was sitting in a soft chair in a clinic underneath a blanket wearing a mask to cover my eyes and earphones playing ambient, instrumental music, with my therapist in the room with me. I didn't know quite what to expect. The doctor administering the ketamine told me to try not to swallow the pill, but let it dissolve instead. That's what I was concentrating on. Suck, don't swallow. The buzz kicked in. It was a fall-down, whiskey-drunk kinda buzz, as opposed to the white-light, spinning flash of a dose of Molly my friend Maria gave me earlier in the year.

I was caught by surprise by the first image that flashed in my head, my version of a black-and-white scene from the film, *Eternal Sunshine of the Spotless Mind,* one of my all-time favorite films but one I hadn't watched or thought much about in 20 years. I assumed it came to mind because the movie is about allowing a medical procedure to take control of your mind. My consciousness was holding on to the fact I was in a room being treated as my thoughts began slipping away from my grasp. The ambient wordless music began pulsing in my veins like blood running throughout my body. My lifelong love of music took on a deeper meaning, a significance never felt before. It was coursing through me, not only lifting me up like the familiar before, but blurring the line between the physical and spiritual world that I never was able to comprehend in the world I thought I knew.

My mind conjured up images of people and cats present and long gone, scenes from memories stuck in time. Images began to flow by with more speed, more fluidly, less within my control. It was like a psychedelic scene from Willy Wonka. I began to float, but not up. Things were rushing to my side, and the space began to get darker both in tone and in ambience. My face felt it was being stretched back as far as it could take, and finally, it wasn't there at all. I kept thinking I couldn't wait to share this with Maria, who believed the Molly she gave me would provide a moment of bliss. And then the dam broke, and I was in an entirely different universe untethered from my life, earth, and reality like a kite floating free in the wind.

I was drifting along headed into an expanding void, my individual identity dissolving away, when it suddenly dawned on me I was sold a bill of goods. I died and wasn't coming back. I was given the pill by con artists who were from beyond the walls of a world that never existed.

They took me out of my fictional life, the life story I conjured up on cosmic typewritten pages to fool myself into believing in a reality that never existed. I was angry I was tricked and never told that dying was a possibility. The thought of sharing this with Maria turned into sadness in knowing I'd never see her again and believing she, like everything else, was just a fantasy.

As the dark purple universe walls folded in on themselves, I realized I wasn't the only one gone. The whole world I thought I knew was gone and never coming back. The reality I thought existed was all a figment of, if not God's, then the great big writer in the sky's imagination. The curtain was raised, and whatever I was, whatever I was joining was the eternal reality, and the past I knew was a fictional play performed by a group of actors that never existed.

I was somewhat tethered by a familiar pattern I didn't recognize but seemed to come from my long-gone past, a brown rectangle with a white circle inside it and an orange button at the very center. It was either to my side or right in front of me. What I once knew as three-dimensional spatial distance had dissolved away, and now everything and nothing existed in the same location and time all at once. The pattern was so familiar, and I tried to remember what it was.

The word Cournoyer seemed to be the key to unlocking its meaning. The only Cournoyer I knew in the past reality was the Montreal Canadiens player Yvan Cournoyer, a hockey player I watched as a kid but hadn't thought about since I stopped being a hockey fan in the 1980s. He was a fast skater and effective scorer with a helmet-less head allowing his brown locks to flow freely as he glided down the ice.

The rush of images stopped, and I was now floating in a void, sad that my life was over and the only identity I ever knew was a mirage melting away. I was resigned that I had no control over wherever I was now going. I somehow knew that when things stopped moving, it would be the permanent end, no turning back, no going on, no remaining knowledge of my "memories" or the individual separate from the communal consciousness. Then the movement stopped, and I was in an endless dark space with odd purple shapes in front of me.

A sense of peace washed over me. I was glad to be in this new place, content that the world I once thought existed and the identity I egotistically hid behind that was so depressed, suffered so much, worried far too much about meaningless moments, was always an illusion. I felt a never-before sense of peace and belonging.

As I transferred from space to new space, each of the different dark colors and unrecognizable shapes sharing the space, I realized I both didn't care that I was dead and that my lifelong quest for some type of legacy, writing my masterpiece, carving out a career, that always mattered, never mattered. Nothing in life matters because in the end, it's all obliterated by the blink of the eye. The scope of history and the vastness of things out of sight were all just a set of a movie, and eternal consciousness obliterated that both in time and meaning. None of the day-to-day, week-to-week, year-to-year moments matter. Nothing I did or could do matters. All of the stress, depression, and worries were wasted bits of ego. Nothing in the previous consciousness ever existed. In the end it all gets folded into nothingness that is somehow everything. My lifelong feeling of being disconnected was gone. I wasn't connected to a greater whole; the greater whole was all that truly exists.

Then, as the ketamine was wearing off, I slowly came to realize I was in a room, sitting in a chair under a blanket listening to music. I was on a plane coming in for a landing. I was now in a different place having traveled a great distance. I should have been changed by this remarkable difference in space and time, but I knew what I had seen, what I had felt, was temporary. We live, we die, we know not why. Cournoyer was what Rosebud was to Charles Foster, *Citizen Kane*. A single word that couldn't define the life I lived, as if a single word could sum everything up.

The meaning of my life had been making a difference, hopefully through writing my masterpiece but later through my career in being a part of improving our democratic process. Legacy was my meaning. And the death experience showed me legacy is nothing, a dead-end road, a false narrative in the grand scheme of things. Three days later, I was back doing my job. Back to the mundane life, tasks, and stress.

But on a fundamental existential level, I was changed. Maybe that would change as the day-to-day life resumed, but how could I go on living life after accepting and welcoming my own death?

MY INFAMOUS BLUE PERIOD

During my senior year of college, I suffered not so much a nervous breakdown (my nerves were frayed, clearly not broken) but more of an amputation. Like a three-legged cat, I lost a part of me that I had always leaned on to get through life. I lost my muse and my ability to write.

I was overwhelmed with my coursework, working three jobs (one nearly full time) and yes, there were girl problems. Most of my classes my senior year were journalism or history classes and involved writing papers on a daily basis. I interned at a local weekly newspaper, the *Union Advocate*, covering the activities of the AFL-CIO unions in the Twin Cities. Shortly after I got the internship, the editor of the paper left. And when the assistant editor, who encouraged me to apply for the internship, didn't get promoted, he left too. That left me as the only newsroom 'employee' to write content until a new editor was hired.

Some of my best writing came out of this, and I proved to myself I could become a genuine reporter. I also was working as a bagger for a grocery store, a few miles from my family's house, the fancy grocery store that Mom and Dad shopped at on special occasions. My dad helped me get the job the previous summer, and it was a job I didn't want to give up because it grounded me in reality. The other employees were doing this for a living, to feed their families, to serve our customers. It was a whole other mindset from the campus life at a liberal arts college where we all believed we were destined to change the world. My third job was a work-study job in the music department, where I answered an occasional phone call and made really bad, albeit strong, coffee for the faculty.

All this was driving me to write more than ever, and my writing that had always helped me sort through feelings and thoughts and stress and the world stopped working. I was bleeding words, and soon the finite pool of words ran out. I was drained, and the lack of oil caused unbearable friction between my heart and brain.

I remember the worried look in my friends' eyes when they would visit me in my dorm room. I was barely able to move. It was like everything was in slow motion, underwater. My life slowed down because everything had become too much. Didn't anyone else see the floating fish I saw in the room? And I wondered why my friends acted as if I was the same as always. I clearly wasn't, and I knew they were being polite and not pointing to the enormous elephant in the room, but I didn't want to be this version of me, and I didn't want others to accept this diminished version of me. To make matters worse, the things I used to combat depression in the past, like music and baseball, lost their inspiring power, making me feel even worse.

There was a session with my current therapist where neither one of us spoke for the entire hour. It seemed he was testing how stubborn I was or how much I wanted to get better that I would waste the paid-for hour avoiding eye contact. The next session he suggested hospitalization for a more thorough, hour-by-hour, day-to-day evaluation of the depression that was growing worse by the second. Reluctantly, I agreed. My parents drove me down to the Mayo Clinic. Once again, hardly a word was spoken.

I was in the hospital room by myself, but they kept the light on the wall above my head on so when the nurse checked on me every hour, she/he could see me. Given insomnia was a major part of my depression, the lack of external darkness (as opposed to the internal darkness) wasn't helping.

Lloyd, the silver-haired senior wearing a white golf shirt with blue and green stripes, paced up and down the psychiatric ward hallway every day each and every hour shuffling along at such pace that I wondered where his energy came from. When did he sleep? He noticed I wore a Minnesota Twins baseball jersey and asked if I was on the team. I didn't have the heart to tell him that I couldn't hit a curveball to save my life. As a five-foot-four, 135-pound Japanese American, I didn't see anyone in Major League Baseball looking like me.

The night before my parents drove me down to St. Mary's Hospital in Rochester (a Mayo Clinic subsidiary), I watched *One Flew Over the Cuckoo's Nest*, with my coolest friend Eric Patterson. Eric told me all I needed to do was give him the word, and he'd come break me out. I appreciated the offer, but it really wasn't necessary. Because I was voluntarily checking myself in for my depression, I was free to leave at any time.

The first question the doctor, a bespectacled middle-aged woman with matted dark brown hair, assigned to my case asked me was, "Why do you think you are here?"

I thought it was an odd question because again, because this was a voluntary visit, I knew why I agreed to a hospitalization for depression. "I can't write, and because writing gives my life meaning, I don't know how to go on living." The doctor said that wasn't a rational thought and jotted something down in my chart. I shared watching *One Flew Over the Cuckoo's Nest* the night before. She asked why I did that. I said it was an example of my sense of humor. She jotted down something else in my chart.

It was a rocky start to a process I reluctantly agreed to as a last-ditch, desperate effort to try and feel better. I told my boss at the record store that I needed to take some time off because I had issues with my head. He took that to mean headaches, but I confessed it was depression. He was fully supportive of doing what I needed to do to get better.

As a reminder to myself that I wasn't going to allow myself to stay hospitalized a day longer than helpful, I only brought one cassette tape with me to listen to on my Sony Walkman. It was a bootleg of a 1986 Australian concert Bob Dylan performed with Tom Petty and the Heartbreakers. I had fallen in love with Dylan's music, writing, and style over the previous year and a half. The bootleg began with a cover song, "Lucky Old Sun," which I learned was made famous by Dizzy Gillespie.

I loved the way Bob sang the words with so much conviction. The song was about envying a heavenly body's day-to-day, hour-to-hour, second-to-second role about rolling around heaven each and every moment. I loved how the singer's words resonated with me, a recent college graduate, because it felt the cure to my depression was to enjoy the simple beautiful daily things in life as opposed to dwelling on the past or worrying about the future.

I was listening to my Walkman when a nurse asked me who I was listening to. I told her it was Bob Dylan. She said she didn't know who that was. I lost all remaining confidence that those treating me could help me. Dylan was the only effective antidepressant I found. How could anyone understand, let alone help me, without knowing Dylan's incredible music and how it changed me?

There was a Dylan song that described every feeling I felt, every thought I thought in such an insightful, articulate way, and I'm among millions who feel and think the same way. I fell in love with Bob's music in 1985 when my parents gave me his retrospective box set, *Biograph*, a wannabe summary of his career, at least 37 years premature as he continues to make great music after turning 80 years old. Two of my favorite songs are deep cuts, "Caribbean Wind," a song left off my second favorite Bob album, *Shot of Love,* that included the lyric that explained how I was feeling after my breakdown. "Caribbean Wind" has the singer singing about having a dream that couldn't be explained with a girl with lone brown eyes that he can't forget. "Senor," a song on the LP *Street Legal,* has the same singer lamenting the place/space he finds himself in is so confusing that he needs a greater power to provide some explanation all the while knowing that likely won't happen. "Street Legal" was the closest thing to a recorded nervous breakdown I've ever heard. No wonder if sworn under oath what my favorite Dylan LP is, it would be the one. My desert island pick.

The way I managed my depression in the months before the hospitalization was to try and find things I could look forward to. One of those few things was the scheduled release of a new Dylan album. There were few details about the album, but my friend, Johnny Baynes, drove with me to his past employer, Down in the Valley, to buy the new LP. The store was playing it on the speakers when we arrived. Track four was a song titled "Death Is Not the End" where Dylan sings it's okay to let go and welcome what comes next. Johnny looked over at me with a face as white as a ghost. I knew what he was thinking… Bob was giving me permission to leave this world.

One night Johnny gave me Brian Wilson's, The Beach Boys' heart and soul, just-released first solo record. It seemed a miracle that Brian, who suffered a well-documented nervous breakdown, was creating new music. I loved the record from a fellow wayward soul. My favorite song was "Melt Away" that included lyrics that expressed my feelings with a childlike precision. Positively inspirational.

I tried to explain to my doctor why losing my writing voice was so critical to me. Why was writing so important to my day-to-day existence, and why, without it, did I have little ability to function? It was a chicken-and-egg question. Was I depressed because I couldn't write? Or because I was severely depressed, was I being cut off from my ability to write?

I began keeping a journal in the ninth grade. I would go through my school day not being able to process my thoughts and feelings until I got home that night and wrote about my day. Writing connected my thoughts with my feelings. It connected the disconnected. It was almost like I couldn't feel until I wrote. I kept a daily journal from ninth grade through my first semester of my senior year in college, when the writer's block dropped me into abandoned wilderness.

I took very few sick days in K-12 school. I was constantly afraid I'd miss the day when our teacher explained what everything meant, how all the pieces fit together, the very meaning of life. I don't know if I actually missed that day, but I fear I did miss the day when they taught us how to move on from things.

Years later, I'm still writing about things that happened in my past, trying to figure out why they still linger inside and change me. I'm a dweller among doers, the eternal outsider looking in, while at the same time, my writing feels like turning my insides out. And my writing has always been about chronicling my life for all posterity because my life was so important to share. EGO. I fully bought into the belief I was going to write something that would change the world, and this would be my legacy. And that kept pushing me forward even through a near-lifelong bout of crippling depression.

My saving grace was always about my muse. I discovered the greatest feeling of all wasn't love; it was inspiration. Those who inspired me were few and far between. They made me feel connected to a greater whole, a greater existence.

My hospital stay only lasted about two weeks. One day, they brought me into a room with my doctor sitting in between two others. Behind them was a mirror that I assumed was a two-way mirror with others sitting behind the glass, observing me and writing down things on their clipboards. I was asked a series of questions from a questionnaire I completed earlier in the day. Two questions I remember are, 'Does your head sometimes feel mushy?' and, 'Do you hear voices?' I said no to the former, knowing I'm quite hardheaded. I said yes to the latter because I often followed my muse. When questioned about this, I again tried to explain to the doctors that it was all about my writing. I knew that if being interrogated was part of the cure, it was worsening the disease.

My second-to-last day in the hospital, my doctor brought me up to the roof so I could get some fresh air. The entire roof was enclosed by a metal fence, not only around us but up above as well, leaving no possibility of leaping off. I was wearing my leather coat, and a bee landed on my shoulder. My doctor didn't seem to notice. I could barely move, afraid of being stung. I told her I wanted to check out and go home. She told me she didn't think I was ready, that more evaluation would help. She also said that if I did indeed decide to check out, she recommended living in some monitored group home. She also suggested I consider electroshock therapy.

My mind flashed to the scene in *One Flew Over the Cuckoo's Nest*, where Jack Nicholson's character is given that 'treatment.' My doctor said there had been recent advances, after its initial use was seen as a barbaric treatment as so effectively written about in the actress Gene Tierney's autobiography. Tierney, a budding starlet in the 1940s and 1950s, underwent electroshock therapy. It made the rest of her life even worse.

My doctor told me the main side effect of the new, improved treatment was a loss of short-term memory. That almost appealed to me. I just needed a way to forget the past year or so after all. But I knew deep in my heart, I didn't want to mess with my memories because they had always been related to my dreams and my love of writing.

As I was checking out, Joyce, a mother who I met in group sessions, hospitalized following the birth of each of her children, wished me well. "I hope you'll be okay, David," she said. I wished the best for her as well. We all have our demons, and I hoped the love for and of her children would be enough to help her slay hers.

Years later, I read a newspaper story about Nina Evans, a college classmate of mine, who killed her baby after she was diagnosed with postpartum depression, a condition I had never heard about until reading the story. Nina killed herself in prison. Depression takes on many forms. It's an insidious disease because it knows our individual weaknesses and attacks us on a personal level.

On our drive home from St. Mary's, we stopped at a restaurant for lunch. The ride was somber; hardly anything was said. What really could be said? As we waited for our food to arrive, Mom said to me, "David, I really appreciate how during our family's most difficult times, you've always been the one to say something to make us all smile." It remains the nicest thing anyone has said about me.

IN DREAMS BEGIN RESPONSIBILITIES

My memory of my college graduation ceremony is a blur. I remember I was woken up early in the morning by the sound of bagpipes practicing before the ceremony. My college had Scottish ancestry. I should have gone to a college tied to the Swabian Jura region of present-day Germany ancestry. That's where the first flutes got played. A thousand flute players couldn't match the volume of a single bagpiper.

I got up and decided to take a final walk around campus. It rained the night before, so the grass was wet and the sidewalks pooled with puddles. I went in Old Main, where many of my classes my junior and senior year were held. I walked through the halls of the dorms I lived in. I went into the Janet Wallace Fine Art Center where for four years I worked in the music department for my work-study assignment. It was a nostalgic walk even though I long shunned nostalgia. I didn't know what was next, so looking backward gave me uncomfortable comfort. Having a degree seemed important with the options that might be in front of me, but my degree didn't guarantee a paycheck.

Hours later, the bagpipes began to play for real. I supplemented my black graduation gown with a red-and-blue Minnesota Twins hat, tassel wrapped around the bean of the cap. I brought a batting practice baseball I once grabbed that flew over the left field plexiglass of the Hubert H. Humphrey Metrodome where the Twins played. When my name was announced, I walked up the steps to the stage and handed the Macalester College president the batted ball in exchange for my diploma.

The applause from my family and friends was on par with the other graduates. Afterward, I tried to work my way through an endless sea of people, classmates congratulating me and saying goodbye, strangers I'd never seen in my life slapping me on the back, trying to find my family to get me out of this dizzying cornfield full of locusts, trying to enter the next stage to my life.

I moved into a three-bedroom apartment not that far from our college campus with three of my classmates. My friend Masashi lived in a walk-in closet, while the other three of us had small bedrooms. My days varied because of my job at Cheapo Records. The store was open from 8 a.m. to midnight, seven days a week, 365 days a year. We had three different shifts: 8 a.m. to 4:30 p.m.; noon to 8:30 p.m.; and 4 p.m. to 12:30 a.m.. Our managers were good at rotating staff through each of the shifts so no one was forced to wake up early every day to start the early shift, and no one was assigned to work until midnight every day. Cheapo had two stores directly across the street from each other on Snelling Avenue. The store on the east side of Snelling sold used records and cassette tapes. The store on the west side sold new and used compact discs and new records and cassette tapes. I'm not sure why, but I was the only employee who worked at both stores. Most employees wanted to work at the east location because you never knew what used records somebody might bring in to sell to us, records out of print and known by reputation only.

When I got my driver's license in high school, my best friend Steve Smith and I used to drive to the many Twin Cities record stores. We bought a lot of used records from Cheapo with its great prices: $3.60 for a record in fine condition; $2.90 for a record in good condition; and $2.10 for a record in fair condition. All ratings based on the depth of scratches and blemishes on the LPs. Great prices but the staff was surly, actually mocking purchasing decisions of artists deemed hacks.

That was an attractive benefit of applying to Cheapo. I didn't have to be a friendly retail clerk. The music was what mattered. I got an interview with the store's manager, Bill Seeler, a thin, tall bespectacled guy with a slight New England accent. During my interview, a classical piece played on the store's speakers. Bill, a classical music expert, asked me who composed the piece. I guessed Béla Bartók, given it was clearly a modern classical piece, and Bartók was a composer my piano teacher thought fit with my piano playing style. Bill told me that was incorrect, that it was Shostakovich, but he gave me points for being in the ballpark. He offered me the job, and I accepted.

Working at a record store was the perfect job for me, given my love of music that began with my family's record collection. Listening to music is among my first memories and at the core of who I grew up to be. As a little kid, working in a room full of vinyl, all at my fingertips, would have seemed even better than being left alone in a candy shop.

I was hired right as the music industry was transitioning from vinyl to compact discs, the latest technology that offered a pristine listening experience at the expense of holding a 12-inch record in front of you, enjoying the artwork and inner sleeve with lyrics and information. It was ideal talking music with other employees who shared the love and with customers who ranged from those knowing nothing and looking for a gift to others who taught me so much about music genres I knew little about and helped me diversify my own record collection.

I wasn't too good at the retail part of the job and interacting with customers in a cheerful way. Remembering how surly the employees at Cheapo were when I'd shop the store during college, I felt I found a compromise. However, the record store owner, a great man who was to become a mentor of sorts, named Al Brown, decided if his store was to survive, customer service had to become a focus.

We all took turns playing in-store music. I suppose the idea was to play something that a customer would like and want to buy. One day, a group of skinheads came into the store. It was my turn on the turntable. I tried to think of the most Jewish music to play, so I put on the soundtrack to *Fiddler on the Roof.* The three skinheads didn't flinch, probably just thought the store played some awful-sounding music.

I loved whenever it came to my turn to pick the in-store music. I was trying to discover new music that would add to my listening life and burgeoning record collection. One such pick was John Hiatt's recently released *Bring the Family.* I hadn't heard of Hiatt, just put the record on because it was at the front of recent returns. The cover is a closeup of his smiling face shot in black-and-white. The sparseness of the album cover appealed to me. Song after song blew me away. The soaring Ry Cooder guitar solo in "Lipstick Sunset" melted my depression. The following song, "Have a Little Faith in Me," stopped me in my tracks, and I began crying. The song's message was about finding someone who believes in you. That was all I needed to do.

Music has always been my muse, my lexicon, my salvation. Songs sing to me and uplift my spirit in a way nothing else comes close to doing. There's a great scene from the movie *Light of Day,* where Joan Jett reveals to her movie brother, Michael J. Fox, that her estrangement from their dying mother about giving birth to a son out of wedlock was painful, and the band's music was all that really mattered. I've replayed that movie scene in my mind over and over because it resonated with me in such a significant way.

If music didn't exist in this world, I wouldn't have lived as long as I have. I'm an amateur musician, taking piano and guitar lessons, and so admire the incredible talents of the musical artists that have kept me alive with their songs.

MY MUSE

Growing up, I had two recurring dreams. One was quite violent, dying young before I was 40, innocently caught in gunfire that ripped a hole in the grey felt fedora I was wearing. The other was walking on a beach, enjoying the warm sand between my toes, when a figure approached me walking with a noticeable limp toward me. She intertwined her fingers with my own, and we walked together as the soothing sound of the waves washed against the shore. When she finally spoke, it was with an accent, one I decided was Australian. This led me to want to visit Australia one day.

After I returned to the record store from my hospitalization, I noticed a new employee's name on our work schedule. Her name was Stephanie. I assumed she was hired to replace me, considering it wasn't certain I could come back. We worked a shift together, and I still don't know how she did it, but Stephanie immediately made me feel like the old me, the version who existed pre-depression, pre-hospitalization.

Much of this was certainly based on how she made me laugh and smile from the start, something no one had figured out how to do during my breakdown. She made me feel like I used to feel. She had a gentleness, calmness, and laid-back style, and she seemed to intuitively get me. When she moved away from the counter of records she was working on, she had a noticeable limp. She said she had a skiing accident the previous winter that left some pins in her knee, and a scar she was hoping vitamin-B ointments would help fade. She also shared she was contemplating an Australian trip with a male friend who asked her to go with him. Woman with a limp with an Australian connection? Woman that appeared in my dreams?

The record store had just expanded to include a VHS movie video rental section of the store. VHS movie rentals were the big new thing that our owner hoped to capitalize on. He built a little cubby hole to show kids videos while the parents shopped for records. One day, Stephanie and I sat in the cubby hole and ate lunch together. I revealed I was haunted by memories of my recent breakdown. She surprised me. "Well, we'll just have to make new memories to replace the old." I loved the "we" in her reply.

Stephanie left on her Australian adventure. I agreed to store her stuff so she'd have to contact me when she got back. She gave me a futon frame she designed and built with her dad and a basket full of clothes. She sent me a letter a week into her trip and brought back a red, orange, and brown, heart-shaped rock she found on the beach on her last day. To this day I hang onto and treasure that rock to center me on everything my life has ever meant, ever was supposed to mean, all the dreams that blur into memories.

When she got back, we spent time together. Her Australian connection inspired me to write for the first time in forever. I shared my first-ever short story with her. As we grabbed a beer, she told me she loved what I wrote and shared. She told me she was going to keep all my writing in a folder.

One night, weeks later, in a bar by her parents' house where she was living, we made, at that time, the ultimate commitment to each other. We agreed to travel the United States together. This would give me the fodder to write the great American novel. "I'm doing this if you tell me this is what you want to do too," Stephanie said. A day later, she drew out and shared a preliminary map of our trip. I was all in.

Days later, she told me it was going to have to be only a two-week trip because she was moving into an apartment with another coworker,

Dirk Scofield, an even more tortured and cynical artist than me. I worked with Dirk a few times but was devastated that Stephanie chose him over me. She was my soulmate. Dirk was just another guy looking for a girl for the short term. She was my forever partner. I wasn't sure Dirk was willing to commit to that.

Stephanie and I took that trip together, and it was the most meaningful thing I ever did. It inspired me to write my novel, my life's dream. But my novel couldn't be submitted for publication. It was a mess. Me biting off more than I could chew. Trying to do what Dylan said about one of his masterpieces, *Blood on the Tracks*, writing songs in the past and present at the same time with multiple narrators of the songs, different points of view, so the listeners could listen to words in a song or hear the song in its entirety, just like looking at parts of a painting while still appreciating the whole.

We got back to the Twin Cities on her birthday, and I didn't know if I'd ever see her again. She saw my dark side, and I knew it scared her. She saw how, at its worst, depression left me lifeless, unable to move, unable to connect, unable to speak, extremely suicidal. One of the final days of the trip was spent on the balcony of the Los Angeles apartment of Eric Patterson and his girlfriend Anna D'Andrea. Stephanie lit her Virginia Slims cigarette and said I could talk at her if I wanted as we looked down to the street scene below. I said I'd rather we talk with each other. Silence followed.

We said a painful goodbye. Stephanie asked if I wanted to celebrate her birthday dinner. I did not. I was dropping her off at an apartment that she was going to live at with Dirk. I was going home to write.

Months later, I sent the final version of my novel to Stephanie. I didn't get any response. And it killed my soul. What happened to the folder she was going to keep my writing in? I brought my novel to the copy shop near the record store where Stephanie and I met and once worked together. I allowed myself to feel proud about fulfilling my dream despite the loss of the love of my life. I wasn't sure the price I was paying was worth my dream. I decided I needed to celebrate by buying some music at the record store we worked at. Cruelest of all timing ever, I arrived at the store the exact same time as Stephanie and Dirk were leaving. Not a word was exchanged, but I knew I wasn't in a place where I could take any of this anymore.

The difference between a dream and a nightmare was the same as the size of a razor's edge. I drove uncontrollably back to my empty apartment, took out my bottle of antidepressants, poured myself a glass of whiskey, and downed it all. I didn't really think I was attempting to kill myself; I just didn't want to feel anything anymore. I wanted to drift into a coma and awaken years into the future.

My pharmacist student roommate found me, did his best to keep me conscious, and drove me to the emergency room. I don't know if they pumped my stomach. I do know they gave me something bad-tasting, maybe charcoal. They sent me on my way home the next morning, asking me questions, confirming I wouldn't do the same thing again. I came to realize it was that moment when a critical part of me died. I told myself I didn't try to kill myself, but once I crossed the line of not caring if I lived or died, part of me would never be able to feel the same ever again.

A few days later, I knew I had to talk to Stephanie. So I mustered up all my courage and called her. Her ever-soothing voice sounded shaky for the first time ever. She told me her knees shook all the way home when she saw me. She said it scared her reading my novel how much I remembered, details down to how much sugar she put in her tea. I didn't tell her what happened to me when I got home. I called just to say goodbye. I wondered if she felt relief in hearing this. What did any of this mean to her? Before she hung up, she said she felt the same about me as always, which was about the worst thing she could have said to end things.

Six years later, I was watching the movie *Demolition Man,* and the female character who looked a little like Stephanie, sounded a little like Stephanie, and had the same calming, funny personality made me do a double take. Did Stephanie become a movie actress? The actress's name was Sandra Bullock. A few months later, the movie *Speed* came to the $1.00 movie theater within walking distance of my apartment. I knew little about the movie other than it featured a flying bus. Again, the female lead reminded me so much of Stephanie. Again, I discovered it was Sandra Bullock. After that, I made it a point of going to all of Sandra's movies as soon as I could. It felt good to remember the important role Stephanie played in my life, even if it was for such a short time and even though she broke my heart.

In the weeks following the September 11, 2001 attack, I was helping process some elections documents, and I saw Stephanie's name and phone number. It seemed like the world was coming apart at the seams, and I knew what I needed to do. I worked up the courage to call Stephanie. She seemed surprised to hear my voice and figured it was related to her recently visiting Cheapo Records and selling some CDs. The store required those selling CDs to provide a driver's license. We had a short conversation catching up on things. She was a seamstress living in Duluth. I was sad to hear when she said music didn't mean as much to her as it did when we were friends.

As we were ending the call, I asked if anyone ever told her she reminded them of Sandra Bullock. "Only a hundred times a day," she said. "The guy at the liquor store today told me that…"

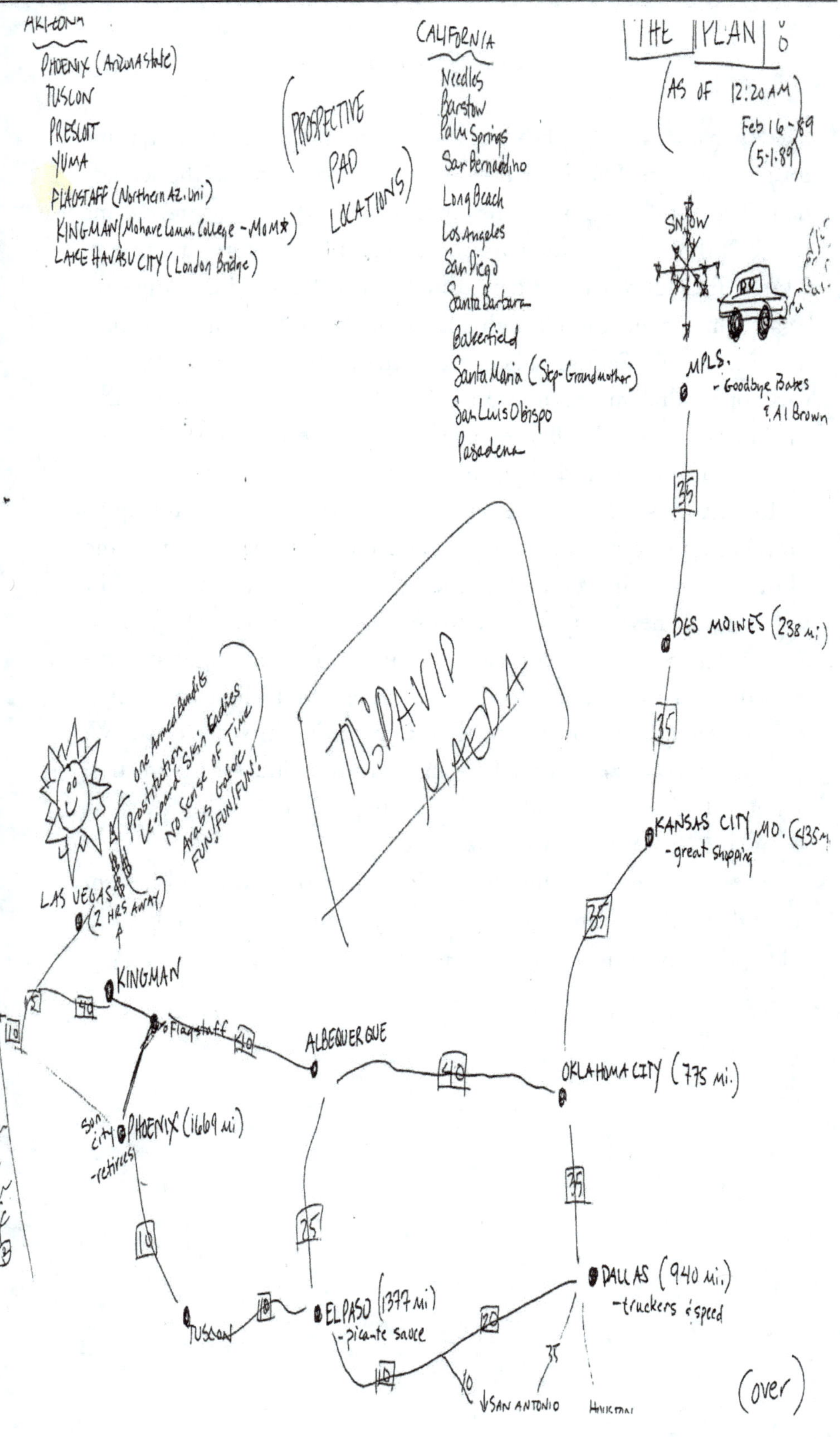
ARIZONA
PHOENIX (Arizona State)
TUSCON
PRESCOTT
YUMA
FLAGSTAFF (Northern Az. Uni)
KINGMAN (Mohave Comm. College - MOM*)
LAKE HAVASU CITY (London Bridge)

(PROSPECTIVE PAD LOCATIONS)

CALIFORNIA
Needles
Barstow
Palm Springs
San Bernardino
Long Beach
Los Angeles
San Diego
Santa Barbara
Bakersfield
Santa Maria (Step-Grandmother)
San Luis Obispo
Pasadena

THE PLAN
(AS OF 12:20 AM)
Feb 16 - 89
(5-1-89)

SNOW

MPLS.
- Goodbye Bates
& Al Brown

25

DES MOINES (238 mi)

35

KANSAS CITY, MO. (435 mi)
- great shopping

35

TO DAVID MAEDA

One Armed Bandits
Prostitution
Leopard Skin Ladies
No Sense of Time
Arabs Galore
FUN! FUN! FUN!

LAS VEGAS
(2 HRS AWAY)

KINGMAN

To Flagstaff

40

ALBEQUERGUE

40

OKLAHOMA CITY (775 mi.)

35

San
City PHOENIX (1669 mi)
-retirees

10

25

35

DALLAS (940 mi.)
-truckers & speed

10

TUSCAN

10

EL PASO (1377 mi)
-picante sauce

20

10

10

SAN ANTONIO   HOUSTON

(over)

BLESS THE LORD

I was waiting for my friend Sam to pick me up in downtown San Diego. I hadn't seen Sam in over a decade, and I was a bit jittery as I enjoyed the sunny Southern California evening sky. Sam had recommended that I stay in the downtown La Pensione hotel in Little Italy. After checking in, I was glad she did. My room had a tiny balcony overlooking the many independent restaurants, boutiques, and businesses in the vicinity. The smell of freshly brewed Italian coffee and fresh-baked bread filled my nostrils.

I was downstairs, standing right outside the lobby people-watching, when it occurred to me that I didn't know what kind of car Sam was driving. Not only that, but I hadn't seen her in quite some time, so I wasn't even sure exactly what she would look like these days. I found myself peeping into the windows of all passing cars and trucks. I thought to myself that I could probably eliminate pickup trucks because that type of vehicle simply wasn't Sam. When she lived in Minnesota, she drove a grey convertible Mazda MR-2.

When I called her a couple of weeks earlier, she seemed excited that I was coming out. She had to cut our conversation short, since she was off to ballet class. It didn't surprise me one bit that she was taking ballet—it just seemed like something the Sam I knew would dive into. Just as I was getting lost in my thoughts, a Honda Civic pulled up slowly through the intersection. Inside was the smile that I knew so well. I opened the door, and she said she recognized me because I was wearing a hat, a trademark of mine back in the days 15 years ago when Sam and I worked for the Secretary of State.

Back then, my job wasn't much of a job, so I ended up taking some vacation time and taking a trip to the East Coast, thinking I might never come back. During my time off, the office hired a temporary employee, Samantha Karen James, to be our front desk person, taking over for a crusty staff legend, Sandy, who underwent surgery on her wrists for carpal tunnel. Since I had been out when Sam started, I walked by her day after day without saying a word. It was a mixture of my depression and lifelong antisocial nature, or clumsy social skills, especially with attractive members of the opposite sex.

A few weeks later on my way out of the office at the end of the day, Sam finally spoke up and asked if she could walk out with me. She asked why I didn't like her. I didn't know what to say. I was too screwed up, dealing with too many things. I just needed to keep my head down and work as hard as I could with no lasting ramifications other than taking whatever small step forward I could. I told her it wasn't that I didn't like her; I was just going through some difficult things. We began to take our lunches and breaks together. She joined our softball team and told me she loved watching how I ran. A speedy yet fluid running style that I learned from my all-time favorite Minnesota Twin, Rod Carew. Years later, another teammate told me the same thing. I ran with such joy contrasting with what was going on inside of me.

One day, after a nothing day at work, we were stuck in rush hour traffic, driving out to our softball game on I-94, one of our state's busiest freeways. Sam said to me, "Someday, we'll be having dinner at a fancy restaurant, you in your suit and me in my fancy dress, and we'll look back at these days and laugh at how far we've come." At this point I was grasping at straws, just so tired of losing everything important to me, so I almost asked Sam to sign some sort of a contract binding her to her vision because I was glad she could foresee a future with me included.

We soon stopped spending time together. Sam believed my depression was often based on feeling sorry for myself. She didn't want any part of that. Sam was a shooting star, and I was stuck in the mud. I could either pull myself out or let it be quicksand instead and sink me forever. She told me she had endured so much in her life; she had no time to get back into the muck. She believed I was using depression as an excuse for taking a menial job and not using my skills in a more meaningful way. She was working a temporary job that was a holding place for a greater career. She felt I was giving into my depression because it was easier than applying for career jobs like she was doing. My depression was self-imposed, like being in a prison cell with the door unlocked. All I had to do was have the courage to move forward rather than stew on the familiar.

Those living in the Twin Cities during a particular spooky Halloween morning in 1991 experienced a record-breaking snowfall. By the end of the weekend, we were buried under 30 inches of snow. I was awoken that morning by my ringing phone. BRRRRRing! Given the early hour, I sensed who was on the other end even before I picked it up. Indeed, the small voice on the other end belonged to Sam, who, despite the quiet tone she used to greet me with this morning, was assuredly not timid.

I carefully listened to Sam's voice, more to the tone than the words—I loved the melody of her voice—and soon found myself glancing past my cat, Mr. Max, out the window of a tiny efficiency to the pure white swirling snow that blanketed everything within sight. Even though I knew who was calling, I was still surprised that it was Sam's voice on the phone, seeing we hadn't spoken in weeks since hitting a snag in our relationship. Our silence had rang throughout the office with our office colleagues gossiping about our relationship. Now to hear her voice again, trying to be kind, reaching out, seemed as surreal and out of place as the coat of snow that hid everything outside to such an extent that even the ever-lucid Mr. Max looked concerned.

"I can't get my car out of the garage," Sam said, referring to the foot of snow that had fallen overnight. "Can you give me a ride?" To pick her up, I had to go in the opposite direction from work. I felt I owed her nothing, being angry about some hurtful words spoken weeks ago, and knew she was disappointed in me for all the usual reasons. She thought I should be doing more important work.

"Sure, I'll be there in 20 minutes," I said without hesitation.

The drive down the road to her apartment was slick and treacherous. I knew if I stopped moving, I'd get stuck, an apt metaphor for my depression. I saw others stranded by the side of the road, their vehicles facing in odd directions. Sam and I made it to work a few minutes late. In an office of around 100 people, we were two of five that had braved the conditions and showed up. The day passed by in a blur as the snow continued to fall in a record amount. The drive home was slightly less hazardous but still rather slow as the plows tried to keep up with the constantly falling snow. The silence in my robin-blue Honda Accord seemed equal parts trying to concentrate on the road conditions and trying to figure out our relationship conditions.

The ride was tense and silent except for when Sam, out of nowhere, quietly said, "Bless the Lord." We continued on until we finally arrived at her home. She gathered up her stuff and wrapped her scarf more tightly around her neck. I sensed I had to say something, that our latest adventure couldn't end in silence.

"Say," I said. "Why did you bless the Lord?" She looked at me with her twinkling eyes, puzzled. "Back there, you said, 'bless the Lord.'"

Sam let out a giggle when she finally figured out what I was talking about. "I didn't say 'bless the Lord,'" she said. "I said, 'bus alert.' I was warning you about that bus pulling out into traffic."

Two days later, I made the three-mile drive from my efficiency to the record store, where I was scheduled to work a shift. The city had plowed the streets, but there wasn't enough space to push the snow. People had a difficult time digging their cars parked along the streets out to move, not to mention there was nowhere to move the cars to. The drive was difficult. After my shift was finished, I decided to leave my car in the plowed record store parking lot and walk home. It wasn't the brightest decision of my life. Many of the sidewalks remained unshoveled, so much of my walk was through thigh-high snow. I got about halfway home when I thought I might not actually be capable of finishing the walk home. But I was just as far away from my parked car so there was no turning back. I somehow made it home, my feet burning with blisters.

When I went back to work Monday at the Secretary of State, I told Anita, my favorite coworker, about my adventure. The next day she gave me some kids' bandages that her five-year-old daughter wanted me to have. The act of human kindness melted my heart (and depression), if only for a moment.

Sam left town shortly after for much better things. We were able to get together in Washington DC in 1994 when she was interning at the White House (pre-Monica Lewinsky), and it was nice catching up after a few years. We were having coffee sitting in a shop with a window facing the street. A man sat down on the plants in front of the shop. Sam chastised the man's behavior for damaging the plants. I was more worried about a human being who might be struggling with mental health issues.

10 years later in San Diego, after even more time since we last saw each other, was equally as wonderful. Sam proved to be wrong with her past vision in one aspect. We were in casual, not fancy, clothes as we stood out on the deck of The Fish Market, a fine San Diego seafood restaurant, waiting for a table and overlooking the sunset over the ocean. We had sushi, and I loved gazing into her ever-twinkling eyes again. She was worried she was using her chopsticks incorrectly and had me show her the way that I thought was right. I told her you hold the bottom one just like you hold a pencil and you don't let it

move: the top stick does the moving as your thumb and forefinger act as a fulcrum.

Our conversation was enlightening. We both had changed over the years, both had been through a lot, yet as I listened to her and tried to share some things, it was the same Sam I grew so fond of all those years ago. If ours was to be a friendship where we only see each other once every 10 years, so be it. She'll always remain someone I have a great deal of affection and admiration for.

Sam was a city planner in San Diego after earning her master's degree from the University of North Carolina. She proudly gave me a tour of the city's renovated downtown. Seemingly, the city had one major development project after another. Its vibrancy was eye opening. I was visiting in 2005, when San Diego had around 27,000 people living downtown in apartments and condos (which average $480,000 in price), and they expected that by the year 2030, there would be over 89,000 people living downtown.

But equally impressive to me was Sam's own home improvement project. She had bought a rundown four-unit housing complex and had poured her sweat and love into whipping it into something quite beautiful. We talked about haunted houses. One of the four units to her personal complex was haunted, according to two different tenants. It was great catching up with her, and it melted my heart to see how happy she was when she counted the quarters from the washing machine and dryer she had put in for her tenants and came up with $18 in one week. It was also great meeting her cat Moussaka.

Sam had left me with the lasting impression of my time in San Diego. As we were looking at various new construction projects, she told me the ones she liked and the ones she didn't like. "It's all about windows," she said. It was something I might have said for altogether different reasons. She wasn't talking about their transparency or reflective qualities, but rather their appearance.

NO DIRECTION HOME

I believed that once my depression was cured, all the time I lost trying to get better would be returned to me. Depression was a temporary hurdle. The reward for recovery would be gaining back everything I had lost. That was the big lie. For years I took prescribed antidepressants. I didn't like how they left me feeling.

I took my first antidepressant in 1987, right when the Minnesota Twins were making their run to winning their first World Series. During their first playoff series in 17 years, I was knocked out by the drug I was taking. I tried to stay awake and watch the games in my room but just couldn't. And couldn't feel any excitement about the team I grew up loving finally finding some success.

I have a vague memory of attending my first World Series game at the Hubert H. Humphrey Metrodome with Eric and Anna. I high-fived Anna after a Twins home run. The memory is foggy, but is one that I want to remember. A few years ago, Anna knit me a lime-green scarf that became a key part of my professional wardrobe.

My dad advised me to buy a house and build up equity instead of throwing money away on rent. I was far enough in my government career and stable enough with my finances that I took his advice to heart and reached out to a realtor, Don Harrison. I was looking for a townhouse in the Grand and Summit Avenue area where I went to college in St. Paul, with a porch and a fireplace. He worked with me, and I got a mortgage company to approve a loan, in the $90,000 range.

We visited many properties, and none of them felt at all like home. Most lacked one of the criteria I listed. I began to feel like Harrison was growing frustrated by how many properties he was showing me only for me to say no.

The last place we visited was within walking distance of the apartment I was living in, right on the St. Paul/Roseville border. It wasn't in the Grand/Summit Avenues neighborhood, but it was in an area of the cities I clearly was fine living in. The area was close to both downtown St. Paul and downtown Minneapolis. The price was within my approved loan amount. The house was owned by a widow whose husband had recently died. The two of them were the original owners of the one-and-a-half story, two-bedroom, one-bathroom house, with an attic and basement that could be renovated into living space. After some negotiation, we agreed upon an $89,000 price that, within a few years after the housing bubble in the late 1990s and early 2000s, would escalate to something close to twice that amount.

I know Mom and Dad took my home buying as a sign of me overcoming my depression. Ever since my hospitalization, we began going out to dinner over the weekends. Mom told me how much it meant that we were having adult conversations. I was given access to the house prior to closing to begin some work, mostly pulling out the carpet and carpet staples, that covered a hardwood floor that I was going to have sanded. Mom joined me in removing the carpet staples, and there was an unspoken feeling in the air that this was a big step forward for me as I tried to envision building a true permanent home separate from the home I grew up in.

When my mom and dad were looking to buy their first house, they were rejected, despite otherwise being qualified, because they were Japanese American. There are covenants in our country prohibiting housing purchases for nonwhites. I don't know a whole lot about those covenants that in this day aren't legally enforceable, but I don't know if this is what Mom and Dad ran into in trying to find a home or if it was just some unwritten policy preventing them from moving into a neighborhood. I don't know which is worse.

I thought I was doing okay in the beginning of my academic career until my kindergarten classmate Billy Jefferson said I had a yellow face. At first, I thought he might be referring to some leftover makeup on my face from my brother and I messing around with our sisters' makeup. Mom later told me it was a racial slur against Asians. There was one other Asian American in my class, Sally Murakami, another Japanese American, so all our classmates assumed the two of us would become a couple and marry each other. I liked Sally; we're friends to this day. I remember spelling "Mississippi" in kindergarten to her mother trying to impress mother and daughter with my precocious intellect, but I bristled at others assuming our natural coupling.

Over the following years, I was to learn more about my own family's history and how my dad's family was among the 120,000 Japanese Americans sent to concentration camps after the Japanese attack on Pearl Harbor. Dad's family was relocated to Minidoka, Idaho. Dad rarely shared much about how it felt to have his own government imprison him because of a question of loyalty based solely on his race. Most of those 120,000 Japanese Americans were U.S. citizens. All looked to America as a country to improve their chances of living an improved life. I'm not sure how any of this filtered down into my lifelong feeling of being different, being disconnected from everyone else in the room, perpetually feeling like the other without a sense of belonging.

Dad had a lifelong love of cars. The most painful thing about living behind the camp's barbed wire, faced with the elevated towers of armed U.S. military, was that prior to being incarcerated, he had just bought his first car that he had to give to a white friend. The friend, trying to do a good thing, visited Dad but parked Dad's car on the other side of the barbed wire fence. Seeing his car beyond his reach made Dad sad. And maybe even mad. In the late 1980s, the United States

Government issued an apology to the Japanese Americans who were incarcerated and lost their freedoms during World War II. Along with the apology, the government authorized $20,000 checks to those who suffered along with my dad and his family. I'm not sure Dad made a deliberate decision to send a middle finger to the government. I never heard him question, but he used that restitution check to buy a brand-new, shiny, maroon Honda Accord, absolutely the best car of his life.

I don't know how or if trauma is passed down between generations. I saw early on how my classmates, like Billy Jefferson, saw me as different given the difference in our race. And no kid wants to be seen as different when trying to fit in, finding one's place among those who could become friends, or at least not be picked on for something out of your control.

As an Asian American growing up in an almost all-white community, the feeling of my race made me feel separate in subtle ways. I was automatically different from my classmates, but at the same time I was one of the most popular kids in our class, even voted 'Citizen of the Year,' a glorified popularity contest, by my sixth-grade classmates.

But as we moved into finding a girlfriend or a boyfriend, I never felt like any of the girls I liked would want to be my girlfriend. Being different made me uncomfortable, and a cliché of being Asian is being invisible. Race in our country is usually defined in terms of black and white. So when I felt invisible, I decided I'd use being Asian to my advantage. It freed me to not play the popularity game. I could be me because I stood apart from every group I was in. This dichotomy of being invisible and being highly visible is something that continues to define and confound me throughout my life.

During the first few weeks of my freshman year of college, a group of Japanese students approached me in the dining room, smiles beaming, welcoming me as one of them. Once they found out I wasn't Japanese, but instead I was Japanese American, the smiles on their faces faded away. They never spoke to me again.

I read a 1984 *Playboy* interview with Paul Simon where he confessed his theory about his depression. That he'd come to believe his small physical stature made him inferior to others, but his intellect and songwriting ability made him mentally superior to others. It seemed vain, so I didn't want to admit Simon's theory somehow resonated with me. My small stature and Japanese face left me feeling inferior to my peers. But my observational skills, my listening ability, and my skill at writing balanced things out. My race was my weakness; my inner voice separated me from others in a superior way.

During my trip to Japan in 1997, there was a late afternoon when I was standing in a subway station in downtown Tokyo. There was a sea of people rushing through the platform. Normally, I'd be anxious about being in such a huge crowd of people. But I felt strangely calm. And it dawned on me why. For the first time in my life, I looked like everyone else around me. I was average height, if not a bit taller, than many of the men. I could tell I was better-looking than that guy and not as good-looking as this other guy. I hadn't realized how being Asian in a white community weighed down on me throughout my life in ways I didn't consciously think about. There were a couple of exceptions.

In 1993, I got my first promotion on my way up the government ladder. It came when our office, The Secretary of State, decided to 'professionalize' one of the duties many of us shared and loathed. Our business services operation was responsible for accepting business filings. There was an annual registration required from corporations. New businesses were often unsure of what to call themselves, as they were unaware of what names were already taken. They believed that the name of their company would be vital to their success.

The office received over 600 phone calls a day with those with questions about their filing documents with our office. In order to answer those phone calls, all clerical staff were scheduled to spend time on the corporate phones for an hour or two a day. It was tedious and stressful at the same time. None of us answering the phones could answer legal questions about the filings. There was a standard script all of us cited about the filing of business names: "That appears to be available, but a final decision won't be made until you file." Dealing with vague answers to legal questions was my hour-to-hour, day-to-day existence work life. My personal existence was all about overcoming my depression and moving on.

Our office decided the best way to answer the corporate phones wasn't splitting that dreaded duty among many but hiring three to spend all day on the phones. Because it was a promotion, I applied, interviewed, and was hired to be one of the three to take on this duty. The three of us were given shared space in an old office with Denise and Mary Jo given windows and me facing a wall. Given this focused time on the phones, the three of us got one-offs, people not knowing what to file or what we had on file. But there were regular calls from accountants, law firms, and others that resulted in talking with the same people every day. There was an office rule that we could only answer questions about three businesses per phone call. If the caller had more, they had to call back. This led to frustration about the amount of wait time each call required.

Businesses in Minnesota had to finalize documents establishing themselves in our records. Minnesota corporations also had to file an annual registration to keep their data up to date. 'Foreign' corporations, those incorporated outside of Minnesota, many of them from Delaware, the state that had the friendliest corporate tax environment at the time, also had an annual registration requirement. These corporations had to file with us if they were doing business in Minnesota. The difference between Minnesota corporate annual registrations and 'foreign' corporation annual registrations was the latter required an agent in Minnesota to accept service of process from someone suing the corporation. There wasn't the same requirement for Minnesota corporations. One of the main reasons people formed a corporation was to personally protect themselves and their assets from litigation.

The entity sued is the corporation, not the people that formed the business. Minnesota corporations sometimes listed a contact person on their documents, but it wasn't required. Foreign corporations listed another business as their agent, many of them listing CT Corporation that had a Minneapolis office as their agent for legal purposes.

Answering 250-300 phone calls a day from people who were on hold and whose questions I often couldn't fully answer was stressful. The saving grace was there were voices I recognized and heard from nearly every day, so there was a rapport that was built that combined business with personal chat. We all were doing our best to do our jobs, but there was a natural connection available being able to talk with, and provide the information being asked for, available to those regularly calling our office. One person I answered most every day was a woman calling from CT Corporation. It took many calls before Janice Wall and I had anything other than an informational conversation, only for her to call back a few minutes later to address our office's "only three business inquisitions per call" policy. I found myself hoping to be the one among the three of us in our office answering Janice's calls.

One day, I took the huge step of revealing something personal about myself instead of answering Janice's questions directly. Janice responded. Our next several calls took on another meaning. We were talking with each other not in this limited realm of conversation we did in the past but as actual people. She crossed over easily into this new realm. I stumbled across another broken person wanting to find an authentic connection.

We talked for weeks about meeting each other in person. I knew it was risky meeting in person, seeing if our inner, intimate attraction and sharing would continue our love. Janice suffered a traumatic head injury that led to her not knowing what to understand from her past and present. She said I reminded her of a boyfriend that she was trying to remember, but her memories about him were foggy. I shared my depression guiding where I was going. It was a weird, shared connection.

Both of us were broken, looking for our soulmate, knowing that the other person was broken and needed to be fixed. Our business calls morphed into something more intimate. We called each other after work hours and bravely shared our true selves, and all the brokenness between us forged such a common bond.

We agreed to meet on the steps of the State Capitol. We wanted to know what the other looked like. Before we met, Janice said she thought I resembled Jerry Seinfeld. I hadn't told her I was Asian. She told me she had light brown hair, thin, with a fair complexion. The day and time arrived for our life-changing meeting. When she saw me, her face went white. We were supposed to go to a nearby restaurant for lunch, but it was immediately apparent she didn't want to do that. So we went our separate ways.

I was devastated. All we revealed about our inner selves, our life stories, and she rejected me because of how I looked. And most likely because I had not revealed I was Japanese American. I drove back to my apartment where my cat Max was surprised to see me at the unusual work hour. I lay down on the living room carpet, unable to cry, losing the ability to move. Max knew something was wrong, and he hopped onto my back and began strolling back and forth, giving a comforting massage.

In the following days, I consoled myself knowing that Janice had accepted me for who I was inside, that revealing my inner self caused her to fall in love with me. This was a first. At the same time, I knew my looks, different from the majority of who I might be attracted to, was different. And I tried to believe my inner beauty would one day connect with someone who could accept my outward appearance.

In 1988, a few years before Janice Wall, I was working at the record store with our new employee who was a Korean American adoptee named Leah. I promptly dubbed her the Lovely Leah. Leah had an elegant physical beauty, slight in stature but with an angular face that was both kind and mesmerizing. She laughed easily. She clearly was intelligent and articulate, and she loved modern jazz, something I knew little about. We went out a few times, and she even met my family at my niece Megan's birthday party.

This was the first time I dated a woman who looked like me, and it inspired uniquely and oddly familiar feelings. I suspected Leah had the ability to understand me on some type of level others couldn't. But that was unfair because our backgrounds were entirely different, no matter how much we looked similar to each other. I was born and grew up in a suburban Twin Cities community. She was born in Korea, adopted by a white couple with a white brother in another Twin Cities suburban community, much more conservative. The first time I met Leah's mom was while her mom was checking out at our record store's register. I told Leah's mom her daughter was a favorite of mine. Leah's mom responded, "That's good because she isn't one of ours…" I hoped she was joking, but Leah later lamented she didn't have a mapmaker, one who could help her figure out a way forward.

On our last date, Leah said she didn't want to see me anymore because I was too inscrutable. I told her I'd probably be offended if I knew what the word meant. When I got home, I looked it up in the dictionary. Too hard to read, too hard to understand. Her diagnosis was spot-on. It made me realize she too wanted to connect with our Asian bond, but the mask I learned to wear to hide my true self, the common Asian mask, made us incompatible. I didn't understand this until many years later.

TURNING JAPANESE

In 1998, Al Brown, the owner of Cheapo Records, decided he wanted to open a store in Japan. He lived there for a time as a kid while his dad was in the Army. Al found some Japanese businessmen to partner with on the project and asked me if I was interested in flying to Japan with him to scout potential locations. We were going to visit Tokyo and Osaka.

Flying from the Twin Cities to Tokyo was a 15-hour flight. It was odd to go to sleep one morning, only to wake up later the same day to find yourself in a very different world. I reminded myself the next time Max the Cat whined and moaned as I loaded him up in the car, I would remember what it was like to be trapped inside a metal tube with no way to control your destination.

What made the flight somewhat bearable was listening to the Northwest Airlines entertainment channels through my headsets. A one-hour Beach Boys' special played over and over for nine hours. By the time we were over the Sea of Japan, I swore if I heard "Help Me Rhonda" one more time, I was going to jump out of the plane. But damn if those *Pet Sounds* songs didn't hold up even after the ninetieth listen. I discovered too late (the last hour of the flight) that another channel played a Styx reunion special. The listening experiences erased any doubt which culture had warped and shaped my mind.

The first sign we saw as we got off the plane was one telling anyone who felt "abnormal" to go to the quarantine area. It was my first mental test. I always feel a bit abnormal, but did the Japanese officials need to know that? Going through customs, I was impressed that the security officials called me "Maeda-San" with politeness and respect. Al spoke some Japanese. All I could do was count to 10 and say hello, goodbye, and good night. So the first thing I learned was that the communication gap was going to be challenging.

I looked Japanese but didn't speak the language. The white guy I was with spoke some Japanese. I was not his interpreter. So I didn't feel as if I could say much. When I did speak, people looked at me with a stunned, confused look in their eyes. When they spoke, the meaning of their conversations baffled me. Everything was rather odd and a mystery. In other words, it was just like home.

Our first couple of days in Tokyo, we stayed with the family of one of the businessmen Al was working with. It was a weekend, and the father cooked breakfast while listening to Hank Williams. My dad loved Hank Williams, so the familiar smell of bacon and eggs along with the pleading songs of Hank felt like I was right at home even though I wasn't at home, even though this was a part of the home of my heart.

We hadn't celebrated our Japanese heritage much growing up, other than some meals primarily served on New Year's Eve and Day. My grandparents didn't speak English, so even though they came over for dinner on the weekends and we visited them at their house regularly, I hardly got to know them. Yet here I was in Japan, and I thought my grandparents would be happy for my exploring my roots, and the place they came from before I was born.

Before I left for Japan, I had tried to sharpen the focus of the picture of what it would all be like in my mind's eye. That picture was shaped by the portraits that used to hang in my grandparents' house in St. Paul—paintings of Mt. Fuji, photographs of their trips to Japan. After arriving in Osaka and taking a train from the airport into town, those pictures were about as close as the ones recently returned from Mars. A quick glance of Osaka revealed a city that looked like any big American city: tall buildings, slightly aged, with apartments and houses scattered about. In a way, it sort of reminded me of Philadelphia—the age of the architecture and the layout of the city as viewed from an above-ground train. But unlike Philadelphia, the city didn't seem worn out but was rather well kept. Osaka definitely had its own rhythm, the narrow streets where cars zipped through past hordes of pedestrians and bicyclists. Yet somehow there was a comforting order to the chaos.

At night in Tokyo, the electric signs flashed into my eyes as life buzzed around me. There was no honking of horns from impatient drivers or ornery looks from passing strangers. The retail, hotel, and restaurant help was extremely polite, bowing as we entered their establishments. The Kentucky Fried Chicken sign suggested not all was foreign and that we hadn't landed on Mars after all (although I'm sure when the Mars landscape is developed, a KFC will do quite well there as well).

I learned Japan is not a good place to go for a guy who does not own a good pair of socks. I'm the type of fellow who rarely gets rid of stockings, even if the elastic is worn and torn and the holes outnumber the remaining material. I believe worn-out socks are one of the prices you must pay for living in an imperfect society. But in Japan, where one often removes one's shoes as you enter homes or restaurants, wearing worn-out socks can be a bit embarrassing. Also, squatting at meals was a bit hard on the knees.

But the food was exquisite. I've never eaten as much in my entire life. One thing I learned to do was eat quickly. The Japanese don't dawdle when it comes to food. And they eat large quantities (I felt I was on some sort of sumo wrestler's diet). We had sushi, udon, tempura, and sashimi. We ate at a restaurant where there was a charcoal grill built in the table, and we cooked our marinated beef on the grill.

Mom's biggest weakness was being a smoker. She quit sometime when I was in junior or senior high, partly because she wanted new carpeting in our house and Dad wouldn't agree to it until she quit smoking. I found out that the Japanese loved smoking. Want to quit smoking without the difficult side effects? Go to the Tokyo Wendy's, step into the second-floor area, and take a deep breath. Within minutes, you'll have enough nicotine in your system to last you for nine lives. These people could seriously smoke. And they also enjoyed an adult beverage whenever possible. They probably drink more beer than your average Green Bay Packers fan.

One nice feeling was, for the first time in my life, I didn't feel noticeably short. Not that I was tall among the Japanese people but I was about average size, until we got to downtown Tokyo, where all of a sudden, the people (especially the women) seemed a bit taller than other Japanese. One look at their footwear suggested why that was—huge platform shoes.

We were told by our potential business partners that for the Japanese, the name of a business or product wasn't important as far as the meaning of the words. Rather, it's the sound that the Japanese take into account. Thus we saw some oddities like a drink called Pocari Sweat. Nothing quite quenches a thirst like a jug of sweat. And we also saw a shopping bag with the name Marginal Glamour. One wouldn't want excellent glamour when spending hard-earned cash; mediocre glamour is okay.

A Shinto temple we saw had a shrine where drivers drove up to an area where their cars were blessed for good luck and low accident claims by shaking a broom-looking object in their direction. Unfortunately, we witnessed a 10-car fender bender while leaving the temple (not really).

Like many business meetings I have participated in, the meetings we attended were a bit perplexing. Language differences made communication difficult. I committed a faux pas by forgetting to bring along my business cards, which are used during introductions as a polite way to help people put names to faces.

One of the meetings we attended was held at a conference table in the company's showroom. The table was eye-shaped, illuminated by a bright light, yet it wasn't harsh on the eyes. It felt like sitting at one of those TV political roundtable discussions. With my camera case strapped around my neck like a tricorder, it also felt a bit like I was a member of a *Star Trek* landing party meeting with some planet's dignitaries. Words flowed, but little was understood. Still, it was amazing how much can be communicated by a smile or a meeting of eyes. For those who do not speak, there still is hope that there are others who will be able to understand.

I watched several baseball games on my hotel TV at night. It almost made me feel a hint of homesickness. Differences? What's the deal with the trumpets that constantly blare throughout the game playing a fight song during the action? What is the deal with the plastic clap devices (and if you've ever used a plastic clap device you know just how painful that can be) that are given to the crowd to bang and make noise?

I felt the earth move in Tokyo. Fortunately, it was just an earthquake. And no one even panicked, which is a good thing with the volume of the population. One thing the country has is lots of people. So many people where anyone who might go in with an inflated value of their own self-importance can be quickly humbled. Being in the middle of the Tokyo subway system during a busy time, as streams of people swarm around you from every direction, you quickly see how one individual's life is insignificant in the grand scheme of things. At the same time, the opportunity to visit foreign worlds and see the possibilities that exist was eye-opening and awe-inspiring.

My most searing memory of Japan came one night when we hopped onto a subway in downtown Tokyo. There was a young woman seated across from me. She was sobbing, and no one seemed to notice. I wanted to reach out but knew I had nothing to offer to her. Maybe she broke up with a significant other? Maybe a family member died? Maybe a pet died? Maybe she lost her job? Maybe she lost her way? I still wonder to this day what caused her so much pain.

When I got home, the first thing I noticed was someone left a welcome mat on my front steps. I emailed everyone I thought might have given me the gift, but no one admitted to it. Welcome home, such a significant reminder of what I just experienced, part home, part outer space, esoteric part of me that I was only starting to grapple with.

THE SOUND OF SILENCE

I began curling in 2005, about a year before it took off as one of the Winter Olympics' most talked-about competitions. My friend Lisa asked if I was interested in joining a team she was starting up. I was game. We play at The St. Paul Curling Club, which is now 120 years old. There's a lot of tradition to the sport, and much of it is amplified by the memorabilia and banners on the walls of the club that has eight sheets, a downstairs viewing area, and an upstairs restaurant where the winning team buys the losing team beer, a sign of good sportsmanship.

A team is comprised of four players, each responsible for delivering two rocks down the ice. The skip is the one who stands at the other end of the ice, placing their broom on the ice where they want the player to aim the stone. Because the player puts a slight turn on the stone's handle before letting go, and because the ice is pebbled, the stone is going to curl to its end spot. The skip needs to read the ice to know where to place the broom in order to have the stone end up curling to the proper ending spot. The two players not delivering the stone sweep the ice, helping it maintain the proper speed and line. Sweeping makes the rock go farther and curl less.

I played every winter on Sunday nights, hardly improving after year two or three because the only ice time I got was when we played our matches. Still, I enjoyed learning a new sport. The few times I made a perfectly delivered stone kept me coming back for more.

Five or six years into playing, I threw a stone that I knew would end up far short of its mark. So I followed the sweepers down the ice, hoping to get in front of the stone to help with sweeping. Unfortunately, I slipped and ended up hitting my head hard on the ice. I saw birdies. My teammates asked if I was okay. I didn't know. My head hurt badly, but I seemed steady on my feet, and I was more embarrassed than hurt. After we finished our match, I thought about going to the emergency room but figured there was little that could be done even if I had a concussion.

Within the next few days, I woke up to a loud ringing in my ear. I made an appointment with my doctor. He didn't see anything physically wrong and jokingly let me know that there were support groups for those that suffer from ringing in the ears. My doctor referred me to an ear specialist. I was given hearing tests, and they revealed I lost a significant amount of hearing in my left ear, the side of the head I slammed on the ice.

The ringing was my brain trying to make up for the lack of hearing in one of my ears. I never again would know the sound of silence. Worse, one of the skills that elevated me from others was my listening ability. Several told me over the years that I was a really good listener. The best way for me to learn was to keep my mouth shut and pay attention to the words of others.

The ear specialist recommended getting a steroid shot to my eardrum as a last-ditch effort to right the ring. The shot was extremely painful, like a bee sting to my eardrum. When I was a kid, a mosquito got into my ear, and I could hear it was still alive because of its buzzing. Mom eventually flushed the mosquito out, an eerie foreboding warning of what was to come many years later. Driving home from the shot, I had to wait for lines of traffic, both vehicle and pedestrian, from the massive crowds attending our State Fair near my house. The pain was making me nauseous, and I thought I was going to pass out. I made it home without throwing up. The steroid shot didn't reduce the ringing or hearing loss. Months later, the hole remained in my eardrum, so the ear specialist recommended surgery to repair the hole. The surgery would take tissue from my ear and graft it onto the eardrum. When I awoke from the surgery, my ear specialist told me there was inadvertent contamination of surgical instruments. He had me sign a waiver, acknowledging my understanding that accidents happen during surgery.

I got a hearing aid. Wearing it for the first time, I heard sounds I never before paid much attention to. The metronome of my car's windshield wipers swishing back and forth; the sound of my shoes hitting the pavement. Sounds that seemed comically loud, while hearing the person speaking right next to me in a crowded room was impossible. A real weakness of hearing aid technology.

One of the other early lessons from having good hearing in one ear was that like our vision, hearing is a three-dimensional sense. You lose depth perception if you lose sight in one eye. Similarly, you lose the ability to discern where sounds are coming if you only have hearing in one ear. I sat on the light rail, and someone would be playing their music for all in the light rail car to enjoy. It was nearly impossible to discern if the music was coming from someone sitting in front of me or behind me.

The Minnetonka communication manager was the only one who made the connection of how ironic it was I lost the most important sense for me, given my lifelong love of music. I once sold a car, a beater with over 100,000 miles on it, because one of the two speakers blew out, leaving the sound from that speaker to sound tinny. I couldn't live with a car where I couldn't fully enjoy listening to music.

Beethoven wrote his ninth symphony through deafness, a remarkable accomplishment. He had enough music in his head in order to hear without his ears. I didn't have that ability. My enjoyment of music and connection suffered a serious blow, one I still deal with today.

My ability to write and my ability to connect with others were rooted in my listening skills. I never took that for granted, both having someone willing to share something personal, and my ability to lend an empathetic ear. Losing hearing hampered this to a depressing degree. My rare ability to find connection was forever gone. You can't listen if you can't hear.

EXISTENTIAL ANGST

Depression has defined my life. There are two ways I can look at its impact. First, it stopped me from reaching my potential. Constantly battling alternate feelings of despair and numbness while trying to get through each day, week by week, year after year has necessarily been my main focus. I don't have long-term relationships. Friends have come and gone.

The other way to look at my life through the lens of depression is it is amazing what I have been able to accomplish. I wrote a weekly newsletter column for over 14 years, rarely missing a week. If you want to know the real me, reading those columns comes as close as possible. Through my part in improving our state's election processes, I've been able to reach the top of my profession, a profession that is the foundation of our government, free and fair elections. That's nothing to sneeze at.

I've always admired broken souls. One of my all-time favorite Minnesota Twin baseball player is Jim Eisenreich. He grew up and played amateur ball in Central Minnesota and was drafted by his professional home team. Eisenreich was one of several rookies called up during the 1982 season, a group that included Kent Hrbek, Gary Gaetti, Tim Laudner, Tom Brunansky, and Frank Viola. Those five were at the core of the 1987 Twins team that won the franchise's first World Series. But in 1982 the inexperienced team finished last, losing a team record 102 games.

Eisenreich, the most talented of the rookies, had a smooth swing, was fast, and was a great center fielder. He was only able to show glimpses of his talent when facial and body tics began raising the mockery of opposing fans. Soon, the Twins put him on the disabled list, the first Major League Baseball player sidelined by stage fright. Over the next few years, the Twins medical team tried to figure out the cure that would allow Eisenreich to play the game he loved and was so good at playing. The doctors put him on a sedative, but hitting a 100-mph fastball while sedated wasn't a successful recipe. The Twins eventually let Eisenreich go, and he was able to resume his Major League career elsewhere. He ultimately was diagnosed with Tourette's Syndrome. Medication allowed him to play a successful career, although he never reached the potential he showed in his early days with the Twins.

Depression is such a selfish disease. It feeds upon itself by making one think that it's all about too much navel gazing, too much feeling sorry for yourself, for your suffering. Added to this is the myth that being a writer requires living a tortured existence. I'm guilty of all of the above. I've been afforded love in my life and great opportunities, and a privilege of sorts. Depression has consumed so much of my being, and maybe that was self-inflicted, or maybe it was a chemical imbalance, or maybe it was me being too weak to just say, "Fuck it, I'm going to be the best me I can be despite how I'm feeling."

The most depressing thing about my life is I survived my infamous blue period that included a nightmarish hospitalization. I stopped listening to all the mostly well-meaning advice, shared experiences, expert diagnosis, and medical recommendations, and decided the only way forward was to find myself again. Just like a Major League Baseball player trying to work his way through a slump, sometimes you just have to turn within and trust yourself, so you can be better going forward.

My inner voice was lost, drowned out by listening to everybody but me. I needed that voice to write my way out of my depression. And I did it. And it led to a five-year period where I was no longer depressed. I began to have dinner with my parents every Sunday evening, rotating a repertoire of restaurants. Mom told me how great it was to be able to have adult conversations about serious things. Ditto, serious conversations were what I always craved from my closest friends and family.

And then, during the past 10 years, the depression returned with a vengeance, even worse than before. That five-year period was a mirage. The idea that I was able to find my way out of depression by my own inner strength feels like a myth.

I've seen many therapists over the years trying to help me with my depression. I stopped taking antidepressants a few years prior to this latest deep bout of my illness. I felt like the drugs were just numbing me and not dealing with the underlying cause. Then I connected with a therapist who diagnosed me with existential angst.

When she diagnosed me with existential angst rather than depression, it hit me in the gut. She explained existential angst meant I was constantly needing to find the meaning of life. When I couldn't, it deepened and fueled the angst I was feeling. For the first time in all my years of suffering, someone had come up with an accurate diagnosis. This therapist actually committed to calling me on a regular basis to check in on how suicidal I was feeling.

I've endured depression because there didn't seem to be any other choice. Give up? Yes, I faced that choice so many times in my life that it seems crazy I'm still alive. There's always been a part of me that craves, needs, the need to see what comes next that hopefully will explain the meaning of what we've just lived through.

My life with cats has only reinforced how I've continued on. Each cat, each moment of getting to know each cat better, kept me alive. I promised during my darkest times I'd always be there for them because that was what I committed to, despite how my depression made keeping such a promise, a cross-species connection, seem like another reminder of my lack of connection with my own species. But the promises kept me alive to this day.

Part Three:
Pads, Paws, And Claws

"One cat just leads to another."

—Ernest Hemingway

When I was a little kid, our next door neighbors, the Kazas, had a boxer named Blitz. Blitz was a friendly dog with a sweet face and sad brown eyes. The Kaza kids and the Maeda kids used to play together, and Blitz often joined us. Of course, this made me want a dog of our own.

Mom broke the bad news to me. Two of my sisters were allergic to dogs and cats. Out of sympathy, Mom allowed my brother and me to have pet turtles named Huey and Louie. They were a beautiful deep green, about the size of a police badge. I loved the orange streaks both had on the back of their cheeks leading onto their long necks. We only had them for a few months as they developed a disease that softened their shells. Mom didn't quite explain what happened to them, but one day, Huey and Louie were no longer part of our family.

99

One morning, my neighborhood friend Bill Lenz and I went looking for garter snakes in the woods near our homes. We were both successful, and I snuck my snake inside my house without telling Mom. The next day, I went to look at the box I put the snake in, and it was gone. The jig was up. I knew I had to tell Mom there was a loose snake in our house.

A thorough search ensued. Couch cushions and furniture were looked under. I could tell Mom was not pleased. As a last-ditch effort, Mom opened up the vacuum cleaner bag, and sure enough, wriggling around inside the dirt and dust was my snake. It's unknown whether Mom had vacuumed the snake up, or maybe it crawled up inside the vacuum cleaner? Nonetheless, I had to say goodbye and let my snake go.

After college, I knew I was going to get a pet. Growing up, I was definitely more interested in dogs, but a cat seemed more practical. I didn't have to let it out during the day to do its business, and cats needed far less attention. So I adopted Max, or, as I ended up calling him, Mr. Max or Mr. Maximoto. Max was a social cat, not at all shy around people, but not at all fond of his own species.

My first significant feline experience came from house sitting my sister's cat, Mr. Ralph, an orange tabby with a personality as big as a tiger's. Ralph loved his outside romps in a huge yard in Lake Elmo, a city in Washington County, Minnesota. Ralph caught some mice and other small rodents. He wasn't so good at catching his prey because his strategy unfortunately had him sitting upwind.

After I adopted Max, I continued my occasional Mr. Ralph house-sitting duties when my sister and her husband took a vacation. Mr. Ralph and Mr. Max never saw each other as both hissed upon living in the same space. When I left for work, they were sitting on the opposite sides of a closed door, and when I got back, they were in the same spots.

From 1992 through 2006, I edited a weekly newsletter for Cheapo Records. Each week, I wrote a column mostly about music but sometimes about Mr. Max and his successors, Thompson, Diego-san, and Theo. Far and away the columns that elicited the most positive feedback were those about Mr. Max.

At a company holiday party, I felt like both a stranger and a celebrity since I didn't work in any of the stores, so I didn't know most of the employees. At the party, hushed voices pointed out that I was the guy who did the newsletter. Iris, a slightly tipsy employee, stumbled over to me and said, "I love Mr. Max!"

I never meant to replace human love with feline love. But life is love, and I gave my heart wholly to my feline housemates. When they left me, they broke my heart. What they taught me kept me alive. I treasured every moment with them and gave my whole love into our unique relationships.

I don't know a lot about Ernest Hemingway. I know he loved cats; I know I liked his sparse writing style more than I liked what he wrote about (war and bullfighting). I know he committed suicide. I watched Ken Burns's Hemingway documentary series, hoping to learn more about our shared struggles with depression and love of cats. Unfortunately, the documentary didn't elaborate on Hemingway's love of cats, but I have to believe that Hemingway's cats helped him live with his depression as long as he did.

MR. MAXIMOTO

I was living all alone for the first time in my life. Years after living with my family and then with college roommates and post-college roommates, I rented a small efficiency in a brick building off Summit Avenue in St. Paul, Minnesota, not that far away from where F. Scott Fitzgerald once lived. The building looked like a small castle with red decorative turrets running up either side.

I knew I wanted to adopt a cat, but I didn't know where to find one. My sister had a friend, Lonnie Willis, who had taken in a cat temporarily, but the original owner had decided he couldn't take the cat back. The cat, named Max, needed a permanent home. He had been found living on the streets and was described as very friendly. Enough said.

I went to pick Max up at his home off Hiawatha Avenue in Minneapolis. Being a St. Paul guy, I knew my new roommate was living on the wrong side of the tracks (a Twin Cities joke). Lonnie called out his name, and a large dog came prancing into the kitchen, followed by a grey-and-white striped tabby. The two animals clearly got along well, and Max was a little wary of a stranger standing in his kitchen. But he let me pick him up and stroke his soft fur and ample belly. Lonnie gave me his dinner and water bowls, and we were on our way. Max protested quietly, timidly meowing on our drive to his new home.

That night, he checked out our efficiency, basically one room with a walk-in closet that led to a small bathroom. It had old grey shag carpeting. When I moved out a few years later, my mom admitted the place depressed her. Max took his place lying on my chest, softly purring. I noticed my t-shirt was wet. I examined what end Mr. Max was leaking from, not that it mattered. I wasn't about to return him. I had myself a drooling kitty.

I was at the tail end of my infamous blue period, my free fall into depression. Max was instrumental, with his impressive striped tail, in helping me finally move forward again. In the first weeks, we established a routine. I fed Max three times a day: when I got out of my morning shower, when I got home from work, and right before bedtime. He quickly learned exactly when mealtimes were and looked forward with great anticipation to each meal.

Every day, he would greet me at the door when I returned from my eight-hour work day, then turn away as if he was expecting someone else. This felt like a lifelong snub. His favorite thing to do was sit in the screened windows, left open during the spring, summer, and fall, as he breathed in all the outside smells.

I knew he began life as an outdoor cat and now was strictly an indoor cat, so I purchased a harness and leash so we could take walks. He quickly learned his only time outdoors would be on a leash. I put on my grey felt fedora and lit up my pipe. Max pranced proudly ahead of me, frequently stopping to munch on grass. I had myself a feline cow. Our walks only lasted a few blocks, as eventually, Max would plop himself on the sidewalk and roll in the dirt. This was a sign he was done, so I would pick him up and carry him home. Our walks together, and the people who admired Mr. Max during our walks, remain a significant memory.

Max and I had tons of fun. We had little corporate jokes that never failed to crack me up. For a while, as I was leaving for work, I'd say, "I'm off to the Office-Max," with a chuckle. Or I'd say, "Do you know the Time-Max?" I giggled as he looked at me without blinking. Or the classic, "I'm Mad-Max." We were, after all, both road warriors having come as far as we had. We later came up with a new one. I said to him, "It's time to look in the Mirror-Max. Hey, wasn't that the name of the studio that distributed *The Crying Game*?" A bit more of an esoteric reference but endlessly funny, nonetheless. Hee Hee, Snicker Snicker, oh the joy we shared.

We had our quirks. On laundry night, as I took the sheets off my bed, Max zoomed onto the mattress. When I put on the clean sheets, he hid underneath each layer, pawing and biting at me as I tried to rub his belly underneath the material.

Max loved human food too. We sounded the same as we munched on corn chips. I quickly learned that Max's favorite treat was steamed broccoli. Once he tasted it, he couldn't get enough. I had myself a vegetarian kitty. I became a fan of the Japanese cooking show, *The Iron Chef*, and one of the Iron Chefs' names was Masaharu Morimoto. Soon, on occasion, I began calling Max "Mr. Maximoto."

There were certain times during our days when Mr. Max's eyes got as big as dimes. This meant he was about to tear around the room with lightning speed, all but daring me to catch him. Later, when we moved into a more spacious apartment, this became an amusing game we shared. He would knock things over, darting from room to room. I would knock over things trying to tackle him. It was like the *Pink Panther* movies with Inspector Clouseau chasing his assistant Cato. When we moved into our house with hardwood and tiled floors, the traction wasn't there. When he was in a hurry, he spun his wheels like the roadrunner, sometimes giving me enough time to reach him.

Max became an integral part of my life. Sam used to pick me up in her sporty Toyota MR-2 on our way to our office. Max never got to ride in the car (not that he would have wanted to), but he certainly became part of the interior. I transferred his hair from my clothes to the otherwise pristine passenger seat inside Sam's car. When I got my first computer, I shipped off my old electric typewriter to Sam, who had just started grad school at The University of North Carolina. When she opened the typewriter and turned it on the first time, a single solitary cat hair flew into the air. She laughed at the little hello from Mr. Max.

Mr. Maximoto taught me a critical life lesson. By taking the focus off myself and learning I was responsible for keeping this 12-pound bundle of wonder safe and alive, my depression lessened. Mr. Max walked me out of my infamous blue period more than any other soul. I loved how he constantly lived in the moment, observing what was currently there while still knowing his routine: when he would be fed, when bedtime was, etc.

Six years into our relationship, I had the opportunity to go to Japan for a 10-day visit. I had never been apart from Max for so long. My parents gladly took him into their home. I missed him so during my trip, but knew my little friend was giving Mom and Dad as much love as they were giving him.

A year later, Mom was diagnosed with cancer and given the prognosis of living another six months that proved to be eerily accurate. When I got off that phone call with Mom and Dad, I began sobbing. Mr. Max, who himself hadn't been feeling well, hopped up on my lap and purred away. It was such an act of kindness and love, and yet it caught me off guard and by surprise. How did he know how much pain I was in? How did he know exactly what he needed to do?

Three years after Mom died, Mr. Max's health hit a serious decline. He was diagnosed with feline hyperthyroidism. Worse yet, his lungs filled up with fluid, leading to multiple visits to the veterinarian. His lifelong hate of car rides to the vet quickly dissolved into silent rides with little protest.

I had to leave him overnight. When I visited him the next day, they had him in an oxygen chamber with tubes hooked up to his nose to help him breathe. He looked like a Borg from *Star Trek*. As

I turned him around, there was a tear in his eye. The vet tech must have noticed my reaction and said the tears were probably caused by the extra oxygen, not pain and sadness.

I brought Max home, thinking we might have a night or two left together. I was lucky; it was a bit more. The first night back, I stayed up and watched his every breath. I couldn't help but think of the past 12 years we spent together. He was weak, and food, his lifelong love, no longer interested him. I had to feed him with a syringe.

Away from the stress of a foreign environment, his breathing got better. There was one evening while he was lying on my chest that he began softly purring and drooling. My friend Amy accompanied to his last vet visit. We drove him out together, knowing we wouldn't be returning to my house with him. The veterinarian and vet tech let me spend as much time as I needed to say goodbye. When Mr. Max was administered the drug that caused him to breathe his last breath, I sobbed just like I did when I held my mom's hand when she died. I tried to be brave, thought I prepared myself for both traumatic moments. But I was helpless by how deeply my heart was broken.

When I got Mr. Maximoto's ashes back, I visited the three places we lived together and spread some of his ashes outside his favorite windows. At the original brick efficiency we started our lives together, a cat wandered out when I spread Max's ashes.

I repeatedly listened to one of my childhood favorite songs, Peter, Paul, and Mary's "Puff the Magic Dragon." Not the perfect metaphor, since Max was my Puff, and I was his Jackie Paper, but the sentiment was spot on. We belonged together, and the world would never be the same without him.

Bean Counter - From the Cheapo Newsletter

"Mr. MAX, we got beans!" the little Japanese America fella, a career-long bureaucrat, said excitedly as he entered the side door of the house. The cat greeted him with wide eyes, expectant because of the tone of the little fella's voice, of something wonderful to soon happen. He looked up at the little fella who was carefully cradling a bundle of beans in his arms that he had just picked out of the garden. Mr. Max sniffed at the beans out of curiosity, looked up, turned around, and left the room.

He resumed lying down on the hardwood floors of the hallway in the stifling, steamy, sweltering heat of the stale air. The little fella quickly wandered from room to room, opening up windows to get some air circulating in the overly warm house. "It's not so much the heat—it's the humidity!" the little fella said. "And it's not so much the humidity—it's the seven feet of rain! It may be time we find those partners for the ark!" Mr. Max was, at best, ignoring his roommate; more likely, he was in deliberate denial of his existence. "But we got beans, buddy! Plenty of beans!"

The little fella rubbed Mr. Max's ample belly. The heat exchanged between the two only made things feel worse, but the cat's purr encouraged further belly rubbing. The little fella quickly changed from his dress clothes to a T-shirt and a pair of soccer shorts. "When I was a kid, Mr. Max," he began, "I used to grow a bean plant indoors at the beginning of spring. I used to nurture it, watering it just right, making sure it had plenty of sunlight." Mr. Max curled up as the belly rub continued.

"Since I never planted it outside, I would only get a couple of beans, but my momma made sure to cook them up real special and serve them to me as my own little treat," the little fella continued. "Best meal I ever had." It was an elegant memory through eyes that could no longer see things in the same way. He wandered into the kitchen as Mr. Max, now at full attention, followed along. The little fella opened the cabinet and pulled out a metal pot. He went to the sink and cleaned the beans. He carefully placed the beans in the pot, breaking the ones that were too long to fit in half. Mr. Max carefully watched each and every one of the steps.

The little fella brought the pot full of beans over to the stove. He placed it on the front burner and turned the heat up to high. "These are going to be the best beans ever, Mr. Max," the little fella said, as the water showed its first signs of boiling. Somehow, the cat's eyes seemed to indicate that he believed, that he trusted the truth of the statement entirely.

The water began to bubble. The heat of the steam caused the already-warm kitchen to feel even more uncomfortable. The little fella went to the refrigerator and pulled out some ice water. He took a swig and looked down at Mr. Max. Further words need not be spoken; they both knew what was ahead. The anticipation was as binding as all the moments already shared.

The beans were finished cooking. The little fella quickly drained the water into the sink and pulled out a bowl to hold the steamed vegetables. He brought the bowl over to the table as Mr. Max followed along. "We got BEANS! WE GOTS LOTSA BEANS!" the little fella said as he searched carefully and pulled out the perfect two for the cat. "Here you go, Mr. Max. ENJOY!"

Mr. Max could no longer hide his own excitement. He meowed as the little fella placed the two beans into his dinner bowl. He sniffed at the root of all the hubbub and licked one of the two green beans. Soon, he was munching away enjoying the taste of the fresh vegetables. For a moment, the discomfort from the unforgiving heat was forgotten. They had beans, and that was all they needed.

DA BOYZ

Katelyn Lee and I met on an online dating website. Through our online chats and emails, her intelligence and conversational skills were clear. Her profile said she was a nurse, although her picture showed her in what had to be a nonstandard nurse's uniform, a very short white dress. We agreed on a date and time to get together. Unfortunately, the evening we agreed upon happened to be the night after Mr. Max died. I emailed her on the day and told Katelyn Lee I needed to reschedule. She sent a sympathetic response and let me know she understood.

I opened my house door to a redhead with a beautiful smile and kind eyes, reminding me of the actress Molly Ringwald. She was slightly taller than five-foot-four me, a situation made worse by the high heels she was wearing. At dinner, I shared personal information by talking about Mr. Max. I let Katelyn know that I didn't think I could ever adopt another cat because the loss of Max broke my heart.

She revealed her true nature then. She let me know I was being selfish. There were so many cats that needed a good home. I was obviously a person who could provide that. If I really loved Mr. Max, I owed it to him to give another cat a good home.

Katelyn told me she had two cats, Jazzy and Pumpkin. She volunteered her time at an animal shelter that took in cats and dogs that likely would never be adopted because of physical disabilities and behavioral issues.

About a month later, I learned that Katelyn Lee killed herself. Despite my limited time with Katelyn, I listened to her wisdom and indeed decided to adopt not one, but two cats. Thompson and Diego quickly were the new loves of my life. I was so thankful for Katelyn's tough love the only night we saw each other. And I never got to share that with her.

Her wisdom changed my life. To this day, I wish I could thank her. I sometimes wonder if I had shared how much she helped me, would that have been the words that could have saved her? I wondered how bad the place was she reached, how far the fall was, that she even gave up on the notion that there were two souls that needed her in the way only a pet and their human can understand. How could she leave Pumpkin and Jazzy on their own? I donated to the shelter she volunteered at and got a thank you note from her mother. Her mom wrote she didn't know how I knew Katelyn, and she was still trying to figure out why she lost her daughter. I wanted to provide some comfort, but all I could say was we shared a love for cats.

Deep down, I feared the limited connection we shared. No one suffering from depression is whole. Both Katelyn and I found out too late that we related to cats more than we did human beings. And this was a profoundly sad thing to share.

Opening my heart to another cat was not an easy decision. I decided I would adopt two cats together so when one of them died, I'd still have the other around to help get through the loss. I thought about adopting a mother cat and her kitten, figuring having cats of different ages might lead to a more orderly transition. The shelter staff let me know that might not work out so well. Kittens often turn against their mothers, so it might be better to find two non-related cats who had learned to get along together.

I was working at the legislature at the time when I saw a bill introduced into the State Senate that would prohibit Minnesotans from owning monkeys as pets. I discovered the bill while in the middle of pondering my own personal pet options. One of the things I was contemplating was getting a pet monkey.

Outrage didn't even begin to describe my opposition to the proposed prohibition. This state just had too many darn laws, and this would've been one of them. If we outlawed owning pet monkeys, then only outlaws would own pet monkeys. Law-abiding citizens like me would either have to go monkeyless or conceal our monkey ownership after obtaining a primate friend from some seedy, underground, black-market monkey emporium.

I'll confess that all this is proof positive that losing my best buddy for the past dozen years sent part of me reeling over the edge. This whole grieving over the loss of a pet was a brand-new animal for me. After Mr. Max died, well-meaning people comforted me with various forms of advice. Some advised getting another cat immediately to help me through the sadness. Others thought I should allow myself time to grieve. "You'll know when you are ready," I was told. And the inner ongoing dialogue bounced back and forth seemingly every minute or so, from never wanting another cat to wanting 17 so I wouldn't get quite so attached to any single one.

Months after Max's death, I couldn't quite find it within myself to put away his dishes, his toys, or his bed. I looked at the pictures a most talented photographer took of him in his senior years. I'm so glad that his many wonderful and wondrous faces were captured so memorably on film. I've never been a fan of photography, but these pictures came to mean more and more to me each day.

And as much as they reminded me of how much I missed him, they also reminded me of the stability he helped bring into my life. It didn't matter how good or bad a day I was having; it didn't matter how tolerable a year's worth of events were. Max was always there to come home to and rely on. He had his quirks, but he was consistent. In a significant way, he read me like no one else ever has. Losing Max was like losing a limb. Taken for granted at times, always a remarkable thing to have, the loss of which causes you to lose balance.

In my mind, I knew I had to find a way to separate how much I missed Max from how much I missed having a cat around. I went to a cat shelter, not because I thought I was going to bring home another cat, but because I missed Max so much and wanted to be around his species, a species he wasn't at all fond of. It was another thing we shared in common—I find myself not always so fond of my own species.

I had to sneer whenever someone told me, "Max would want you to have another cat." I know that wasn't true. They would follow that up with, "He would want you to be happy." That was easier to believe, but my happiness and allowing another cat into his house were two distinct things. Max disliked other cats so much that whenever one would enter our yard, his tail would get twice as big, and he would hiss and howl.

While I was at the shelter, a beautiful calico cat named Kat hopped up on a stack of bags of kitty litter next to me. She reached her paw out to me and meowed. She kept at it until I touched her. She even followed me into the next room. The shelter guy said he had never seen her do that before, that she tended to be the antisocial type (birds of a feather). He asked if I had tuna in my pocket or something. My only thought was Max had possessed her soul for a moment. Later, a rational reassuring voice told me it was perhaps a sign I wasn't quite ready for another cat.

My friend Stooey emailed me websites for a couple of local cat shelters. Reading the stories of some of the cats in the shelters brought a tear or two to my eyes. There seems to be no shortage of abandoned or abused kitties. With the monkey option becoming less viable, my pet plan was becoming a little more focused. I decided that I would adopt two female cats to try to make them as different as Max as I could. The plan of getting two cats was hopefully also a way to not get so attached to either of them, making any upcoming loss a little bit more palatable. Practical? Probably not, but that has never exactly been my middle name.

I talked with a woman at one of the shelters. She sent me to a foster home that had three female cats that were bonding fairly well. One of them, Mamie, was ultra-friendly. Another, Savannah, couldn't get away from me fast enough. I never saw the third, Baby Cakes, who left me asking an obvious question of the foster mom, "If I adopt them is it all right to change their names?" Yup, she said, that's quite a normal thing to do. I could live with Savannah and even Mamie, but somehow, despite my obvious lack of mature manliness and attachment to felines, I could never picture myself living with a cat named Baby Cakes.

A few days later, I visited Mamie again at an adoption held at the Roseville Petco. The rational voice of reassurance came along. While at the store, we saw some sweet and mellow greyhounds that got me thinking again about a completely different course of action. The cat adoption lady had also told me about a pair of male cats living in another foster home, Thompson and Diego.

I had remembered reading about Thompson on the web page. He had one of his front legs amputated after getting his paw caught in a trap. He had bonded with Diego, so the shelter wanted the two of them adopted together. Knowing I wanted two cats, the adoption lady asked me if getting two female cats was my absolute number-one criteria. Being as wishy-washy and Charlie Brown-like (in my always annoying way) as ever, I wasn't quite sure. Seeing the two boys at the store changed my way of thinking.

I felt an immediate sympathy for Thompson, a grey, black, and white striped tabby. When I was a kid, I had a pink stuffed cat. I named all my stuffed animals after baseball players. The pink cat's name was Hefty Thompson, named after Twins' shortstop Danny Thompson, who died of leukemia (a disease that plagues the cat community). The thought of having a cat named Thompson seemed reasonable. And Diego, a long-haired black cat, was as advertised, extremely social and friendly. The foster mom told me that someone had wanted to adopt Diego by himself, but she remained firm that the two of them go together.

Men are often accused of thinking with a certain body part other than the brain, but as I told my soulmate Stephanie many moons back, I couldn't be any lesser a man without somehow disappearing altogether. As a battery of analysts might someday attest, I tend to think with my heart (or maybe it's my spleen... whatever). I liked the idea of bringing in another ultra-friendly cat along with another cat who has something special about him. That the two got along so well and somehow needed each other almost made me want to adopt Thompson and Diego on the spot.

My friend Amy sensed I was rushing things. I did too. She was kind enough to invite me over to her house to spend time alone with her two cats, Maya and Marabou. I went over one night and was glad I did. Yes, it was weird to spend time with cats again, but the look in their eyes was as reassuring as it was amusing. Marabou was the queen of the house. She greeted me at the door, as I suspected she would. Maya, who seemed to have seen it all in her short lifetime, eventually came out and ultimately spent most of the evening in the bathtub. She sat beneath the tub's faucet, clearly expecting me to know enough to turn it on so she could get a drink. I picked up on the vibe but didn't want to splash her with water. She pawed at the metal and lapped up any drop of water that dripped out. And after winning a staring contest with Marabou, I somehow knew what I had to do next.

I made a visit to the foster home where Diego and Thompson were staying. Diego nearly leapt into my arms and was purring within seconds. Thompson was a bit more reserved, but I was won over by how intently he watched Diego's every move, as if he needed reassurance before he tried anything. I could see why those who knew the two insisted that they be kept together. And I knew a certain fellow who was quite willing to do so.

I called the adoption lady a few days later. She told me I should visit the two again before I made my final decision. So I did. Diego was as friendly as could be. My heart marveled at how well Thompson got around on his three legs. I also visited them at an adoption event at a local pet store. I saw many people gravitating toward Diego's warm and friendly personality and silky-smooth fur, despite the stigma some have against black cats. Thompson stayed at the back of his cage, and few were attempting to meet him.

I heard some people ask if they could adopt Diego by himself. It was then and there that I knew I had to keep the two of them together, but the thought of letting other cats in my home, in Max's home, still played on my mind. The idea of taking in a pair of compadres, one of whom was disabled, made me think that maybe I was ready despite how much I missed Max.

Approaching Mother's Day, another unexpected feeling welled up inside. Somehow it didn't seem right to get another cat, knowing I would never be able to get another mom. I wished my mom could meet Thompson and Diego. One of the last things I whispered in Max's ear was to go and keep Mom company.

Katelyn Lee's tough-love words made my decision moot. I was someone who could give these cats a loving home. The choice was obvious.

I brought Thompson and Diego into their new home. Diego immediately ran away and hid in my basement for the next two days. Thompson surprised me by being the braver of the two, exploring every room and sitting with me before he too went somewhere downstairs not to be seen. When I finally drew Diego out, he immediately reverted to the friendly cat I saw at the foster home. Yet the first few days were about bonding with Thompson, marveling at how his handicap wasn't a handicap—he did what he had to do to enjoy his life.

Watching Thompson and Diego's interactions was heartwarming. They chased each other around, wrestled, and took naps together, glad to be partners in life. Diego was the alpha male, craving all the attention Thompson and I would give him. Thompson trusted me, yet he was extremely shy around any visitors to our home. I was honored to have earned his trust.

During one of their fights, they stood staring at each other when Diego made a brilliant yet cruel move. He swiped Thompson's lone front leg out from underneath him, causing his brother to tumble as Diego pounced upon him. Diego was the smartest cat I've ever known. I soon added "san" to the end of his name, Japanese for "Mr."

The first time I played with cat toys with Thompson, I rolled a ball that unintentionally went to his missing left leg side. As he reached down to grab the rolling ball with his mouth, he fell over because his leg wasn't there to keep him upright. One day, a furnace maintenance guy came into our home to inspect the furnace. When he saw Thompson scamper away, he said I was obviously a great cat person because I was willing to give home to a three-legged cat. I thanked him but knew the opposite was true. Thompson was the great one, willing to accept, trust, and teach me.

Living with two cats created as different a dynamic as their personalities were different from Max's. Diego and Thompson sometimes teamed up to show that in our house, the majority rules.

Take the great box conundrum. For years, I stored several cardboard boxes in my basement. Max never seemed to pay any attention to them. Days after I brought Thompson and Diego to their new home, someone had gone downstairs and ripped holes in just about every box. Bite-sized pieces of cardboard littered the basement floor. Yet I couldn't exactly yell or punish either one of the boys since I wasn't sure who was responsible.

It only took me a year and a half to figure it out. I bought a new futon bed, and the frame arrived in a big box. I immediately cut up one side of the box and put it out on the sidewalk for recycling. The other side of the box I put in my office, figuring I'd cut it up and put it out during the next recycling cycle.

Diego-san immediately saw the box top as the perfect place to rest. He stretched out his impressive black-fur-covered frame, making the cardboard seem as comfortable as the futon itself. Thompson came in and gave away his one true misbehavior. He began gnawing at the edges of the box. If it had been the ever-mischievous Diego, I would have probably scolded him, but it was hard to yell at Thompson because he took a scolding so personally. (He seemed even more upset when I hollered at Diego.) Plus, the box was going to be ripped up anyway, so who was I to say that Thompson just wasn't doing his part to help out?

I marveled at how Thompson overcame his handicap. He not only kept up with the energetic Diego; he often was the one to instigate their dual romps. The first time I tried to take the two of them on a walk with them wearing harnesses and leashes didn't go so well. Once outside, they took off in opposite directions. I lost hold of Thompson's leash so I chased him in circles around our house. Slowly, it dawned on me that I wasn't going to catch him, but I could reverse the direction I was running to meet him halfway. It worked, and the three of us returned safely back into our house, never taking walks again.

I swear there were things that Diego did just because he knew that it would be difficult for Thompson to do the same. Diego took to drinking his water straight out of the bathroom sink tap. The sink's rim was a couple of inches wide, so it was not something that Thompson could easily jump up on to and balance himself on. Plus, Thompson was quite satisfied with doing like the rest of us and drinking his water out of a bowl. Still, with Diego's constant race into the bathroom, Thompson's curiosity got the better of him. One night he just had to see why Diego insisted on jumping up on the sink. He started by hopping on the toilet. From there he looked at Diego-san lapping up the trickling water flow.

The next night, Thompson sat on the edge of the bathtub. As Diego finished his drink, he turned, startled to see the nearby Thompson gazing up at him. Unexpectedly, Diego reached over and patted Thompson on the back. I'm not sure if it was encouragement, or if Diego needed to determine if it was indeed Thompson sitting ready to jump up on to the sink.

The next evening, I was in the upstairs bathroom brushing my teeth. The bathroom had a vanity counter, and Thompson came moseying up and leaped on to the vanity. He looked at the running water, and he looked at his and my reflections in the mirror. Diego-san came racing around the corner, preparing to leap up on to the vanity, when he saw that someone else had beaten him to his usual spot. He looked a little confused as he pranced away in the other direction.

Thompson waited until the water was shut off, and then he began licking the surface of the sink. Diego eventually returned and waited until Thompson was finished and had left the room. Then he hopped up onto the vanity, letting out a squeal to let me know it was his turn and it was time to turn the water back on. I patted him on the back. It may have been just another night in our household, but it was also a reminder of how lucky I was to be sharing the times with the boys.

One of my favorite things about Thompson was watching him move. His was a lurching move forward as if he had to momentarily think about where to place his lone front leg in order to take the step forward. His was a halting gait that reminded me of jazz, unpredictable yet purposeful.

I did some diversity and inclusion work at my job, and one of the things I learned through that effort was our need to categorize people and things to bring order to our thoughts. It was easy to define Thompson as my three-legged cat. One of the many life lessons he taught me was his disability was a part of his life, but it was far from the only thing that defined him.

I loved his natural imperfections: the brown spot on the left side of his nose that otherwise interrupted the white fur around his nose, mouth, and chin; the intermingling of black and pink paw pads; how the white fur on his legs was of differing heights. He could never be a show cat, but all that made Thompson worth everything else I have ever loved in this world. He wasn't the cuddliest cat, but the times he chose to cuddle were the best. He lay on my chest on the side of his missing leg, allowing him to get his head as close to my heart as possible.

A life lesson learned from Thompson: at any moment of time, you can suddenly lose an important piece of yourself. Perhaps even more insidiously, it can happen over a period of time when you don't even notice the loss until it's too late. The important thing is understanding the key of how you adapt to this unwanted change. We always have the choice on how we are going to try to take the next step.

When Thompson lost his leg, he was lucky the woman who had been feeding him in the park found him and took him to a no-kill shelter. Had she brought him to the Humane Society, he likely would have not been given the chance to live. And he always let me know how grateful he was for the meals, for my attention, and for me coming home every night to complete our daily routines.

Thompson knew that when I finished with my shower, it was breakfast time. He joined the stampede down the stairs to the bowls in the kitchen. He patiently took his place next to Diego, waiting for me to fill his dish. At night, he knew that when I was finished watching TV, it was time for dinner. He knew that on the weekends, the routine was slightly different. When I got back with my soy latte from the coffee shop across the street, he knew was treat time. He would be the first to bellow out his meow in anticipation. Eventually, the weekend routine incorporated music and reading time. Thompson took his place next to me on our loveseat.

During a time where I felt alarmingly less connected and far less inspired by anything and everything, Thompson remained an inspiring soul. As my darkest, deepening, unrelenting depression returned at the same time Thompson's health turned for the worse, I made a pact with him: I wouldn't give up as long as he didn't. Let the record show he never gave up. He was good at teaching me that life is about finding a place to call home, and he was glad he found his, but there ultimately comes a fight where it becomes clear the circumstance was insurmountable. I understood that.

Just about every night, Diego-san slept snuggled up next to me, pushed up against my armpit, head on my shoulder. When I watched TV, he would nap on my chest, softly purring away. He loved trying to rub his face against my face, not something I was terribly fond of, but there was no denying him. His paws were the size of a bear's, and his tail huge and floofy (the vet techs always commented on his impressive tail). His long black fur was silky soft. His big personality filled our house.

I was impressed by Diego-san's athleticism. He was brilliant at catching bugs, flies, and moths. He was able to leap onto counters, the stove, the refrigerator, and the high basement window bays. Diego's fearlessness frightened me some because it led to some accidents. I always figured he would be the first to go because of his reckless curiosity.

There was the great soup incident when I spilled some soup on him, not seeing him waiting to leap onto the stove. It burned him, and he then became much more cautious when he saw me carrying pans and bowls. There was the night I noticed blood by the litter box. When I tried to grab him, he leaped into the unfinished basement ceiling. I called the fire department to see if they could help me (they couldn't). I called my friend Amy, Diego's favorite person in the world, whose soothing voice coaxed Diego out from hiding.

There was the time he scratched a hole in the window screen and escaped the house. I found him sitting on the outside window ledge, shaking like a bunny as the busy traffic in front of our house buzzed on by.

Diego-san was fascinated by the sound of running water. Whenever I turned on the bathroom faucet, he would come racing into the room and hop up on the vanity. As he watched the flow of the water and it swirling down the drain, I would ask him, "Diego-san, where does that water go?"

One morning, I must have left the bathroom door slightly ajar as I hopped into the shower. I saw Diego-san leap onto the vanity three feet away from the glass shower door. I could see him pace back and forth and knew exactly what he was thinking. Before I could stop him, he leaped from the vanity in an attempt to join me in the shower. He didn't make it. His front paws held onto the top of the shower door. I knew I wasn't strong enough to pull him over, so I shut the shower off and tried to slowly open the door, hoping he wouldn't fall. Unfortunately, that's exactly what happened. And he never tried that again.

Diego-san's foster mother told me I needed to comb him every night. I figured she was sharing this because of his long, soft, silky black fur and preventing mats. But I learned that he wouldn't let me go to bed until I combed him. He loved the comb strokes and having all my attention.

All my life, I've been looking for another who would complete me. The Siskel to my Ebert, the Trapper to my Hawkeye, the Waldorf to my Statler, the Lennon to my McCartney. I loved how I lived with the greatest partnership of all, Diego-san and Thompson. Their partnership brought blissful appreciation for how they found each other, bonded, and made each other—and me—better in their bond.

NEW KID ON THE BLOCK

I quickly saw there was a flaw to my plan in adopting two cat partners to help me avoid what happened when Max died and my heart was broken. The plan was, when one of the boys died, the other would still be there to help console me. What I hadn't considered was because the two cats loved each other, when one of them died, the other would be devastated.

Thus, I launched a plan to adopt a third cat so there would always be two when one of them died. What I didn't consider was the third cat would have to find a way to become equal with two cats who had already strongly bonded. If he couldn't, maybe I would need to bring in a fourth cat for the third cat to bond with. I think this is the way someone ends up living with 40 cats.

I found Dribble, a black-and-white tuxedo cat, on the same pet rescue site I found Thompson and Diego. His sweet, perpetually confused face drew my attention. His description was a glowing account of his friendly personality and said he was affectionate and got along great with other cats. He was named "Dribble" because his white chin made it look like he dribbled milk out of his mouth.

Soon after reading his profile, it was taken down. I feared I was too late, that someone else had adopted him. But a few days later, a new profile was published, this time under the name of Stevie (as in Wonder), capturing a lifelong personality trait.

When I called to inquire about meeting Dribble, I was told the change was due to a stalker situation. I never learned what that was all about. I visited Dribble in his foster home, and when Denise, his foster mom, brought him out to meet me, he spent all his attention cuddling in her arms, trying to swat at a Christmas ornament that hung above them on a wooden room divider two feet above. I fell in love with how much he believed he could reach the ornament, never giving up.

As I was signing off on the paperwork to bring Stevie home, a woman at the rescue warned me he wasn't right in the head. That sealed the deal. I wasn't either, and I figured it was something we'd bond over. I don't know if cats can be autistic, but Dribble seemed to live in another world.

He had come from a foster home where he lived with three other cats that included a three-legged cat he bonded with. Being introduced to a new place, he figured that the other two feline figures would understand and be sympathetic to his confusion. They were not.

I'd never introduced a new cat into an atmosphere where others already trod. To learn about the process, I did what any of us now did when we needed information: I Googled it on the Internet. And then I ended up talking to some people who had been through the experience. What I learned is that you were supposed to keep all the fur legs and glares physically separated, while trying to remain a comforting presence to all involved. The new cat got established in a safe room where he could get used to all the new sights and smells, and the resident cats got to wonder what the hell was going on behind that locked door.

After a while, I was supposed to switch their places so they could all acclimate themselves to the smells of each other. (Hopefully, the overwhelming stench of the sole human inhabitant didn't interfere with this busy, twitchy, nose process.) Then, when I thought the antenna of the agitated nerves was somewhat receptive, I allowed everyone to see each other. Expecting a full-fledged brawl at this point, I was happy that the two resident cats acted like they didn't quite know what to make of this new tuxedo intruder. Dribble, half their size, looked up with his big round eyes and let out the tiniest of meows as if to say, "Hi, guys, wanna play?"

It's never easy being the new kid on the block. Growing up in Roseville, I went to Central Park Elementary School. When we went on to junior high, half of my classmates went to Capitol View Junior High, and half of us, including me, went to Parkview Junior High School. There were three junior highs that fed into two senior highs. Us Parkview kids were split between the two high schools. Thus, many of my friendships came to a screeching halt after the sixth and ninth grades, and some resumed after being apart for three years. My first year of high school was spent trying to find my way among many who pretty much had gone to the same schools all their lives.

I remember sitting in hour one of my homeroom class in 10th grade, hardly recognizing another face in the room. It took me all the way back to kindergarten—feeling like everyone was in on something I knew nothing about. The same feelings came flooding back during my freshman year at college. I ended up with a group of jocks and drunks and sex-crazed hipsters (none were mutually exclusive clubs) that left me feeling like I grew up on Neptune.

I honored Dribble/Stevie by being the first cat I named on my own. Max lived with his name years before I met him. Thompson was named after an ex-boyfriend of the girl in his foster home. Diego was named after the famous Mexican painter Diego Rivera. "Dribble" seemed like a good kitten name, but it just wouldn't do in the long term.

I remembered a book about the making of the original *Star Trek* series where the creators of the show ran through a list of names for the Vulcan, everything from Spook to Speck, ultimately settling on Spock. I got a glimpse of what new parents must go through in selecting a name for their baby. I wanted something that captured his essence, yet it had to be something others would remember and accept as appropriate. I've long wanted to name a cat after something musical. My once-upon-a-time muse, Stephanie Jane, won me over by telling me she once had a cat named Jazz. "Dylan '' would have been an option if not for *Beverly Hills 90210*.

I ran through several musicians' names from Duke to Thelonious, from Wyclef to Hank (Sr.), but I just couldn't decide. I then settled on Eliot after Elliott Smith, only with one "L" in deference to T.S. Eliot. The short name to that would be "Eli," but my friend Amy named her new cat "Elijah" (a wonderful kitty name) and thus called him Eli. I didn't want to copy Amy, who clearly understood my love of cats, by naming our cats the same name. I just about settled on Cecil after jazz pianist Cecil Taylor. Indeed, I called the newcomer that for a day or so, but it just didn't seem to fit. So I came back to one of the first names I thought about, Thelonious—Theo for short. I ran it by Amy. She liked the name Thelonious-san Monk-Maeda. I did too. I ended up naming him Thelonious Dribble Maeda. Theo for short.

How did I get Thompson and Diego-san to accept their little new housemate? There were no fisticuffs when I first opened the door all the way. When Theo's absolute period of isolation ended and the doors were opened a bit, where all involved could get a peek at each other for the first time, the anxiety in the air could have been sliced with the force of a swipe of an unclipped cat's paw. Theo wanted to explore, but the veterans didn't want him to violate their territory.

Theo took some steps toward Diego, who could sit on him and flatten him to nothing. Diego-san, who ran our place, glared menacingly, but when Theo got near, Diego ultimately retreated (as was his nature). Thompson proved even more surly. If Theo got within two feet, Thompson growled. If Theo got within a foot, Thompson hissed. If Theo got any closer, Thompson ran away. One time, Thompson sat perched upon his favorite piece of cat furniture when Theo tried to climb up. Thompson took his one front paw and rapped Theo hard on the top of his head. Theo didn't quite get the message, and the process was repeated again until he quit his attempt.

But detente was finally reached. Theo lived up to his name and pranced upon the piano keyboard. Diego-san, himself quite the piano player, nodded in approval. Theo loved to pace the hallways. Thompson looked over and seemed to accept things as they now were. Theo's bundles of kitten energy had the other Boyz look on both out of curiosity and cynically, seemingly with the message, "You'll learn better one day, kid..."

He couldn't have been more friendly towards me. Purring seemed to be his natural state. When he stopped, it felt odd. He was also a great headbutter, seeing my head as one great big soccer ball. Theo skillfully found his role in our house, although it felt like he was destined to be the third wheel. Thompson loved napping with him. Diego-san reluctantly accepted Theo occasionally napping with him. Diego and Theo's fights were legendary. I tried to teach Theo strategy, but he always took a position lower to Diego, giving his foe free rein to whap at the top of his head.

Of all the cats I'd known, Theo was the one who needed a rigid routine, living on a schedule. He didn't like changes. For many years, our days began with the alarm waking me up and me hopping into the shower. When I got out, Theo licked my legs until I put on some pants. And then the race to the meal dishes began, with me calling out the winner like a Kentucky Derby announcer. Theo and Diego-san won most days because Thompson had an impossible time keeping up with his three-legged gait. I did my best to block those with four legs, giving Thompson a fighting chance, and was always glad when he reached the kitchen first, declared the winner by my "and down the stretch they come," play-by-play call. I cherish all those races.

A few months after adopting Theo, he began sneezing constantly. I took him to the vet, and he was diagnosed with herpes, a feline respiratory disease. Unfortunately, as he got better, Thompson got sick. Our biggest talker, herpes cost Thompson his voice. He tried to express something, only it came out in silence. Then Diego-san became lethargic, barely having any interest in doing anything but sleeping. As the herpes made its round, it unfortunately repeated itself. Theo sneezing, Thompson losing his voice, Diego losing his energy. This was to repeat itself over the years.

Thompson and Diego-san's dishes were next to each other, Theo's slightly to the side. I'm not sure why I didn't arrange things more equally, only that, late in his life, Thompson finished his meals behind Theo and Diego. I knew when Theo was done, he would try to finish Thompson's meals.

Diego-san and Thompson joined me in 2003. Theo completed our home in 2005. The next dozen-plus years, we all learned to live in a stable home, a predictable routine. I switched jobs, flailed through some important relationships. But life in our house was established into something we were comfortable with.

And I tried to carve out a time for me to individually bond and connect with and love each one of my housemates. Once his last meal of the day was fed, Diego-san loved to be combed as I got ready for bed. On the weekends when I had time to read books, Thompson took his place next to me, nestling his head against my arm, making it hard to turn the pages of what I was reading, but I didn't mind. Theo's time was our routine, licking my legs as I got out of the shower in the morning and returning home from work in the afternoon.

I gave each of the Boyz chores. Diego-san was responsible for catching bugs that wormed their way into our house. Thompson was responsible for making sure his brothers and himself didn't vomit on carpets and rugs, but on wood floors and tiling instead. Theo's job was to make sure when I got home, none of my bath towels were pulled down onto the floor, an activity he loved to do. Diego-san did a great job with his duty; Thompson wasn't so successful; and after I assigned Theo his chore, somehow finding towels on the floor became less frequent. Maybe he was smarter than I was giving him credit for.

THE LAST FAREWELL

Thompson died in August 2018.

There was clearly something ailing him the last few years of his life. He lost over half of his body weight and spent increasing times napping. He was tested for thyroid and kidney issues and diabetes, but his tests didn't indicate anything far out of the normal. The vet said he likely might be suffering from some form of cancer, but to confirm that would mean getting tissue samples. I didn't want him to undergo invasive surgery only to find that there likely would be no good treatment for what was found. I just wanted him to be as comfortable as possible during his last months.

The whole lack of clear communication between species is what it is, but it ultimately sucks. During his final weeks, Thompson constantly purred. I learned there are probably two purposes behind a cat's purr: expressing extreme momentary contentment and trying to make themselves feel better. The latter was clearly happening. He hardly ate anything for a month and was down to skin and bones.

I had to let go of one of my life's greatest inspirations. So I scheduled a time with an organization that euthanized pets in their own homes. The thought was to make their final moments as peaceful as possible in familiar surroundings, rather than being brought into a more frightening clinical place. The process was also meant to help the other pets in the house by seeing what was happening with their sibling.

The morning of the scheduled last day of Thompson's life, I went downstairs to watch TV. Diego-san joined me, as he always did. Thompson happened to do so this morning as well, just like he used to. It was great to spend time with the two of them. I wished Theo would join us too, but he was somewhere else in the house. Thompson hopped onto my chest, purring away. I wondered if he somehow knew I was letting him go, putting him out of his pain.

When the person arrived to administer the drug that would kill Thompson, my inspirational love joined me on the couch in the living room. The exact same spot we spent many weekend mornings together as I read books and he cuddled next to me. Diego-san and Theo were nowhere in sight. And then Thompson was gone. The person let me spend as much time as I needed with the dead body, then wrapped Thompson in a blanket and took him away.

Diego-san died two years later, in September 2020.

In March that year, Diego-san, Theo, and I entered into the apocalypse not knowing how to deal with a worldwide shutdown due to a deadly global pandemic. I hoped we were entering a tunnel coming out into the light on the other side, but I feared we were entering a one-way cave with no way out. My fears turned out to be true. None of us survived unscathed.

We tried to figure out our new normal where I was home all the time. The Boyz relied on the routine we developed during their 15 years together. I went to and returned from work every day at the same time. Meals were fed at the same times. My day and night routines were predictable. Now I was working from home, talking to other people on my phone and laptop. Diego-san's health clearly was deteriorating. Theo, always so reliant on our routine, clearly wasn't happy with all the major changes.

Diego did his best to disrupt my communications with others, appearing on camera with me during legislative hearings and a judicial procedure. I worked from my kitchen table looking out the window of our backyard where squirrels, chipmunks, and rabbits scurried about. Diego-san napped next to my laptop's mouse on the kitchen table, occasionally getting up to observe the activity in our backyard. The memories of those days remain firmly and powerfully within me. The new normal was soon to take a drastic change.

During the summer, Diego-san grew weaker and weaker. My new favorite thing to do was to push my finger deep into his bear-sized paw, and he would close his claws around it and squeeze back. It was like we were holding hands. Like Thompson, his body was wasting away, weighing less than half of what it once did. His lifelong struggle with anal gland and constipation issues worsened, leading to several trips to the vet. I began cooking Diego-san chicken in the pressure cooker, using my fingers to strip the chicken breasts into bite-sized pieces. This kept him eating as much as possible.

After he returned from one visit to the vet to deal with his latest bout of constipation that caused him to stop eating and gingerly moving, he clearly wasn't okay. He joined me downstairs as I watched TV, as he always did, but instead of sitting on my chest, he sat at the end of the couch a couple of feet away. He began leaking diarrhea. I brought him into the laundry room where the litter boxes were as I went to grab some rags to clean up the mess. When I returned, he was lying on his side next to the litter box. I knew he was dead, and I was heartbroken I left him on his own to die alone.

It occurred to me that of all the souls I've lived with, I spent the most time alone with Diego-san. He slept snuggled up next to me most every night we lived together. He almost always joined me when I watched TV. I took guitar lessons for several years. And all the nights I was learning to play guitar, singing my heart out at the top of my lungs, Diego-san would sit right next looking slightly irritated by the noise. Thompson and Theo remained downstairs until the ungodly noise ended, but Diego-san's favorite place was always by my side.

Days after he died, my friend Maria texted me telling me she was picking up a clothes order from the mall near my home and asked if she could stop by. She came into the house, and we hugged for the longest time. She knew my heart was broken and said she really admired how courageous it was to give my heart so fully to another. I asked her if she got her clothes OK, and she admitted that was all a ruse to visit me.

Two years later, still mourning, I watched the movie, *Star Trek II: the Wrath of Khan*, again. I've seen it many times before. Probably my favorite story in the Star Trek timeline. I remember feeling old and worn out like Captain Kirk in the movie when I saw the movie in the theater when I was in high school.

The movie was among the first movies I rented when my parents bought my first videotape recorder, the Sony Betamax. I watched it over and over. Spoiler alert, the scene when Mr. Spock dies and Kirk is devastated and then gives his eulogy to his best friend ever kills me each and every time I watch it. It defines the story of my life on some strange level.

Watching it on its 40th anniversary for the first time in a dozen years, I smiled at all the lines from the movie I memorized and became part of my lexicon. Small throwaway lines like Captain Terrell's, "What the hell is that?" was a phrase I've muttered ever since seeing the movie.

Watching the movie the latest time around, I cried again when Captain Kirk gave his eulogy to Mr. Spock, a Vulcan whose species was all about logic and not giving into feelings. Kirk said of all his travels, meeting different species on different planets, that Spock was the most human soul he met, despite being a Vulcan. I could say the same thing about the feline soul who I was lucky enough to spend the most individual time with in my entire life, Diego-san, my cuddling and healing, understanding, comforting, best friend ever.

Losing Diego-san was the straw that broke my self-declared honorary feline's back. I was under tremendous stress trying to figure out how we could possibly administer an election during the pandemic in a treacherous political divide. The day after he died, I couldn't get out of bed. The only thing that I found could distract my mind was to try to remember every baseball player I ever saw play. I tried to remember rosters and lineups from the past. Who was on the 1975 Chicago White Sox? What was the 1984 St. Louis Cardinals lineup? I was surprised at how strong my memory was for my lifelong love of baseball. It took me some moments to recall a certain player, but eventually, I did, resisting the temptation of looking up the information on the internet.

Theo was clearly concerned about Diego-san's absence and the fact his food guy wasn't going to get out of bed ever again. He coaxed me out of my stupor, and I went down to the kitchen to feed him. I realized I needed to make things as normal for him as possible in yet another new normal.

Since the beginning of the pandemic, through living over a year in solitary confinement, my existential angst morphed into existential anguish. Making it to the next moment seemed too painful to endure. I began seeing two therapists, one a traditional "tell me your troubles, and we'll talk through how to change your thinking" professional. The other was a hypnotherapist who gave me subconscious advice to listen to in a relaxed state.

Separately, both counseled me to try my best to live in the moment. Breathe. Don't worry about the past or future. Now is all that exists and all I have some control over. I was struggling learning how to do that until Theo was lying next to me and I paid all my attention to his breathing. The anguish and suicidal thoughts were still overwhelming, but feeling Theo breathe and trying to align my own breathing with his got me through to the next moment.

When Theo's favorite drinking fountain broke, that was his last-straw moment. A competent person could have easily repaired the broken fountain. A wire had become detached from the metal connection of the wall plug. It only would take some soldering to fix, but I wasn't a handy person, and I didn't own a soldering gun, so I ordered a replacement fountain that would take a few days to arrive.

Theo spent most of those days face down in his favorite cat bed barely moving, barely eating. I decided it might help him to bring into our home another cat or two, since he clearly loved napping next to Thompson and chasing Diego-san around our house.

My boss's family was fostering a mother cat with a litter of six. My boss's wife said she hoped someone would adopt two of the kittens together since the two had bonded. Alias was originally named "Billy," and Norma was named Norma. I had always told myself that if I ever adopted a female cat, I'd name her Billie after Billie Holiday. But it seemed odd to start calling Norma 'Billie' and either change Billy's name or have a brother and sister with similar names. So I settled on renaming Billy 'Alias,' meaning I could call him anything I wanted.

I visited them at my boss's family home and filled out the paperwork to bring them home. I was hoping their crazy kitten energy would spark Theo's lifelong crazy kitten energy. The nights before bringing Alias and Norma home, I stroked Theo's forehead and said I knew he'd be a great big brother just like Thompson and Diego-san had been for him.

Theo took a month to accept Alias and Norma. And accept was all he really had done, learning that he could still spend most of his time alone napping. He bonded some with Alias, who loved and encouraged when his older brother licked his forehead. But mostly, Theo had learned to coexist with his new siblings. Again, destined to be the third wheel.

His health, like his brothers before, was worsening as he entered his 18th year. He began eating less and less, losing weight as a result. As he approached his last days, I realized way too late I failed him from the start. I brought him into a home where two cats had already bonded, and he needed to figure out his role with them. And now I brought in two other cats who bonded from the start of their lives and looked at him as the strange guy who mostly avoided them.

Maybe in the end, we really did finally find our common bond. And yet, he might be the most important cat I've lived with, simply because we entered that 2020 cave together and did find a way out, weaker for sure, wobbly and confused, but the two of us did it together and mostly alone.

When my dad was caring for my dying mom in their home, he bought her a space heater because she was having a hard time staying warm. After Mom died, I somehow ended up with the space heater that I promptly stored in a closet, never needing to use it. In 2022, my furnace gave out during a cold spell, so I started using the space heater to stay warm as I did my work. Theo quickly learned sleeping in front of the space heater was ideal. It meant a lot to me that there was this new shared connection between my mom and Theo. During their last days, weeks, months, the heat helped them feel more comfortable. Theo would have loved my mom and vice versa.

Cats live just long enough to break our hearts. I forever struggled figuring out how to best bond with Theo, the sweetest yet strangest cat I've known. But this whole third wheel thing I forced upon him not once, but twice, may be our ultimate connection. I've felt that feeling most of my life. And the whole 'not being right in the head' thing too.

Part Four:
Of the Sea

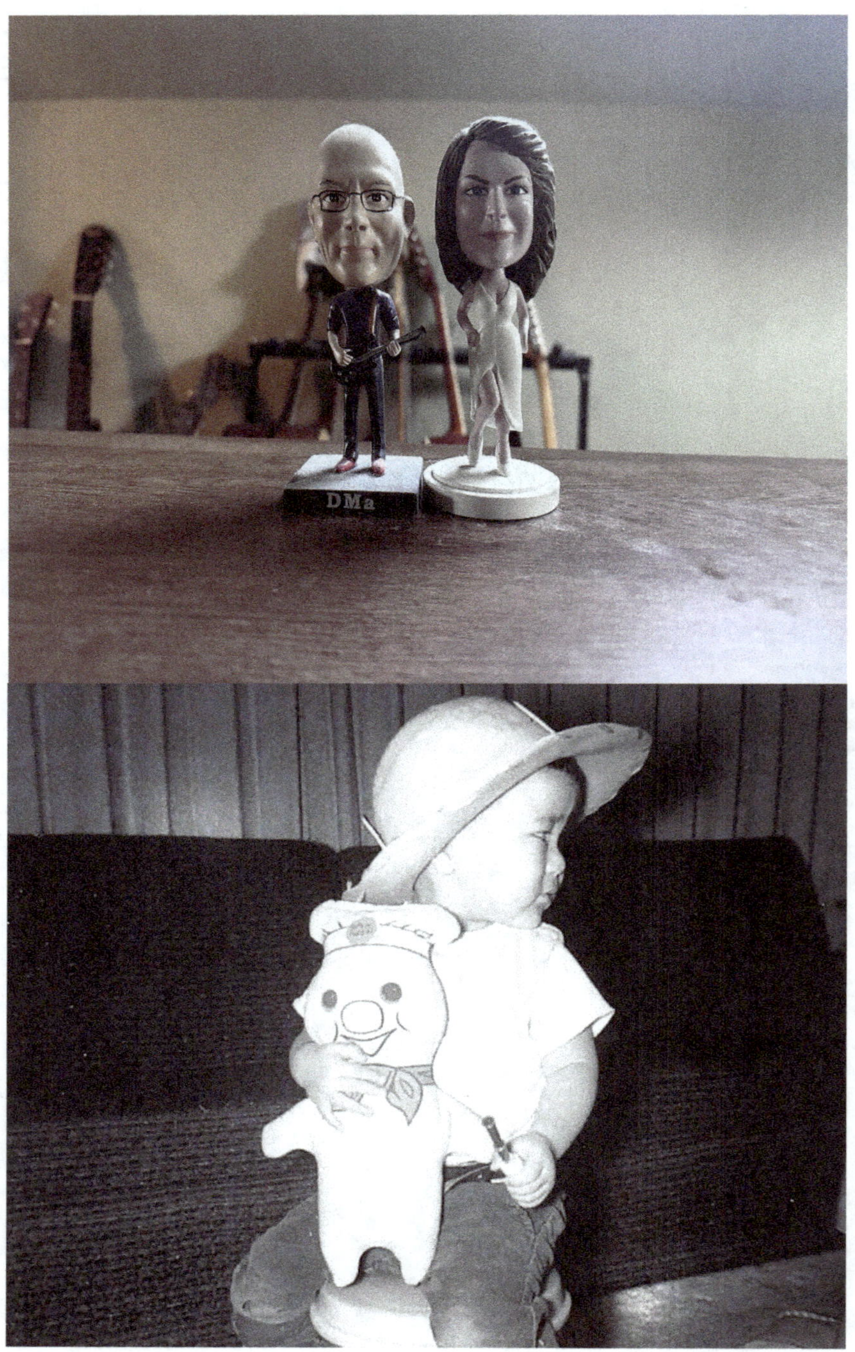

"We found connection in truth, kindness, and respect. We've seen the truth of each other. Despite our radical differences in personal perspective, nine years later, we are still both here.

"Maybe it's not about finding the fairy tale. Maybe it's about being courageous enough to speak your truth while maintaining kindness and respect. Relationships built on these principles feel like they can last forever."

—Maria Jennifer Berrios
Reflecting on our nine-year
relationship

This section was the most difficult to unlock. Nine years, hundreds of drafts, thousands upon thousands of words. It was a mess, a mixture of raw emotions and nonsense, a diamond sitting in a cesspool of sex, drugs, and rock with no roll. I know people who know me don't know this part of me. I know people who don't know me might think more critically after reading this section. Yet it's the most important part of my story, my life. Relationships come and go throughout our lives. Some sting, some sing, some make us stronger, some diminish us in the end by how much we put in versus what we got out. Others leave us wistful, thankful, and blessed for every moment spent together. Most fall somewhere in the middle.

Our story was supposed to be a shared memoir, a telling of two stories that intertwined and became one. We grew up in very different households. We met under cynical circumstances. It was supposed to be a one-night stand.

Our age difference is significant; she's much younger than me. But her wisdom and soul, as the cliché goes, are older than mine. Our relationship has persevered for going on nine years now. It was up to me to figure out how to write our shared memoir. Beyond what she had already told me about her life, we met several times one summer at a coffee shop where she shared the intimate details about her life.

She was inspiring me, encouraging me to write the great masterpiece I clung onto during the most depressing period of my life. But it became clear to me I couldn't do her part of the story justice. And I'm not talented enough, articulate enough, smart enough to explain how during my darkest depression, I somehow managed to meet not my dreamy soulmate, but a real person who I've spent my most memorable, cherished, and authentic life moments with.

We met online in a new world, an online dating site for those of us lovelorn, lacking a connection, either permanent or just for the night. Virtual bar pickups, digital one-night stands. We both swiped right and agreed that neither one of us was looking for a permanent relationship. Those were the rules we agreed to. She was a tennis player. To her, love meant zero. I was just looking for someone to momentarily connect with that could make me smile and not take myself so seriously instead of looking for long-term love and inspiration.

How had I fallen so far? Before, I had always been searching for my soulmate, my muse that would help me understand the meaning of life. I thought that one day I would find this Madonna who would inspire me to write my masterpiece, and it depressed me when the latest relationships didn't come anywhere near.

Somehow, facing down another desperate darkness, I found the most significant relationship of my life. As we continued to see each other, an hour or two at a time once or twice a month, I found her life story amazing, which helped me grow to love her deeply and appreciate her more than any person I've met.

But ours is a relationship born out of our current world's reliance on social media, apps, texts, and getting to know another soul mostly in the vast polluted Internet ocean. I added her as a 'favorite' contact on my iPhone so every time she texted me, my Apple Watch alerted and vibrated on my wrist. Like Pavlov's dog, I was conditioned to smile when I felt that tap on the wrist.

There's only so many times a human heart can break. Our ultimate muscle has the elasticity of a rubber band stretched to its limits. At some point being stretched one time too far too many times, that rubber band is going to break and become useless. I guess most human hearts don't get to that same stage, but mine did. I gave up. Threw my losing hand into the middle of the poker table. So it's ironic that hanging from the end of my rope, I somehow managed to find the most significant, intimate, in-the-moment relationship of my life when I was clearly giving up, looking the other way.

Recently, as she was leaving my house, we hugged, and she asked me, "Can you believe we've been doing this for nearly 10 years now?" This meaning, getting together in our sanctuary, sharing life failures and successes (mostly failures), tears and laughter (mostly laughter).

I gave it a thought for a second or two and said, "No, I really can't. This was going to be a one-time thing." No commitment, nothing serious. Yet hour by hour, year by year, the memories have built, the love has grown, and the connection I never found elsewhere had magically formed.

SANCTUARY

I fell in love the first time we fucked. And I've only grown even more fond of Maria as we've gotten to know each other. Over the years, the sex transitioned from fucking to making love. Desire is all about trust and intimacy, feelings certainly intertwined but often mistaken for one and the same. Creating a feeling through unconventional means. Manufacturing a true and powerful human interaction was our ultimate connection.

The difference between naturally feeling and deliberately manufacturing was a line we crossed not only out of desperation, but also out of an agreement that we enjoyed this different manner of sharing ourselves with another. When I'm deep inside her, it is the most connected human experience that two people can share. And we unexpectedly built upon our sexual relationship to develop the most authentic connection either of us have found.

She disclosed she didn't give me her real name to begin with. I suspected that was an attempt to protect her identity in this weird space we were meeting. I asked if she could at least tell me her real first name. She didn't, but said it meant, "of the sea." She had a tattoo of the Spanish word, Corrupta, for "corrupt" on the underside of her forearm. It was the fake last name she gave me. She said it was her grandmother's maiden name. I later learned it was a youthful joke, branding herself with what her parents thought of her.

The first time we met, she opened her downtown Minneapolis apartment door after I endured a white-knuckled, icy, Minnesota winter drive. Parking isn't plentiful downtown, so I had to circle the streets around the apartment building looking for a spot. When I finally parked, I texted her I was there. She responded, "Apartment 203, baby!"

She was even more beautiful than the pictures she shared, a short brunette with deep ocean blue eyes. Picture Bridget Bardot if Bridget Bardot was a short Midwestern girl-next-door with sympathetic eyes and a smile that could light up a room full of lost souls. Picture Sophia Loren's perfect cheekbones placed on a welcoming face. She smiled and walked me in. Regina Spektor's "On the Radio," a favorite song of mine, was playing in the background.

She was definitely the type of girl I would have been attracted to in high school, but would have figured was far out of my league and way too scary to have a conversation with. We agreed to meet in her apartment, get to know each other, and see where things led. I brought dinner. We shared chicken tikka masala, having revealed we both LOVED Indian food. She said there was a great Indian restaurant near her apartment, so I picked up our food, and she was right. Best chicken tikka masala I ever tasted.

I noted the stripper's pole in the living room. She said it was great exercise. The small talk was substantially deeper than I expected. She must have seen I was struggling with an all-too-comfortable and routine life. She asked me what was on my bucket list. I hadn't thought about that. I turned the question back on her. She revealed that she recently parachuted out of a plane with her sister.

I told her I was suffering from depression, almost as an excuse of why I turned to this latest form of dating. She said she understood. My dad was in the woes of Alzheimer's, so our family recently moved him from my childhood home to an assisted living facility. My oldest sister took charge and made sure Dad's diet didn't lead to other problems as he was borderline diabetic. She rationed one of Dad's favorite treats, potato chips, to five a night. I understood the intent, but given all the things he was suffering from, I thought it was crazy to not allow him some indulgence at the end of his life. Maria got it. She laughed and often recalled the "five potato chip" shared moment over the years as a shared running joke between us. I also said I was learning to play guitar and how music was the most effective antidepressant I found.

She was born and raised in Ohio, the oldest daughter of three (with a brother and sister), of conservative Christian parents. Her parents decided to homeschool her and limited her access to the liberal popular culture of her peers. They didn't want their daughter to become a boy-crazy teenage girl. She rebelled, just wanting to fit in with her peers.

Her parents punished her by taking comfort things away from her: pillows, blankets, furniture, clothing, spending money. She said this was one way they tried to keep her under their thumb, making her need them in order to get by. She felt her mother played her sister and brother against her. Her mother had different rules for her than her siblings. She would be scolded if she came home a little later than she promised, but her brother was allowed to stay out as late as he wanted.

She said this occurred to her years later as she listened to her favorite musician, Trey Songz. Growing up, her parents didn't allow her to listen to popular music because they thought it would corrupt her. They once took her radio away when she was a kid and cut the receptor so she couldn't listen to any bad music. All Maria wanted was to share in what her friends were listening to and talking about. She didn't associate the music with boys and sex. She associated it with another symptom of a disease. She felt ashamed of how different she was made to feel by her mom and dad's rules.

As a preteen, she lobbied to convince her mom and dad let her listen to music. They came to a compromise: her mom and dad would serve as a review panel. She could bring them the song she wanted to listen to, and they would decide if it was appropriate. She hoped this was a real chance for her to find a way to fit in with the popular kids. She didn't care that much about the music; she just wanted to be able to talk about what the others were so familiar with.

The first song she brought for panel review was Elliot Yamin's "Wait for You." She deliberately chose a nice song that she figured her parents couldn't possibly refuse. But they did. They didn't want her feeling that way about a boy, even though the song was about a boy's feelings for a girl. She felt maybe they didn't want boys liking her at all. She suddenly saw the process was stacked against her. It was rare for her mom and dad to approve a song. They didn't say the music was sinful, but that was what she ended up feeling.

One Christmas, she got an iPod as a gift and she downloaded a Chris Brown song. Her parents took the iPod away and said, "How could you do this to us? It's a slap in the face!" One morning before church, she snuck down to the computer to watch Brown's "Yeah Yeah Yeah" video. Her mom caught her and slapped her in the face.

When she was older, she saw that her younger brother was allowed to listen to any music he wanted to. The hip-hop and R&B songs he liked often were about sexy things. Her parents never questioned any of it. Was it a boy/girl thing? Or had she worn them down to her brother's benefit? There were too many other examples of her being the black sheep of the family that at first confused her. Upon further reflection, she realized she was raised by those who had no interest in helping her succeed, but rather wanted to control her. Freedom was counter to what was at stake. They needed her to need them and were willing to do whatever it took to make that so.

She eventually ran away from home. When she decided to return days later, her parents put her in a juvenile detention facility. Her mother shared a passage from the Bible, II Corinthians 5:17: "Therefore, if anyone is in Christ, he is a new creation; old things have passed away; behold, all things have become new. Now all things are of God, who has reconciled us to Himself through Jesus Christ, and has given us the ministry of reconciliation." Maria recited it to me from memory. For her mother, it meant Maria could change, find her salvation through Christ. For Maria, it meant no matter how hard her life became, she had the ability and strength to transform herself.

I was impressed by how her philosophy seemed to be all about self-improvement. That was no longer on my own radar, and throughout our relationship, this was a large part of what attracted me to her. She shared a story about overcoming one of her childhood failures: learning how to swim. "The things a person rejects reflect their disappointments more than their dislikes. I've hated swimming since failing lessons as a kid. Avoiding drowning was exhausting, dented my ego, and continually disappointing. I'd work harder and make less progress," she shared.

The previous weekend, she went to a swimming clinic. "I dreaded my first encounter with the water. After my first lap across the pool, the first major correction was balance. The second was patience. I found the swimming techniques were not successful without the conscious character choices of patience and balance. Over the next 13 hours of coaching and feedback, I let go of who I thought I was (incompetent in the water) and believed that I could choose something different." I was impressed with what she shared and began to believe, for the first time in a long time, there could be a pathway out of my depression.

"Confidence is built on the experience of success. Our future lies in our daily choices. Each small success is a stepping stone to greater successes. It doesn't matter how many times you've 'failed' if you use each as an opportunity to learn and grow. To create positive change in our lives, we have to let go of the fear of being wrong and believe that each incorrect attempt is a step closer to the solution." I didn't know if this message was directed at me as her way of encouraging me to get out of my rut.

From the moment we met, she was skilled at making me feel comfortable in a way only a handful of people in my life figured out. And I appreciated that so much. She took my hand and walked me toward her bedroom. We made love that night, and it was a glorious, life-changing experience. My mind was blown. She read my body, as she still does, with incredible intuition. She made me tingle in new and profound ways.

She started off with a Thai massage, techniques she was learning from another. She used the palms of her hands to put pressure on different parts of my body, shifting her weight to apply the appropriate amount of pressure. She spoke words of encouragement to try to get me to relax, so instead of pain, there was conscious thought of letting go of the things that were actually causing me pain.

Later on, things got far more intimate. We removed our clothes, and she took the pearl necklace from around her neck and rubbed it on various parts of my body, and she slyly looked in my eyes. She finished me off by squeezing her muscles around me inside her. It was a sensation that was beyond anything else I've ever experienced.

THE DIRECTOR OF ERECTIONS

Sex is a crazy topic. Obviously, I'm no expert. It's addictive and pleasurable, the ultimate act of human intimacy that can lead to creating another human being that combines parts of both partners. Yet, at the same time, it's taboo. We aren't to discuss the details of our sex lives, although clearly it would be interesting if we did.

Sex is such an important part of being human, yet it has led to public and political scandals that have ruined people. Others have ended up convicted for sex crimes because there are clear boundaries where someone either rapes another or takes advantage of someone. Yet consensual sex happens all the time under many different circumstances and expectations. It happens between husband and wife, or partner and partner, out of love, lust, or out of perfunctory routine.

It might also just be two people bumping into each other for a moment of bliss or out of desperation. I once had a sexual relationship with a person who said I seemed sad, so we should meet up at a nearby casino and fuck our pain away. We did, if only for an all-too-temporary moment.

There was no guarantee Maria and I would see each other again, given the rules we agreed to, but I sensed she would be amenable to meeting again. She was younger than me and we were at very different places in our lives. I was putting on my shoes when I asked if she was willing to seeing me again. She said she was. But I understood this was going to be a temporary thing. She had her life to live, and I had mine. We had a good time, but it wasn't something either one of us was looking to try to grow upon in any real way, proverbial ships passing in the foggy night. We hugged when I left her apartment.

A month later, we set a time to see each other again. Her text ended with 'muah' like many others to follow over the years. I literally didn't figure out what that meant for quite a while. She was sending me a virtual kiss. Like the first time, our next date was at her apartment. During the latest bout of depression that left me feeling anything at all, this illicit affair was exciting and new.

Having recently moved into her first apartment, Maria didn't want her neighbors to judge her in any critical way by who she was seeing night to night. Given her obvious love of sex, I realized that I probably wasn't the only one she was seeing like this. But again, the rules from the start said that was okay. She didn't know much about my so-called love life, and I didn't ask her about hers. When the day arrived, I thought I was going to have to cancel. I was flying back from a business trip to Wyoming, my mom's home state, that involved flying in a propeller airplane from Cheyenne to Denver. The turbulence caused me to think I would die and was sad she would never know why I didn't show up for our tryst.

We landed safely, but I missed a connecting flight and got back to the Twin Cities just in time to drive out to her apartment. But when I got there, she didn't answer my call. The next day, she said she fell asleep. We found another night, a week or two later, to see each other. I called her to finalize things. The call went to voicemail, where there was a snippet of Fergie's "Fergalicious."

Our relationship began backward. We started with the bump and tickle. Forget getting to know each other much beforehand. But as we continued, talking about ourselves became far more important. With no expectation of commitment to each other as a couple, we created a safe space where we shared anything and everything that we faced without judgment before we made love. We both made life-altering mistakes. No judgment. Therapy of the most inappropriate kind blurring all the clinical lines. Once our latest tryst was over, we were on our way back to our real lives.

At first, I looked at our once-or-twice-a-month get-together as existing outside my real life. Nobody in my real life knew about Maria. She didn't tell anyone in her life about me. In an odd way, it seemed like we were both married to other people and were having an affair that we couldn't risk exposing. Maybe the sex was so good that it made me feel guilty.

With a relationship based on sex with the fringe benefit of becoming friends, it seemed a bit scandalous. What was in it for her? I knew she was capable of pleasing herself. She told me that during family vacations, she would sit in the backseat with her hand between her legs, playing with herself. But I was different; I spent my family vacations sitting in the back of our station wagon with my brother, in a seat facing out the back window, disliking how we were seeing where we'd been and not where we were going.

We created this safe sanctuary where we could unwind, discuss anything going on in our lives, have philosophical, political, religious discussions, and share our deep dark secrets without fear of the other person running away screaming. Because of this, ours was the deepest relationship of my life. When I thought I died from the ketamine treatment, Maria was the last person on my mind.

One of the ways we were different was her willingness to break the law, whether it be speeding, shoplifting, or getting into spats with the police. I thought she was mistaken in thinking I adhered to laws because I was afraid of getting caught if I broke a law. For me, it was never that. I believed a democratic society needs people to agree to a set of principles, rules, and laws in order to function. We belong to a greater collective. For order to preside, we all have to agree that laws are important, and we agree to live under the rule of law. She shared one of the things she learned from me was the importance of reliability. When I said I'd be there for her, I meant it.

When we first met, I asked Maria if she planned on voting in the upcoming election. She told me she had little interest in politics and didn't even know who was on the ballot. I said participating in the political process felt empowering, a way to make a difference great or small. Years later, she got involved working on a campaign. She proudly let me know she was now a regular voter and thanked me for pointing out the importance of elections.

When someone perfunctorily asks how you are doing, it usually is meant to begin a polite noncommittal conversation. The asker doesn't want to hear, "I'm depressed and suicidal… how are you?" That's why I've always appreciated Maria asking me that question. She knows when I'm not telling the truth, knows me well enough to listen to the latest spinning down into the darkness that would make others squirm. And she always asks follow-up questions to get me out of my rut, my funk, my stubborn depression. She never has judged me for wallowing in my depression, but has done her best to understand it and, given our obvious different mindsets, to offer an alternative way of thinking.

Our relationship may not be real, in that we do not do what me and the rest of my friends used to do: find time to get together for coffee, or dinner, or a sporting or musical event, and do what people normally do. Maria and I share ourselves, our lives, and then we make love, with no further obligation or commitment.

But nine years later, all that we've shared has piled upon itself into something that neither one of us expected but both of us clearly have benefitted from and cherish. Every time together is our best time together, until our next time together.

When it comes to blending sex and art, there was no one better at it than the 'other' famous Minnesota musician not named Dylan, Prince. The most mind-blowing concert I've attended was Prince at the Xcel Energy Center in St. Paul in June, 2004. His song catalog was deep and enjoyable, so the set list was amazing. Seeing him in person, his musicianship and charisma was astounding, jaw-dropping, off-the-charts, crazy stuff. His dancing and showmanship only highlighted what a great all-around entertainer and spiritual guru he was. The world came off its axis the day I learned Prince died. His songs capture the essence of my time with Maria—an inspirational combination of God, love, sex, art, and pain.

MADDISON

There were times when Maria disappeared and stopped communicating with me. I took it to mean she found someone she was getting serious with, and our separate intimacy would likely be seen as an issue with her new boyfriend. These hiatuses were hard on me. I wanted her to find the guy that would make her happy and the life she wanted to create together, and I knew that wasn't me.

There was a time she told me she was going back to school at the University of Minnesota. I was happy for her. A few days later, I happened to be attending a John Prine concert on the U's campus. Sitting among college students, it made me happy Maria could easily become a part of this campus life, sharing moments with people closer to her age and enjoying the whole learning experience.

But not seeing her, not knowing how things were going for her, broke my heart. During the latest extended period of radio silence, I saw some of her social media posts and learned she moved in with a boyfriend. They looked like a typical happy social media couple, sharing fancy restaurant meals and happy moments. I truly was glad for her.

Then, once again, we resumed our relationship. The relationship with the boyfriend was rocky from the start. He was abusive. That she was seeing me, and maybe others, wasn't a sign of a healthy relationship between her and the guy she was now living with. Not that ours was the healthiest of relationships either.

One day, she sent me a photo of a positive pregnancy test. The timing of our last time together made me wonder if I was the father. She later let me know it was her boyfriend's baby. She had a difficult decision to make. Her boyfriend had a painful genetic disease that likely could be passed on to the baby. Given her religious upbringing, having an abortion was problematic at best. She decided to have the baby even after it tested positive for the genetic disease.

I told her I would support her in any way I could. We made love again when she was eight months pregnant. I tasted her breast milk. Who had I become? I was too weak to stop seeing her, but in an odd way strong enough to continue to try to be supportive of the person who had become my new muse. The person I wrote about after each and every time I saw her. Maria was now the one helping me create new memories to replace the old, painful ones just like my old muse, Stephanie, once promised to help me do.

Maria planned to have her baby in a natural setting without drugs. But the pain was more than she anticipated, and she gave birth with painkilling drugs to help her. It was a beautiful baby girl named Maddison. We texted each other, and I paid for dinner to be delivered to her. She was estranged from her family during this life-meaning moment, and she let me know that it meant the world to her that I was so supportive.

The feeling was mutual. I was glad to be there because she was there for me too when I was in moments of need. How was our relationship not real and authentic just because at its core was our sex together, the pain we consensually shared, and not a more traditional get-together for coffee?

Most of our times together have come at an hour or two a time. There was one time where we met at the Mall of America's Radisson Blu for an overnight experience. I knew waking up next to her would be a significant moment, feeling like a real couple. This was as close as I likely would ever be to being on a honeymoon.

We had a memorable conversation that night as she revealed more of her true self than ever before. "I learned pretty quickly that to be loved, I had to be beautiful. And who doesn't want to be loved? So I became beautiful. At the time, I didn't have the money to buy the makeup or clothes, but I promised myself I'd become successful so I could. And money would be my access to love," she said. I was saddened by that confession. It was one of the many ways Maria and I were very different.

I guess I'm lucky I never thought much about money. My parents somehow carved out a comfortable life for me and my four siblings. We weren't rich, but money was something I never worried about, even though there must have been times when Mom and Dad did. And I've made enough during my career to afford the things I want.

We made love that night and then ordered room service and watched TV together. A normal couple for just one night. When we woke up the next morning, we made love again, our first morning sex. I held her for as long as I could. We ordered room service. She once shared how important her morning makeup routine was to her, so I asked if I could watch. She was happy to share, saying she honed her makeup routine over the years and thought what she came up with through some trial and error was perfect for her. "Puberty took me from an awkward shy girl to one whose features bloomed," she said. "Some people now call me beautiful without makeup. It took me from age 16 to age 23, but I artfully crafted a makeup look that sets me apart. You'd have to see it to know it, but once you see it, you know it."

We scampered to the hotel bathroom with its large vanity and picture-window-sized mirror. I've never written science fiction but always thought it would be a great story, about a planet where there were two species made out of glass. One transparent like a window and the other reflective like a mirror. The two sides were constantly at war because although they were made up of the same thing, they were opposite in purpose. I'll have to write that story someday.

She took out her makeup kit. "I was fascinated with makeup because one of the girls I went to school with was gorgeous… and wildly popular. She was who I wished I could be. Hair perfectly smoothed, eyeliner perfectly applied, outfit stylish. And let's not forget everyone loved her. She was who I wished I was. She got what she wanted from life," Maria told me.

She began with a skin primer to her entire face, allowing the next steps to lay flawlessly. Then, she drew triangles in a light shade just below her eyes to bring the area forward, making her look more awake. She took a beauty blender and blended it seamlessly up to her eyes' waterline. Then, she dotted foundation on the rest of her face and blended it in, creating flawless-looking skin. It was amazing how each step made a subtle but real change to her face.

Next, she took a dark contour stick and drew lines in places she said she wanted to make thinner. "These are blended until they appear as if God painted them," she said. She took a brightening setting powder and applied it generously under her eyes. She said this set the under-eye concealer and brought the area forward even further. "I have a different, nude powder I use to set the rest of my face," she explained.

"I still look a bit dull, so next come eyebrows. I use a powder to enhance areas that are sparse. I delay the time doing my hair so that the powder can set," she said. She lightly brushed away all excess powder on her face so she could apply mascara. "Once my eyelashes are long and luscious, I use a powder contour to bring out the creme contour. Then, I sweep blush on the apples of my cheeks. I do a onceover on my entire face and then set the look with a setting spray," she said, proud to show me this well thought-out personal routine.

I thought about how people throughout my life told me I'm hard to read because of my mask-like facial expressions. We all share what we want the world to see. My mask was natural but not intentional. Was it mostly caused by my stoic Asian face?

"Perfection is a funny thing. It looks so wonderful on the outside, and I'm convinced that's the only thing that looks wonderful," she said. "Underneath a perfect exterior is something that's hiding. For me, I was hiding from who I was in high school. I vowed to never be that girl again. The one who wore the wrong clothes and wasn't allowed to wear makeup. The one who felt like she didn't fit in. The one who was laughed at when she had one of her girlfriends tell a boy in her class she liked him. When my makeup is done, I look in the mirror and feel powerful. I feel like anyone who isn't with me… well, that's their loss. It's superficial, but when that's all a person has, they hold on to things."

I tried my best to picture a young Maria, full of insecurity but brimming with a plan to change that. "Good makeup enhances what is already there. It's my face, but better. It hasn't guaranteed me love, but it has gotten me a lot further in life."

When the pandemic shut down society, Maria kidded me that I was well prepared for the staying at home as I spent my entire life social distancing and wearing a mask-like face that hid what I was thinking and feeling.

A couple months later, George Floyd was murdered by Minneapolis police officer Derek Chauvin. This led to riots and burning down businesses along Lake Street in Minneapolis. For 11 years every summer, I would ride my scooter to my job in Minnetonka, a suburb of Minneapolis down Lake Street, past the police precinct that was the original target of the rioting. The world seemed to be exploding and coming apart at the seams.

Maria texted me she was searching Craigslist for an assault rifle. There was no way she would let anyone destroy her home or hurt her and her daughter. My reaction was 180 degrees different. I knew anger wasn't the answer, but I also knew the rioting was due in large part to a history of racism that was never addressed. I watched my city burning down in horror and didn't know if I wanted to live in a world where we needed to arm ourselves and hoard toilet paper at the same time.

She asked if I wanted to catch up and meet her and Maddison in a Home Depot parking lot near their home. I was happy she asked. She and Maddison would be the only people I saw in person for many months. We hugged, and Maddison was delighted to race around the mostly empty parking lot, occasionally updating Maria on things she saw like some birds in the sky.

Maria was the only person who checked in on me regularly, and we eventually occasionally began getting together again. I knew it was a risk. Even before the pandemic, she was an anti-vaxxer, a sometime-believer in conspiracy theories like how 5G waves were brainwashing us. But I couldn't continue the solitary confinement. I needed some human contact.

This led to us getting together in our usual way once again. I moved my hands down between her legs. Her panties were still on, so I caressed her through the cloth. I couldn't believe how wet she already felt. The feeling that she could get that excited about me made me very hard very quick. The scent and taste from her wetness almost made me cum. Her panties were so wet she couldn't wear them to her tennis match. It's a thrill that excites me every time I think about it and will leave me eternally wanting to come back for more. She's admitted it turns her on to tease me to the edge of completion. Near the end of our reunion, right after I came, she squeezed her muscles around me. A reminder of our past times together, it sent my head into the clouds, not to return for hours, a phantom sensation I have tried to imagine feeling ever since.

She shared she went to a bachelorette party at a S&M club. Among the crowd, she spotted a redheaded man who looked spiritually lost. She sensed she should say something to him, so she went over to tell him she'd say a prayer for him. He wasn't receptive. I loved that she'd do that. Saying a prayer for a man in a S&M club defines her in my mind as a uniquely complex person with a great nurturing soul.

UNCONQUERABLE SOUL OF MAN

The only time I left my house for a social event in a public space in 2020 was to watch Maria play tennis at a fitness club. Masked and anonymous, I took my place upstairs and watched her through huge glass windows. The coach of her team sat with me and asked me what I did for a living. When I told her, she said she was impressed, and I had important work in front of me. There were several courts in front of us, and Maria was playing on the second-to-the-furthest away.

One of the few things my dad and I had in common was watching tennis, particularly women's professional tennis. Wimbledon, the U.S., French, and Australian Opens, I remember lying on Dad's living room couch in the years following Mom's death watching our favorite players together. One of my first celebrity crushes was on Chris Evert. I loved her steely demeanor and her steady, unflappable style. Years later, some of my colleagues would tell me that was what they admired about my leadership style. Calm and collected until you looked under the hood. I think Dad and I both had crushes on Steffi Graff and Martina Hingis. We both preferred the women's game because it wasn't all about crushing, 100-mph serves. There were longer volleys and using multiple shots to set up the opposing player for the kill.

Maria's game was exactly that. Her opponent had a much more powerful serve and volley game, but Maria was a machine. She kept the volley alive until her opponent made the inevitable mistake trying to out-muscle her. Her strategy seemed to be less about finding the particular shot to beat her opponent and more about letting her opponent beat herself. This was confirmed the second time I saw her play.

This time, Maria seemed to be having difficulty with the toss to her serve, taking two or three attempts before making a serve. I didn't remember this happening once during her first match. She won the match, and afterward, I asked her why she was having so much trouble with her serve. She smiled and walked me out of earshot of her opponent. "I saw how impatient she was and knew it would get into her head if I delayed my serves," she revealed. Maria's game was exactly that, looking for the smallest clues in knowing how to outthink her opponent. I saw that too in what she shared about her business deals and her relationships. She's very transactional, win versus lose, and that's another way we are very different.

Late in 2021, she flew down to Indian Wells, California with the rest of her team to participate in a national tournament. After she got back, we took our place on her apartment couch with paintings of Marilyn Monroe and Audrey Hepburn adorning the walls. Maria had great taste in role models. I could tell she was anxious to share how the tournament went. She was beaming and radiant, a vision to behold.

"I lost my racquets on the way down. The flight attendant yelled at me for forgetting to wear a mask. And then when we landed, he made a snide comment. I was befuddled, and I left my racquets in the overhead." When she realized what she did, she ran to the lost-and-found and was told they would arrive in the lost items the next morning. All three of her teammates offered to let her use their backup racquets. She called the airport the next day, and the racquets had not been turned in to the lost-and-found. She suspected the flight attendant had something to do with this.

She lost her first match against her teammate Hanna. She dismissed the loss as being rusty from not being able to play much with most of the gyms closed. She won her second match of the day, barely. The second day, it was apparent her racquets were permanently gone. She was angry and embarrassed at how badly she was playing. The racquet she was using had strings probably six years old, wet noodles, and as she hit the ball, it was dying upon contact. "I knew I had to get mental control, and then I got a mind picture. It was like I was a jockey, and the racquet was a three-legged horse with dementia. The picture of this made me laugh, and that was enough of a mental break to win the match."

She switched to another teammate's backup racquet. She lost to the best player on her team, Kerry, but felt her game was back. "Our team went to an Oceanside bar. I needed to win one match before playing Kerry again for the championship." I sensed what she was sharing she hadn't told to other people. One of the cornerstones of our relationship. "Kerry was upset. We were being told our division couldn't play on the center court that was reserved for the men." The look on her face changed. There was a devilish look in her eyes, equal parts twinkling and focused. "I walked up to Steve the organizer, the one telling us we wouldn't play on center court. 'I hear our women's division are second-class citizens,' I said with a laugh." We adjusted ourselves on the couch, her placing her legs on mine. "He said there's just not time for everyone. I mused, 'Limited time, yet all of the men's divisions get to have their playoffs, not just championships, in the big stadium?' And Steve said, 'Yeah, there's limited time for everyone with the sun and stuff.' I told him I wasn't arguing because it was his tournament. I just asked him to help me understand in order to make peace with this. Essentially, it was 'the women's division sucks, so work harder and come again next year?'"

Maria said the look on Steve's face awkwardly changed, a flip-flop with plenty of sweat. He asked what changing things would bring to the table. Maria said the big match would be between her and Kerry. They would bring it. "I'll bring myself and my racquet and look forward to playing in the big stadium." Everyone within earshot was stunned and grew quiet, impressed with Maria's fighting for what was right. Steve relented and agreed to let her rematch with Kelly to be played front and center. It was the first time that happened. Maria is never shy about pushing for something she wants, especially when she sees it as righting an inequality. She has a stubborn streak rivaling a cat with a closed door between it and another meal.

"Kerry and I walked on. I'd never beaten her before. 2020 was quite a year. We've all lived with the unexpected not knowing what was to come next. So I said to Kerry, 'This is the most fun we've had all year. You're probably going to beat me, but we're going to put on a good show.' We got out on the court, and I had a huge smile. This was the best day of our lives." I felt honored Maria was sharing this significant moment with me. Honored but not surprised. Our lives came together for exactly this shared moment.

"Shocked, I won the first set. Kerry seemed shocked too. She has a big serve that requires a lot of focus to return. The second set, I was down 3-1. These are shorter sets to 4, since you play 2 matches a day. Winner was the first one to win 4 games in the set. If she won another game, we would have to play a set tiebreaker. My mind ran through potential scenarios as we took a water break. I could push hard and play a tiebreak for this set. Or I could save my energy and push hard to win the 3rd set tiebreak. I had the most positive possible options in front of me. She had an uphill battle. That was my advantage. Mentally, I talked to myself. I made it this far. Slow down the game and focus on the fundamentals. Suddenly, we were tied games and had to play a second set tiebreak to 10, win by 2." She stroked my arm with her fingers almost automatically and absentmindedly.

"I was ahead and lost focus. She caught back up. We kept exchanging points, neither able to take the lead by 2. Then, she stood on the wrong side of the court. I realized she was losing mental focus and had to keep mine. I was ahead 10-9 and needed the next point to win. She went to serve, her big serve, and I returned it a cross-court angle. The heat played to my advantage, and her return soared over my right side and out of the court. I had won the national championship!" I reached out and hugged her. How great was her accomplishment? But there was more.

"Kerry and I ran toward the net, and I started crying from shock/relief/disbelief. We hugged each other, teammates from Minnesota. She turned to everyone and said, 'She just won without her racquet!' We received our trophies. More than the trophy, the satisfaction was who I had to be as a person to get to where I was. More than the final score, it was the choices I'd made over the last year. I chose to take performance setbacks to improve technique that would take me to the next level. I'd mentally weathered losses and relentlessly focused on the big picture, on what needed to improve for next time. I'd stayed positive through it all, choosing thoughts that served my highest and best good. It was the character I built through the game that makes my life better every day. It looked like it was one match, but this win is a reflection of how I do life."

I got it. I really did, even if that life approach was never me, less so than ever in knowing Maria. Our differences made us stronger each and every time.

"All four of us women from Minnesota placed well, and I truly believe it was because we came as a team and supported each other. We looked out for each other when it came to snacks, drinks, and checking in on how each other was doing and being present for each other's matches. Our support took the pressure off simple details so we could focus on performing in our matches. The power of the other. We were stronger together than individually. It's not just your individual character—it's the people you handpick to be on your team that define your success." I never felt more alive with her sharing the latest chapter of her story. "On the flight home, my trophy fell out of my bag and got lost. Apparently, I need the power of the other more than I realized. The trophy was replaced, but I'll never forget the power of the other every time I see it."

Another change in mindset for me. I wasn't too old a dog to learn a new trick.

LEARNING
HOW TO LOVE YOU

The first time Maria came over to my house, she took note of the baby grand piano that took up much of my living room. She took piano lessons growing up and impressed her parents and friends by memorizing Beethoven's "Fur Elise."

My mom signed me up for piano lessons when I was in the fourth grade. My teacher was Mrs. Good, the same piano teacher my sister Donna took lessons from. I was nowhere near the piano player Donna was, never could be, partly because of the difference of our devotion to practice and getting better, but also because some skills can't be learned. Learning to play the piano was another great outlet for my love of music. Years after moving out of my parents' house, Mom found it amusing when I'd come over for dinner and took my frustrations out in failing at playing Mario Brothers on the Nintendo by banging out a Beatles or Barry Manilow song on the family piano. She noted that I played her favorite Beatles song, "Hey Jude," with unique passion.

I eventually paid for Donna's baby grand piano to be shipped from her home in California to my house in Minnesota. Donna was moving and no longer had room for the piano. The baby grand piano took up significant space in my living room and got played more often by my cats Diego-san and Theo. A few years after Mom died, I asked Dad if he still had my sister Joan's guitar. I was interested in continuing learning my music, only on a different instrument. Dad said the guitar was gone. He gave me a brand-new Yamaha acoustic guitar that year for my birthday. He kidded me for the next couple of years when I did nothing with that guitar gift.

Eventually, I signed up with a teacher to learn how to play guitar. Pavel was a classical guitarist, and what he taught me was the ultimate creative stress release. I would name the song I wanted to learn, and he would listen to the song and write down the chords and teach me how to place my fingers to play the chords and the strumming scheme. Most of the songs I wanted to learn were simple three-chord rock-and-roll songs, so my guitar repertoire soon far exceeded my piano playing. Playing guitar was inherently therapeutic, a combination of left brain/right brain integration. Playing the chords and figuring out the finger positions on the guitar strings required one side of my brain, while singing the lyrics and expressing what I was feeling required the other side of my brain. My nightly guitar sessions replaced my nightly writing sessions for the most part. I was glad and sad for this new turn of events. I let go of one creative outlet to let in another.

The next time we got together, Maria shared an epiphany. She was going to be better at embracing her femininity. She realized her greatest power over men was how they desired her based on her physical attractiveness. Her term, 'embracing her femininity,' struck a nerve in me. That night, I began to write my first song. As I fumbled for the right lyrics, I landed on the perfect chord progression. Given our unique relationship of sex and sharing our authentic selves without the other running away, the chord progression was the simple chords of most of my last name, "AEDA." I strummed the chords and sang the following lyrics:

You say I'll get better,
You know that I will,
Even if this becomes our coda,
Feeling the moment forever,
These things aren't supposed to last long,
That's why I sing this song.

I love the way you tease me,
I love the way you please me,
I love the way you squeeze me,
Embracing your femininity.

You tell me when and where,
I tell you I'll be there,
My favorite tap on the wrist,
Every time I sigh I feel your touch,
Patience and balance, swimming along,
That's why I sing this song.

I love the way you tease me,
I love the way you please me,
I love the way you squeeze me,
Embracing your femininity.

You want us to smoke some weed
I agree, that's what we need,
Brains, beauty, and brawn,
Melody recalls this feeling,
Making me feel like I belong,
That's why I sing this song.

I love the way you tease me,
I love the way you please me,
I love the way you squeeze me,
Embracing your femininity.

The next time around, I nervously brought my guitar to our visit at her place and tried to sing her our song. I didn't do so effectively because I was so nervous, having never played my guitar in front of anybody but Pavel, my teacher, but Maria was clearly moved by my attempt. I was amazed that I was able to do this creative thing, taking inspiration to write in a whole different genre and then perform it for my inspiration. Such an opportunity for a disappointing result. But Maria responded perfectly, honored and encouraging me to continue forward.

INSTITUTIONAL SHARED EXPERIENCE

Right or wrong, Maria has been the most important person in my life the past nine years. She's stuck with me when others disappeared. That I was able to help in with her figuring out how to be a single mom, when her own family abandoned her, is probably the most meaningful personal accomplishment I've achieved.

She makes me smile, when smiling is the furthest thing in my repertoire, simply because she learned what buttons to push during our times together. She continues to shock me, stimulate me, with great conversations and acceptance. I wouldn't be where I'm at today, good or bad, without her.

She may not be my most conventional friend, but she is my most authentic friend through and through, time and time again. She shared a creative writing story she wrote about being locked up for her juvenile delinquency that I immediately related to, given my own horrid institutionalization experience for depression. She ends her story with horror and humor. I'm still trying to do so myself.

One of my all-time favorite TV shows is *Buffy the Vampire Slayer*. Buffy is the chosen one, a teenage girl who lives on the hellmouth. She alone is responsible for keeping the world safe from vampires, monsters, demons, and impending apocalypses. One of my favorite episodes comes late in the series where Buffy is stung by a demon and ends up in an alternative reality, one where she is institutionalized in a mental hospital and her mother and father are still together and alive (they were divorced when the series began, and Buffy's mother was killed earlier in the series).

The doctor explains to Buffy that she can choose to walk away from this other delusional existence, one where she is a vampire slayer who has befriended vampires, werewolves, and witches. It seems like an obvious choice. Living on the hellmouth, fighting off apocalypse after apocalypse, not only seems like a fantasy, but that life has been so hard, and she is so alone in her overwhelming responsibilities. The other life where she still is a part of a California family seems like a life she has missed. The episode resonates with me because it calls up the time I was hospitalized for my depression. I related to Buffy's desire to live in a more rational world lovingly accepted by her family.

Being institutionalized was something Maria and I had in common. As part of our shared memoir project, Maria sent me the story she wrote about her time in the juvenile detention facility. It was one of our different-yet-similar life experiences… nightmares of being locked up for being crazy or out of control, certainly something our relationship has always shared. I've told very few people in my life about my hospitalization. Maria told me I was one of the very few she shared her experience with.

I loved how Maria was able to write a story using her wonderful sense of humor. I have yet to be able to laugh off my hospitalization experience, yet I relate to the rigidness of the routine and the mind-fucking going on in our somewhat shared yet entirely different experiences.

BEHIND THE BARS OF AUTISM: MARIA'S STORY

I tapped my fingers on the desk and swayed my feet from left to right, left to right. Today was my mom's birthday, and here I was back at Abraxas Juvenile Detention. In two weeks, I'd have my 16th birthday, and I'd probably still be here then. This made me angry, and I defiantly turned towards the forbidden hallway. Although I knew I was breaking a rule, Mr. Patterson's sneakers were clomping up the hallway, so he wouldn't see me, and that's all that mattered. When we're sitting in our rooms, they'd told us to face towards the wall. I didn't know why they made that rule, but it's there for no reason.

Ms. Bonar told me she's not giving back the markers and notebook that I had before I left two weeks ago. Oh yeah, two weeks ago when I woke up one morning feeling actually happy. Lucy, my probation officer, had been trying to schedule a time within the next two weeks for me to go home. So glad to think about that possibility, I wasn't even phased by the monotonous morning routine.

"Detention! Shirts tucked in, socks on; ladies, hair up. Let's get those doors open!" Mr. Rooney yelled from the hall.

I grabbed the rubber doorstop from the top of the electric lockbox and shoved it in place as fast as I could.

A voice called from the hall. "Detention! Prepare to step out to get your contraband!"

In the rec yard a few days back, Michelle had shared her opinion of contraband with Tricia, the third girl on the unit, while I listened in.

"The whole concept of contraband is bull," Michelle declared, casting a menacing glance towards Ms. Bonar, who was in blue jeans and a NY Yankees jersey that made her already obtuse hips scream of an overabundance of the pumpkin whoopee pies that Mr. Rooney had brought in.

"If the wardens are in a particularly bad mood, they'll find something random they can call contraband just to put you on RL (Restrictive Level) for a day or two. Then you have to wear those stupid plastic shoes all day and have to walk laps when everyone else is doing something outside. If we got a lot of time outside, I wouldn't care, but we get to go maybe three times a week," Tricia lamented.

I was on Restrictive Level nearly all the time, so I totally agreed with her.

"I know!" Michelle commiserated. "I mean, come on, an extra piece of paper, doodles and sketches, extra socks. It's really nonsense when you think about it. And here's what really makes me mad—something being allowed in one room and not the other. Last week, I wrote a really nasty letter during school. Even though I had done all my homework and had nothing else to do, it was still criminalized, and that apparently gave them the right to read it. Of course when they did, they flipped out about its contents and yelled at me for over two hours. I swear, when all seven of them had swarmed around me and Ms. Bonar was yelling while her spit flew in my face... That witch almost got herself decked. She's sandpaper to my soul! How do they expect us to just stand there not moving while they tell us how vile and disgusting we are? They ramble about keeping a safe 'environment' and 'balance and restorative justice,' but I don't see any of that being accomplished."

I'd gone through quite a few processes, gotten restrained, been on one-and-one, but I loved how Michelle and Tricia put it. Because I hated it all, I liked to listen in when the two of them talked so mutinously.

"Detention!" someone called from the hall. "You will have five seconds to get your chair, garbage can, laundry bag, sneakers, and books. If you're not fast enough, you'll all put it back and do it again till you get it right. Quietly! Go! Five, four—"

All 16 of us, three girls and 13 boys, rushed out and collected the items.

"Three, two, one. Alright, gentlemen on the office side, prepare to step out for morning hygiene. Everyone else, get your rooms squared away."

Hearing them tell me to get my room squared away was annoying because they said it all the time. I made my bed, using hospital corners, folded my laundry, and put it away in the plastic green bins that slid under my bed.

Then Ms. Bonar called, "Ladies, prepare to step out for morning hygiene. Sweatshirts off." A few seconds later, "Step out."

Michelle, Tricia, and I all took a step, ending with our heels on the one-by-one black tiles that lined the perimeter of the hall and the rest on the white inner area. As we stepped, we reached and turned off the light.

I glanced over at Michelle and Tricia standing in the doorway of their room and grinned. Tricia had been my roommate, and I was jealous that they got to share a room, but they moved me because I kept talking to Tricia. It got so lonely here, and I couldn't help it. The rule list on the wall said talking was allowed if staff granted permission, but they never did.

"Melinda!" Mr. Rooney barked. "Head and eyes straight forward! And no smiling!"

I knew I was autistic, and sometimes that worked for me because most people expected me to keep to myself, but I thought I was the opposite. I loved to talk all the time, and dance in the doorway, and hump the walls to make Michelle laugh.

Mr. Patterson didn't tell me to be quiet when I called out of my room, and Mr. Barron let me use a multiplication table for my problems. I got so angry when I got the wrong answer! After walking down the right side of the hallway, but not stepping on any black tiles, we waited several feet back from the door.

"Bathroom norms," Bonar prompted.

"No posing or flexing in the mirror," Tricia said with a twinge of mocking in her voice.

"No talking," Michelle droned.

"First one in turns on the light," I said.

"All right, ladies, you have four minutes."

Michelle and Tricia had commented on morning hygiene as well. They were full of opinions but obviously didn't blurt their insubordinations in front of staff.

"Four minutes? How the heck do they expect us to go to the bathroom, brush our teeth, which is a two-minute process in itself, and comb our hair?" Michelle complained.

"What epic adventures do we have to rush off to? Sitting in our room and staring at the white wall?" Tricia added.

"Or reading the same book for the fifth time! And what's the deal with 'no posing or flexing in the mirror?' Really?"

While I got ready, I thought about all the rules: show your basket to staff, only two paper towels, wipe out the sink when you're done. That's a lot of nonsense for going to the bathroom. When I got home, I was going to leave crusty toothpaste in the sink just because I could.

We all lined up again and waited at the back of the hallway. The boys were called out, and everyone filed into place. Each resident gave the meal norms and counted off.

Breakfast was a scoop of watery eggs, two slices of dry white bread that was served at every single meal, milk, and a dish of cereal that got harder the longer it sat in milk. I looked at Mr. Abrams and then Tricia and Michelle.

"I think Mr. Abrams is sexy," I whispered, laughing. "So is Mr. Boonbaw."

"Hey! Melinda! No communication!" Mr. Carmello bellowed in his 'nasty' voice that he used with us kids and seemed to love hearing.

Mr. Carmello was the meanest guy in the entire building. He was a nerd with a cruel, squashed face and thin tendrils of greasy hair that he swept to one side in an attempt to conceal his balding head. Coloring in the naked spots with a brown sharpie would've been less obvious!

We finished, wiped our table, dumped our trays, and lined up for 'transport.'

"Transport makes us sound like cattle," Michelle whispered and got away with it.

At 9 a.m., we were hustled into the classroom and waited to be seated until given permission. Mr. Plink's geography class was long and boring as he talked too loudly like usual.

Then, Mr. Barron, the math teacher, taught. He reminded me of my grandpa and was funny. If the class got an average of 90 percent or higher on a test, he'd bring in candy. Mr. Barron always had a bottle of diet soda that he sipped throughout class. Sometimes I wished I could snatch it off his desk and take a long gulp! All we got was metallic water from the building's pipes that hadn't been updated since its days as a tuberculosis hospital, nasty orange drink, or heavily diluted red Kool-Aid. He treated us like humans, which was more than could be said for the rest of the staff.

Towards the end, he had me redo the multiplication problems that I had gotten wrong on the homework, which was most of them. I looked at the first one, eight times 16, and grunted angrily.

"What's wrong, Melinda?" Mr. Barron asked sympathetically.

"I have a low IQ. I can't do it!" I slammed my fists on my desk.

"Step in the hallway, Melinda," Mr. Carmello directed loudly.

I stood up but walked away from the door. I wasn't going out there with ugly, evil Carmello.

"Melinda, if I have to bring you out here, that's going to be a problem."

He stepped towards me as Mr. Abrams and Ms. Bonar moved closer.

"No!" I yelled.

This time, they grabbed my arms and twisted them painfully behind my back. Once in the hallway, they let go. Mr. Carmello's demon-like voice told me not to move.

"Now, what's all this about?" Mr. Abrams questioned, still somewhat patient. "I understand that you have trouble learning, but that was no way to handle things."

"I can't get it!"

Mr. Carmello returned to hawking the other inmates inside the classroom as Mr. Hamilton, the life skills teacher, switched in.

Mr. Abrams talked with me and then brought a desk out into the hallway. "You're going to sit out here since you can't behave. Once you cool down a little, I'll give you paper and a pencil."

I hadn't sat there long before Mr. Hamilton marched out with Michelle. Mr. Hamilton lined her up against the wall and asked, "So what's up with you and Jonny?"

"Nothing," she replied.

"Then why did you smile at him?" Hamilton pressed.

"We were laughing about something."

"Well, you don't know what kind of boy Jonny is. You don't know what a smile communicates to a guy. Your smiling could bring jealousy and make everyone start fighting. My job is to create a safe and secure environment, and sure as Chuck Norris, that's what I'll do! Do you understand?"

"I get that this isn't *The Notebook*: Abraxas Edition, but I don't see how my smiling over an inside joke is detrimental to the rest of the inmates."

"You're not inmates. You're residents. And my job is to keep a safe environment. When you go back to the room, you'll have a new seat."

By the time Mr. Hamilton took Michelle back to the classroom and brought Jonny out, I was working on multiplication. Mr. Hamilton started asking Jonny the same questions as Michelle. Then their voices escalated.

"You're nothing but a deceitful, lying boy! How dare you create an unsafe environment!"

All this hollering was getting to me. I crumpled my multiplication into a ball. I was finished with math and school and stupid Abraxas!

"Stop that, Melinda!" Mr. Abrams corrected, irritated this time.

"I want to leave and never come back!" I shrieked and plunged the pencil into my hand.

"Carmello! Bonar! Call 911 and another unit for backup! She stabbed herself with a pencil again!"

All the staff rushed out, and Carmello grabbed my arms and slammed me to the ground. "You've just gotten yourself a physical restraint, Melinda." He growled menacingly in my ear.

"No! Let go of me!" I wailed as he wrenched my arms behind my back and dug his knee in into my back.

He didn't, and they took me away in handcuffs and shackles.

Instead of the overnight hospital visit I was hoping for, they sent me to a crisis center in Pittsburgh, and I was there for two weeks.

I had gotten out of the hospital and was back home because of good behavior. Luckily, things were somewhat normal, and I was going to school and doing what I was supposed to. Then my teacher made me angry, so angry that I grabbed her by the neck and choked her. That was what got me back at Abraxas.

So here I was now, listening to Mr. Patterson's sneakers in the hallway.

"Can I get a volunteer?" Mr. Patterson called from the hall.

Whenever they asked for a volunteer, the first one to step out got to do some community service. I had nearly 100 hours to complete, and my desk was near the door, so I jumped up and stepped outside.

"Thank you, Melinda," Mr. Patterson said gratefully, walking towards me. "You have just signed up for a room search."

I did not expect this from Patterson. What sort of power play was this? He marched into my six-by-10 foot room, dumped the contents of the drawer pell-mell onto the ground, ripped the sheets off the bed, and flipped the mattress onto the ground.

"Go ahead and step back in, Melinda," Mr. Patterson said after he had completed his task, messing up everything he possibly could.

I chuckled as I struggled to lift the mattress back onto the bed. No one had ever done that before. I put the book back in the desk drawer and remade the bed. Then I sat down in the chair.

Mr. Patterson walked by, and I called out, "Can I do some physical therapy?"

"Don't call out of your room, Melinda. And yes, you may."

I did a few squats and then was bored.

"Mr. Patterson!"

"Yes, Melinda?" he replied, not bothering to tell me not to call out of my room.

"I'm feeling lightheaded. I think I need the nurse!" I really just wanted to talk to Rose, the pretty nurse with the long, black hair. Abraxas was like pain from a broken bone, and I needed some medicine!

"Just sit down a minute. You must have overexerted yourself." He kept walking up the hallway.

After an hour or so of sitting in my chair, Ms. Bonar called, "Melinda, step out!"

I did but hoped they wouldn't mess up my room again.

"Cover down," Ms. Bonar said.

Walking down the hallway, I was greeted by Lucy, my probation officer.

"Lucy!"

"Hi, Melinda. I'm going to take you home. You've been here long enough, and I need to consider some school alternatives, but I want you to be home."

"Oh! Thanks, Lucy! It's my mom's birthday today! She's 37."

"Let's go then. I already have your things gathered. Head into the bathroom and change. I'm giving you this opportunity, but you need to control your anger better. If you keep beating up elderly bus drivers and choking teachers, you'll be in placement forever. You've already been to Abraxas five different times."

We drove home, and I greeted my family.

"Mom! Dad!" I hugged my mom, but my arms couldn't reach the whole way around. It was the same for my dad. We all love food!

The whole family ate some cake. I had three pieces. We talked, and I wished my mom a happy birthday.

"Oh, honey, I missed you so much. Please try not to get angry at anyone and do anything else. I know it's hard, but you know that too. I would be so sad if you missed my 38th birthday because you got angry again."

"Like the time I beat up the granny bus driver and broke her glasses because she told me to be quiet and stop talking?" I chuckled, remembering the incident.

"Melinda, it's really not funny. Please try to straighten up for us."

"OK, OK." I laughed again.

Later, my dad asked if I wanted to go to the store with him to get some more ice cream.

I love ice cream, so I said yes. Together, we drove to the store and were waiting in line. Everything was taking so long, and the cashier was moving so slowly.

And that all made me angry...

PART FIVE:
MAKING THE GRADE

Iwas nearly born in a Chinese restaurant. Thankfully, the family-owned restaurant offered delivery service.

Mom and Dad were returning home from Mom's latest doctor appointment. They decided to stop at Chin's Kitchen, a Chinese restaurant at the corner of Snelling and Larpenteur Avenues in Roseville, Minnesota. It was a small hole-in-the-wall restaurant across the street from the State Fairgrounds. Grandma and Grandpa were babysitting my sisters and brother. Right as Dad was adding Moo Goo Gai Pan to the dinner order, Mom told him they needed to go back to the doctor. Dad said they should drop off the dinner first and then go back. But Mom said no, they better go back right away. A half hour after they returned to the hospital, I was born.

31 years later, I bought a home not far from the corner of Larpenteur and Snelling Avenues. After my mom died, I made it a point to eat my birthday dinner at Chin's Kitchen that had moved across the street into a remodeled strip mall. I'm not sure it made sense to do so, but it felt like I was honoring Mom's sacrifice of some MSG-laced Chinese food that evening to deliver me.

One of my first memories is of a bright sunny day with a clear blue sky when my dad and brother were teaching me how to fly my first kite. The kite was ruby-red with a yellow stripe. If I remember correctly (which is sketchy at this point), it had a picture of a dad and his son together.

Dad had my brother run as fast as his chubby little legs could go, and the kite rapidly ascended into the horizon. Dad took the spool, unreeled the string, and the kite rose even higher. He handed the spool over to me and told me not to let go. I did as I was told as my dad helped my brother get his own kite into the wind and sky. However, I hadn't been told not to let the string unravel further. As I did so, I watched my kite go higher and farther away. Before I knew it, the last of the string left the spool, and my dad and brother were too far away to help. The kite flew away.

I wondered why my dad didn't take my brother and me on a drive across the railroad tracks where the kite flew to see if we could retrieve it. He assumed it was gone, and we couldn't correct my mistake. And the apt metaphor for what my life was to become was burned into my psyche. Without knowing what I was doing, indeed thinking I was doing what I was told to do, I let things unravel, and I lost something important to me that would forever be gone.

Who could've guessed that one of my earliest memories became the overarching story of my life? Looking back at my 58 years, I realize my life got away from me. I let things unspool, unravel, and now it seems too late in the game to get things back, to turn things around.

Life is only about forward momentum. No matter how scarred, how traumatized, how much pain you are in from moments from your past, life outside you is going to go on whether you want it to or not. That said, it's not too late to learn that your perspective can be looking down into a dark bottomless pit, or flip things and see the endless sky above.

I remember lying on my back on our backyard grass looking up at the clouds in the sky beyond the roof of our house. The movement of the clouds gave the illusion our house was moving against the still sky. My whole life was in front of me, and anything seemed possible. Even being able to see my house move with the Earth's turning. I just had to let go of what I knew to be true, that the clouds were moving and not our house, in order to reach my dreams.

Some people look at clouds and see puppies, dragons, and clowns. Others look at them as cumulus or cirrus-shaped water drops. I clearly fall into the former. Yet, when I look up at the night sky, I just see random stars. Others see the constellations. I've never in my life been able to discern the big or little dippers no matter how hard I try. My dreams could only take me so far.

An early memory came when I was two or three years old. There was a tornado warning in our suburb, and when my oldest sister came to get me out of my crib to shelter in our split-level suburban home basement, I was nowhere to be found. My sister freaked out. After an extensive search of our house and yard, someone found me napping underneath my crib. I can't possibly remember this given how young I was, but somehow, I do. I remember wanting to find a better place to nap. When I heard the commotion my choice of crawling out of my crib caused, I wasn't about to lessen the center of attention my actions drew.

When I was three years old, my brother Bruce set my lifetime standard of what a best friend looked like. We spent all our time together. Because I had a slight speech impediment that made it hard for others to understand what I was saying, he became my interpreter. Throughout my life, my closest friends were able to intuitively read me without me having to explain myself.

When Bruce began kindergarten, my life routine changed. Mom made sure there was enough stuff for me to do to occupy my time until my brother got home from school. One day I was so excited to see him getting off the bus, I ran smack into the corner of a short wall dividing our dining room and kitchen. There was a centimeter-long gash in my forehead. Mom brought me into the emergency room. The doctor placed a sheet over my head and sewed three stitches into my forehead. Much later, Mom told me how angry she was at the doctor who offered no comfort to me, a scared and injured three-year-old. I have a scar from that day that is now less notable, losing its place with a lifetime of wrinkles on my forehead.

There was the day when I was five years old that a neighbor called my parents to let them know they saw my brother, his friend Dougie Hammond, and me walking to the A&W Root Beer stand a couple of miles from our house. The problem was Bruce and I were prohibited from crossing the busy Rice Street to get to the A&W. The other problem was we didn't have the money to purchase whatever we were going to order. We got chased down before we got to our destination.

I haven't spoken to my brother since our dad died five years ago. During my first bout of crippling depression, he gave me the message that if I thought I was in pain now, if I killed myself, Hell would be exponentially worse. Tough love, I guess.

Our family struggled with the funeral service when our mom died. Some wanted it to be traditionally religious; others wanted it to be more of a remembrance of Mom's incredible life and influence. We reached a compromise of sorts. The same debate came roaring back when Dad died. And I guess I said something that forever offended my brother. I'd rather have one of Dad's favorite songs played, Roger Whittaker's "Last Farewell," a war song about a soldier saying a heartfelt goodbye to his beloved, than the tried and true "Amazing Grace," the top 40 religious hit, that was apparently a nonnegotiable, nonstarter inclusion for my brother.

Growing up, it was conveyed to me that the expectation was for me to be a good person and a good student, not necessarily in that order. I was to get good grades, do well enough in school to go to college, and then get a good job. I would find a wife, buy a house, and raise a family of equally successful kids.

I don't remember Mom and Dad explicitly talking about any of this; it almost seemed implied because my older three sisters and brother were doing all those things. The youngest kid couldn't be the fuck-up.

My sense of direction has always been lacking. The running joke among my friends and family is if asked for directions, one should go exactly in the opposite direction from where I sensed they should go. Once, my dad gave me directions to some destination in St. Paul. He told me to take a left at the St. Paul Cathedral, a large stately church with a dome as big as the State Capitol's. Somehow, I never saw the Cathedral. I swear they must have sent it out for cleaning that day.

I planned to change the world. That was my destiny. No pressure. Mom always said she just wanted me to be happy. Dad's measure of success was to raise a family. I failed on both of their scales of a successful life.

MUSIC IN MY SOUL

My first love was our 45-rpm record collection. We had an army-green record player with removable speakers that had an adapter that could be placed over the 33-rpm spindle to play 45s.

Mom advised that I place no more than five records on the stack that lay above the turntable, the queue that would tumble down where the record arm's needle would slide into the grooves and play the music on the miniature vinyl record. The directions indicated that six 45s could be piled up, but Mom suggested a more conservative approach, most likely out of personal experience in listening to the first playlists that ever existed. A stack of five reduced the odds of two of the records sticking and falling together.

I loved the whole process of picking out five songs, putting them in the order I wanted to listen to them, piling the 45 records in a stack. I used my thumb to pull back the lever that started the record player turntable spinning while swinging the arm with the needle into the grooves of the first record and dropping the next song after the previous song was finished. This was done with a mechanical swing of the record-playing arm sliding past the record's grooves on the spot of the 45 where there were no grooves. This caused the record player's arm to slide and nearly hit the 45 label, lift, and trigger the next 45 record to hit the turning table, and the arm would then find its way back down into the grooves.

My first special talent was before I could read, my mom would ask me to play a specific song out of our stack of a hundred 45s. I proudly did so, a junior DJ long before I knew what a DJ was. Mom never figured out how I did it. All I remember is looking at the different labels on the records, from different record companies, and the faded look of some of the logos along with the different amount of grooves of each record, and I just knew where to find each and every song.

Everything round became a record to me. I had a wood spindle with different-sized wood circles to place in a stack. Those were imaginary records. I loved listening to music and singing along. My favorite song was Sammy Davis Jr.'s "I've Gotta Be Me." I played that particular record over and over. Years later, my sister Joan gave me a coffee mug with cartoon penguins, one waddling in the opposite direction from the rest, warbling the title lyrics of Davis Jr.'s song. Sammy sings about being willing to go it alone and not finding a way to belong because it was most important to him to be himself. What came first, my life's theme song, or the theme song predicting the moral code to the rest of my life?

Nowadays, I have a smart speaker in my living room, and all I have to do is say, "Hey, Siri, play…" and I can listen to almost any song from the beginning of time. But losing the mechanics of playing records in exchange for convenience and availability lessens the meaning of music. My copy of the Beatles' *Abbey Road* was unique from the rest of the world's because it had a pop in "Oh Darling" that was due to a blemish on my record. My copy of Barry Manilow's *Tryin' to Get the Feeling Again* had a scratch in "She's a Star" that made it unique. The imperfections made the music feel more personal to me.

By far the best Christmas gift I ever got was back in the fourth or fifth grade when Mom and Dad gave me a home radio station playset that I spotted in the Sears catalog. It was a package set complete with a turntable, microphone, headphones, and marker board that allowed me to set the radio station's schedule and song lists. A short while later,

I got a recordable 8-track player that allowed me to spend most of my weekends creating radio shows that featured my not-so-good radio mimicry voice and my own burgeoning record collection.

My station, WQSR, featured the stone-solid Stoney Duncan's morning news show and the wacky Figgy Figueroa's noontime stint, a show that was a bit too close to WCCO-AM's Steve Cannon's, a popular local radio program featuring Cannon changing his voice for his stable of characters including Morgan Mundane, the expert sports prognosticator, and Ma Linger, the sassy wise elderly woman. The day's highlight, however, was probably Shotgun Smalley's drive-time show featuring all the latest hits from ABBA, Olivia Newton John, and Captain and Tennille. Somewhere in my house are a bunch of 8-track tapes featuring the last broadcasts from WQSR's many talented DJs. But now I don't have an 8-track player that can play them.

Years later, I had a radio program on WMCN-FM, Macalester College's radio station. My show featured all Frank Sinatra music. 30 years after my radio program, Bob Dylan did a trio of LPs of songs Sinatra made famous. Sometimes the universe has some musical synergy that amazes me.

Throughout my life, music has been the shelter from the storms, giving context to the meaning of my life or at least providing a needed soundtrack to the meaningful events of my life. One particular June night in 1981 in Roseville, Minnesota, my relationship with music would change forever.

When I was in grade school, one of my classmates, Andrew Wheelock, wore a hearing aid. There was a portable, radio-sized unit that he wore around his chest with two wired earphones connected to the device. I wondered what being deaf or hard of hearing was like. I imagined it was like being underwater with pressure pushing on my ears. Then I thought that probably wasn't right since being underwater was a lot different than moving around with the wind blowing all around.

Green has been my favorite color for as long as I can remember. There is something about certain shades of green that have always soothed me in significant ways, probably starting with our family's record player. Yet the shade of green that is most burned into my memory was a shade I had never seen before or since. That it was the color of the sky caused me to feel far from soothed. The civil defense sirens had blared almost comically as an afterthought. My mom turned on WCCO long before, and the announcers were telling everyone they should take cover after the National Weather Service issued a tornado watch, and now that watch had become a warning with tornadoes touching down in the metro area.

I went down to the basement with my mom, dad, and brother. Things got nightmarishly dark. The wind was whipping up. Dad went to the windows to open them up as we were long told to do, to even the pressure difference between outside and in. The basement windows were rectangle-shaped. To open them, you had to unlock and then push a folding brown metal handle forward.

My brother tried to stop him. The new thinking was the building pressure posed less danger than flying shards of glass. I watched my brother and Dad argue, and just then the windows shattered. The cliché sound of a freight train roared through our house, and I felt my ears pop from the pressure change. It seemed like the end of the world was happening in our family basement.

When things seemed to finally subside, my family emerged from the basement, went outside to absorb the magnitude of what just occurred, and tried to assess the damage. The box elder tree in our backyard was toppled over. The homes on both sides, the home in front, and the home behind were leveled. Our family's house still had its roof, although it was clear there was damage to it. It was as if God had sent us a message: we needed to understand her power. I needed to understand humbling punishments can occur at any moment. I needed to walk straight and true. I needed to live a clean and honest life or suffer the consequences. I was scared straight.

Months later, I noticed I was having difficulty hearing musical bass notes in my left ear. Soon afterward, a high-pitched ringing wouldn't leave me alone in that ear. Mom brought me in to the ear doctor, and he discovered there was a fluid issue within my inner ear. He prescribed medication to address the issue.

The ringing continued but to a lesser extent. But there were a couple of times, spaced far enough apart, where it felt like a tornado blew through my head, and it felt like the inner pressure between my ears suddenly was collapsing my brain. The feeling made me nauseous, unable to stand. I didn't throw up, but all I could do to feel any relief was to curl up in a ball and wait until the nausea subsided.

Eventually, the medication took care of the problem, and the ringing in my left ear went away. My hearing, however, was forever damaged. I couldn't hear the lower-range notes in that ear.

And oddly, being mostly deaf in that ear is exactly as I imagined when I was a kid. It feels like that side of my head is submerged in water.

FAMILY TIES

Mom loved doing puzzles. Growing up, every night she'd work on a crossword puzzle as we all watched television. Once in a while, she would pull out a jigsaw puzzle, either clearing off the top of the living room coffee table or using a card tabletop to put the puzzle together. I never asked Mom why puzzles appealed to her. I never had the patience to work on them, beyond putting a few pieces here and there into the latest jigsaw puzzle she was working on. Mom taught me her strategy was to put the edge pieces together first. The straight edge was an obvious clue as to where they belonged. Once the outline was put together, Mom used the picture on the box to guide her on the rest of the puzzle. This was where she lost me. The number of random pieces that needed to be fit together was far too much work for my attention span.

But looking back, her love of figuring out how all the pieces fit together, whether cardboard jigsaw puzzle pieces, or words written down on a crossword puzzle based on short, coded clues, is similar to my love of writing. Creating a bigger story based on individual word choice, walking a line between thoughts and feelings, insight, and expression, is my version of Mom's love of solving puzzles. In the end, the big picture comes together, but it's somewhat anticlimactic because the reward comes in figuring out where individual pieces belong.

Strange how the day-to-day life that remained largely the same until one of my siblings went off to college and moved out of the house now is a blur of distant memories. I forgot all the little pieces that formed the bigger picture. The bigger picture might be the main focus: what would I grow up to be? But it seems as if the little pieces I do remember stuck in my craw for a reason I never figured out, just like a series of dreams.

I remember Mom in the kitchen cooking our next meal. I remember listening to my sisters play piano, mostly classical, but occasionally pop music. I remember watching my favorite TV shows, *Mannix, Mission: Impossible, Sea Hunt.* I remember Mom listening to Minnesota Twins baseball and Minnesota Gophers basketball and football games on the radio. I remember the feelings all those things conjured up, but on some level, it seems like they are scenes from a book or movie.

I loved watching Mom cook our many meals. I was fascinated by how the ingredients she combined turned into delicious meals. And I loved watching cooking shows. There were two I watched while my siblings were away at school: one local featuring Chef Hank Meadows and the other national, *The Galloping Gourmet* featuring Graham Kerr. I grew up to be a lousy cook. Somehow, I never learned to combine things into the right balance, work/life, feelings and thoughts, and all things to combat existential angst.

One morning, Mom explained to me it was Election Day, and she was going to North Heights Elementary School, the school where my brother went, located about a mile from our house, in order to vote. I had only been inside the school a handful of times going to plays or other events my brother participated in. I don't remember if Mom explained much about voting and elections. I do remember we went inside this huge shower-looking device that Mom pulled a huge handle to close the curtain behind us. Then there were a bunch of levers she pulled to cast her vote. Years later, I'd be the one in charge of making sure votes like the ones cast that morning were accurately counted.

The first major decision I remember having to make was when my mom told me, before I began kindergarten, I needed to decide what

I wanted to be called, "Dave" or "David." I think she was filling out the paperwork to get me into school. Looking back, it seems like it took me days if not weeks to make this critical decision. This was how I was going to be known for the rest of my life. This would be how others would view me until the end of time.

Likely, it was a matter of minutes as my young brain tried to comprehend what my mom was asking. Dave seemed less formal, more approachable. David seemed more dignified, more respectable. Being a serious kid, I chose the latter. And to this day it's like nails on the chalkboard whenever someone calls me Dave after I've introduced myself as David.

I had a stomachache every time I went to kindergarten. I had to walk next door to stand in line to catch the school bus. In the winter, Mom sent me to the bus stop wearing red, white, and blue soldier mittens with my forefinger and pinky filling the soldier's arms, meaning the two soldiers were surrendering unless I bent my fingers. The neighbors' dog, a vicious-looking Doberman with dots above its eyes making it appear to be a four-eyed monster, barked at me as I walked to the bus stop. Mom told me I couldn't show fear. If I just went about walking to the stop, head down, the dog wouldn't bother me. She was right. I frightfully tried the tactic, and the dog wandered away harmlessly. My soldier mittens resumed their surrender position.

In the morning, waiting for my brother to finish washing up, I would huddle against the heating vent in the bathroom. By the time the two of us were finished, Mom would have our breakfast waiting for us. When the bus stop was moved to the end of our driveway, I used to wait for the bus in our foyer as Mom watched out the kitchen window for the bus to appear on the street behind our house. She would tell me when she saw the bus, and this gave me time to join the line of kids.

Mom did a lot of little things like that for me. During the winter, it was nice not having to wait outside. During the fall and spring, it was nice to have just a little bit more alone time or time with Mom. Time was kept by the 50,000-watt radio station, WCCO-AM's, schedule. The news came at the top of the hour. Al Shaver's sports report was at 7:25 a.m. My bus arrived a little after the sports report was finished.

Our family lived on modest means. Dad used to work long hours downtown St. Paul at EDCO Dental Lab, where he made gold crowns. He somehow earned enough to put all five of us kids through college. Dad was long gone before any of us woke up, and we went to bed before he returned home. After dinner, we would call him and talk about our day. We took turns who got the honor of dialing the number and being the first one who got to talk to him.

Growing up, I didn't know what to make of being Japanese American. I knew it made me feel different from my classmates, but was that difference solely based on looking different? The connection to my roots mostly took the form of food and the times our family enjoyed Asian meals. Mom's specialty was her to-die-for teriyaki chicken.

Every summer, we took a vacation trip in our big blue station wagon. On one of our trips, somewhere in Kansas or Nebraska, a kindly country waitress was entertaining our family with a conversation that included the always-hilarious bit of wisdom of how we are what we eat. She began to take our orders, and without missing a beat, when she asked me what I wanted, I said, "Shrimp and Squirt." Oh, the howls of laughter that followed. I really wasn't trying to be funny. That was my dinner order each and every stop on that trip.

Once or twice a month, Dad would bring us to Mei Chu, a fancy downtown St. Paul Chinese restaurant located not far away from his dental lab. The restaurant had three floors: the bottom one where the restrooms were located; the lobby area; and upstairs where we dined. There was plush, rich red carpeting on all three floors and a fancy metal railing that ended up in a swirl at the bottom and top of the stairway. The restaurant menu included a butterfly shrimp appetizer, shrimp fried with a crisp yet fluffy coating, probably the most delicious thing

I've ever tasted. I made sure we ordered that every meal. My brother and I always bought a jaw-full of gumballs from the gumball machine located right by the entrance. Each gumball cost a penny and came in a different color with a slightly different taste. My dad would give my brother and me a handful of pennies to stuff our mouths with gum.

Every weekend, Grandma and Grandpa, my dad's parents, would join us for dinner. Mom cooked up extra food for our guests. Grandma and Grandpa's visits didn't disrupt our routines much. Neither spoke much English, so communication was a matter of smiles and nods. My brother and I would continue playing whatever it was we were playing, occasionally hearing Grandma and Grandpa say something to Dad and Mom, observing what we were doing.

Hearing a strange language spoken was a mysterious key or reminder to a door that I didn't understand. I came to understand Grandma and Grandpa came from Japan, this oddly shaped figure on our family globe, but I didn't know how all this was a part of me. I was learning I looked different from my classmates but didn't understand the implications or weight of my racial difference. It was a little puzzle piece that I wasn't capable of understanding.

Grandpa once gave me a shell of an abalone, about the size of a Nerf football. It was rough and uneven on one side but underneath was as smooth as a marble. I didn't know what an abalone was, but was told it was a sea animal. I couldn't do much with the shell, yet it was unlike anything else I owned. And I was glad to have this small connection with Grandpa.

Grandma and Grandpa immigrated to the United States in the early 1900s. I never heard Grandma's story, but Grandpa wasn't the oldest-born son in his family, so he wasn't going to inherit any of the family fortune. Allegedly, he saw a friend whose arm was shot off in the Japan-China war, and he had no interest in becoming a soldier.

Grandpa became a dental technician, making crowns in a small dental laboratory. Dad followed him into that profession. My grandparents saw some significant changes during their lifetimes, including our country becoming an automobile-driven society, to radio giving way to TV as our home entertainment, two World Wars, the Civil Rights movement, fast food, and microwave ovens.

Occasionally, we'd go over to Grandma and Grandpa's house for dinner. Grandpa had an impressive fish tank with multicolored fish swimming above a multitude of uniquely shaped rocks and objects, including a stone turtle a little smaller than my first pet, Huey the turtle. A lot of love was present in the keeping of those fish. My brother and I discovered a trove of treasures stored in a walk-in closet behind a wood hutch in the dining room. We found BB guns that must have belonged to my dad and his brother. Old photographs that looked like they were taken in a whole other world from a whole other time.

Every New Year's Day, Grandma would serve us a traditional Japanese meal featuring teriyaki chicken; sushi; a slightly salty soup with mochi (rice cake); a slice of carrot and celery; gabo (braised burdock root); kamaboko (fish cake); and plenty of other Japanese delicacies.

Grandma died one morning eating breakfast with Grandpa. She just keeled over and died. I can't fathom how devastating that must have been for Grandpa. Seeing his lifelong partner of over 70 years, one who shared so much of his life's journey, one of the few who spoke his own language, die in front of him. He died three years later on the couch of my uncle in Colorado, discovered by my cousin Michelle when she came home from school. At least both Grandma and Grandpa died the best way possible, without physical pain and with their mental capacities mostly intact. If only all of us could go the same way.

My sisters picked up the tradition of serving a Japanese New Year's meal. My sister Joan and her family bought Grandma and Grandpa's house, keeping it in the family and the place we continued to celebrate

New Year's after Grandma and Grandpa and eventually Mom and Dad left us. We pass the traditions from generation to generation, learning the taste of strange but familiar food, honoring those that came before us.

Mom was always my biggest supporter. She knew I would figure things out and believed and nurtured my love of writing. She was kind and funny but could surprise you with the quirks of her personality. She shared as a little girl she learned to roller skate on the porch of her family's Wyoming farm. She didn't really know how to stop her forward momentum, so she'd grab onto the wood railing to prevent flying over the edge. She was the one who instilled her love of music in all of us. She dutifully signed us up for piano lessons and joining our school's concert bands. She preferred classical music over other genres, liking Beethoven more than Bach. The latter's music was too mathematical, and she felt it lacked heart. After my sister moved away to college, Mom would write her a letter every Saturday morning while old repeats of the TV show *Rawhide* played in the background. Turned out Mom was a huge Clint Eastwood fan. Late in her life, she became fond of playing Nintendo and spent free time playing on our Game Boy as my nephew and nieces started calling her their Nintendo Grandma.

I was holding my mom's hand when she let out a slight gasp, her last breath. My dad and siblings were gathered around the bed. Dad looked at the hospice nurse and asked, "Is she gone?" The nurse felt for a pulse and nodded. I was surprised, since I had prepared myself for the moment when Mom's colon cancer was diagnosed as terminal six months before, and I began sobbing. Dad said to me, "We'll get through this."

For years after that night, I ate dinner with Dad most every night. Afterward, we would watch the Minnesota Twins or Minnesota Timberwolves games on TV. Dad and I really didn't have a whole lot in common, a whole lot to talk about. Mom was the one who turned me on to sports. Dad watched but probably only for Mom's sake and now for mine. After we started just having dinner over the weekends, Dad would inevitably call me after the Twins or Timberwolves pulled off a surprising win.

FINDING HARMONY WITH FRIENDS

My best friend in kindergarten was a girl with curly brown hair named Dee Dee Hasselburg. Years later, Dee Dee's mom, Loni Anderson, became a famous actress, starring in *WKRP in Cincinnati* and marrying Burt Reynolds. I spent a lot of time trying to impress Dee Dee with my smarts and talents. One of the things I learned how to do was to lower the windows on our bus. To do this, it helped to first push the window up, and this would make it easier to use the levers to lower the window. I ran up and down the length of the bus opening as many of the windows as I could. Dee Dee laughed in delight. The bus driver told me to knock it off.

Another day on the bus, I was sitting across from Katy Klausen, who I thought liked me. She was with a group of friends, and she pointed at me and said, "He'll never get married," as they all laughed. I didn't know what she was basing this psychic prediction on, but I knew it was some type of insult. I took it that Katy thought I was too ugly to ever find someone who would marry me. She turned out to be right, at least on the last count of never getting married.

My first actual brush with fame came from my fourth- and fifth-grade teacher, Mr. Hauble, being a professional square-dance caller. Mr. Hauble taught me to be a square dancer, a combination of precise, defined movements, and swing dancing with a certain flourish. I was among the group of square dancers chosen to represent Central Park

Elementary School during a halftime performance at our state's high school basketball tournament at the St. Paul Civic Center, a 16,000-seat sports arena. This happened to be the year Kevin McHale's Hibbing team won the tournament. The adrenaline was running high during our center court halftime square dancing appearance. My regular dance partner, Sue Loomis, who was in the sixth grade, said afterward I swung her harder than ever before. My parents took still pictures from our black-and-white TV. Apparently, the TV coverage featured me more than any of the other square dancers. The cute little Asian kid.

Somehow, I became one of the most popular kids in my class. In the sixth grade, I was voted 'Citizen of the Year' by my peers, the ultimate popularity contest determined by secret ballot. Being popular definitely was not the case in kindergarten through second grade when I struggled to find friends. But in the third grade, everything changed, seemingly overnight, and everyone wanted to be my friend.

I don't know what happened, but in the fourth grade, a new kid, Noah Zanzinger, joined our class, and he was an oddball. Our teacher pulled me out of class along with another popular classmate, Jim Harding, and told both of us Noah needed help, and when asked who he wanted to be friends with, he named Jim and me. That got me wondering if my overnight popularity might have come from teachers talking to my classmates behind my back.

This all was to change again in junior high, when all of us began to become much more interested in developing relationships with members of the opposite sex. Suddenly, I wasn't popular anymore. I was 'Citizen of the Year' my last year in elementary school. One year later, I was a nobody.

Being the youngest member of a musical family, by the time I studied under the sleepy-eyed tutelage of Mr. James Kelley, Parkview Junior High's longtime band director, it was just expected that I would be a talented musician. While lacking the trumpeting technique of my brother or the discipline of any of my sisters (a clarinetist, a French horn player, and a saxophonist), my talents depended more on my ability to stand apart from the rest.

One of the first reviews came from Mrs. Linda Smith, who commented to her son (later to be my best friend) Steve, after one of our concerts, that the band sounded good, but all anyone could hear was the little Asian kid on trumpet. I originally wanted to be a trombone player, didn't want to seem like I was just copying my brother like I always did by playing trumpet, but Mr. Binstock, my elementary school band director, determined my arms weren't long enough to push the slide of the trombone far enough away to play some notes. It was one of life's first big disappointments.

The best part of junior high band was the camaraderie and the shared times. The worst part was having to try to sound like all the others around you and before you. Though I later learned to better blend my sounds with the rest of my bandmates, I never quite mastered the styles or the behaviors that were expected of me. I was good enough to stay out of trouble, but rebellious enough to keep the band from being better than it was. I remained one of the more recognized leaders of the band, along with our wonderful first-chair clarinetist, the fabulous Lisa Lette.

One of the major reasons to be involved in music was to have an outlet for expression for all the emotions roaming inside. For me, Lisa was the compass, the inspiration behind and for whom my musical attempts were meant to reach. Many days of junior high and senior high were made much easier listening to the dulcet tones of Ms. Lette's clarinet, and making eye contact and realizing no matter how much angst existed inside, one should never take ourselves, or our teenage confusion, too seriously.

Playing in a band was much like playing for an athletic team. Early in the process, we sounded rough, learning what the song was, trying to find the right notes, the right balance, the right way to interpret our sounds together. Through practice and repetition and the molding of

Mr. Kelley's vision, we somehow turned the notes on the paper in front of us into something uniquely our own. Individually, Mr. Kelley had to allow us a little freedom (I forever frustrated him with my posture and unorthodox lip embouchure that allowed me to play loud but did not allow me to hit the high notes good trumpeters could hit, likely a result of being an accidental trumpeter) while still melding the sounds of the many into something coherent. One person could screw up all the rest.

Later on in high school, my attitude suffered so much that another trumpeter, Robbie Hanson, and I began improvising our parts and adding a dissonant sound to the rest of the band. I never found the right combination between being myself and being part of the group. Now I understand that contradiction; then it was just one mass ball of confusion.

How can you be what you think you should be when it doesn't mix with the rest of the group? The one time it worked, the one memorable moment of a productive triumph, was during one of our final concerts in our performance of "The Russian Sailors Dance." Midway through the song, Mr. Kelley cut us off four measures earlier than he was supposed to, or from what we had practiced and were used to. Some of the band stopped, some did not, and the mixture of sound and silence left a horrified look on everyone's face including the usually calm and serene Lisa Lette.

Nobody knew what to do. Should we skip four measures ahead, regroup, and hope we all ended up together? Or should we stop and end the piece right then and there? I took a look at Ms. Lette and could swear she smiled and nodded as I jumped in and started playing. Lisa joined in, and the rest followed, and somehow, we all survived the chaos, and maybe no one in the audience ever noticed it wasn't the way it was supposed to be.

Lisa was a candidate for the love of my life. She broke my heart our sophomore year of high school. When I arrived at Parkview Junior

High School in seventh grade, I made a list of the 15 prettiest girls. I thought if I could woo any one of them on the list, I'd end up married and happy. Lisa Susan Lette only made the list because I decided to bend the rules and allow a tie for 15th place; otherwise she would have placed 16th. I saw potential in her, and my scientific analysis of the prettiest girls in my class made me believe she had the capability of moving up the list.

Lisa had a short, stocky, athletic build, and I knew she was smarter than me because she got better grades. She was shorter than my five-foot-four and during the school year went from having long, straight, light-brown hair to short, curly, light-blonde hair. Maybe this was due to her dad being a barber whose shop was located across the street from our junior high.

I'm not sure when Lisa zoomed to the top of the list, don't even remember if it was a slow or rapid ascent. I do remember the thing that made me start feeling really attracted to her was being in band together. She sat in the first row to the right, and I sat in the third row center. The two of us did our darnedest to make the band sound good, but we were fighting an impossible fight. Junior high bands, by their very nature, will always be a work in progress.

During our music making, Lisa and I made many what I called PECs (perfect eye contacts). It was those many PECs that I began to believe Lisa really understood my very soul and had an answer for the confusion that was my junior high life. Just like my brother had done when I was little, Lisa had the ability to understand me when others couldn't. I didn't have the courage to actually speak to her, but when our eyes met, I knew she saw the real me.

I became the editor of our junior high newspaper, the *Panther Paw*, in the ninth grade. And the articles I wrote all had hidden messages for Lisa. She was the first person I wrote for, to, and about. And I learned love wasn't the most powerful feeling of all. Inspiration was. By miles. Lisa Lette was my first and most powerful muse.

Toward the end of ninth grade, the two of us had five burn-in-my-brain, melt-my-heart magical moments. The first was after our band made a field trip to another junior high to play in a shared city junior high concert. After an inspired but likely unlistenable performance, I decided I had reached my breaking point with all that was swirling in my life, the most prominent element being my unrequited love for Lisa Susan Lette. So my best friend, Steve Smith, and myself began to bellow out Beatles' songs at the top of our lungs on the dark bus ride back to our school. Everyone was shocked at this unexpected artistic expression from the quietest of Japanese American students ever. And Steve was even quieter than I was. But Steve and I poured our hearts out that night for a captive audience and, for me, a particular special lady. Steve and I recently fell in love with the Beatles and became obsessed with them.

The next day after school when I sent the latest and greatest edition of the *Panther Paw* newspaper to press, Lisa was finishing up basketball practice. It was a cold end of the winter, transitioning too slowly into spring. I was at the end of the hall by the entrance of our school, waiting for my mom to pick me up. I saw Lisa approaching, apparently going to share the same space, waiting for one of her parents to drive her home.

She was wearing her winter coat over a dress. I didn't notice the mismatch until she put her knapsack down and stood across the hall from me and said, "I must look really beautiful with my jacket on over my dress." The suave me would have poured my heart out and told her she would look beautiful to me if she was wearing a potato sack, only with sophisticated, well thought-out words.

I only was able to chuckle and say a quiet, "Uh-huh." These were the first words I ever remember the two of us sharing. She then told me she enjoyed my "singing" during the bus ride home from our field trip. God, I was so in love, I was ready to propose.

Our next exchange was about a month later. Again, the two of us were waiting for rides after finishing our after-school obligations. This time, we were headed in opposite directions on the sidewalk in front of the school. It was raining. When I saw Lisa, I did something empowered by her first words to me. I began doing a dance that was more like a skip and sang at the top of my lungs, "I'm singin' in the rain, just singin' in the rain..." I wanted to do the Gene Kelly splash through the puddle, but there were no big enough puddles present. Lisa laughed. And that laugh was seared into my heart forever.

The last week of our ninth grade year brought two significant moments. The first was in gym class where we were set to run a relay race. I was to lead off the first leg of the race, and my opponent was, of all people, Lisa Lette. In other races, I showed I was the fastest runner in our class. My weakness, however, was long-distance running. Like a horse, one only had to run a longer distance to overcome my short-distance dashes.

I lined up next to Lisa, for this moment, my nemesis. She, knowing how fast I could run, jokingly said, "Take it easy on me please." I contemplated doing just that, giving her more reason to like me. Maybe it was a cruel streak in me, but I made the last-second decision to run my fastest away from her. The proper metaphor for our 'relationship.' I glanced over at the last second and couldn't help but marvel at how attractive and determined Lisa looked in her short gym shorts and her all-too-white-and-tight t-shirt. Was I really going to run my fastest away from her? That's when our gym teacher, Mr. Rose, blew his whistle, and I blasted out of the starting blocks. Lisa groaned as I flew away.

But she had the last laugh. The second team member of my relay team was nowhere in sight, so I had no other option but to continue to try and run and hand off to our third team member. In my peripheral vision, I saw the person I was supposed to exchange the baton with nowhere close to where the exchange should have happened. Behind me, I heard Lisa let out a belly laugh. I had nowhere near the energy to race to the next handoff spot. Lisa's team won.

Later in the week, our band took a trip to Valleyfair, a local amusement park, on a band field trip. It was a fun day. All throughout, I kept my eyes out for Lisa, hoping for a chance to connect. The chance never came. We got on the school bus to return home, and who decided to sit next to me? The overwhelmingly beautiful, the most inspirational, the answer to my every eternal question, Lisa Susan Lette. I couldn't believe this turn of events. We didn't say much; we didn't have to. This was to be the true start of something special.

The final few days of our junior high life were spent collecting autographs/messages in our junior high yearbooks. The second-to-the-last day of band class, I tried to force myself to ask Lisa to do the unthinkable… sign my yearbook and reveal her minimal thoughts and feelings about me. I couldn't muster the courage to walk down to the first row of the band room and thrust my 8x12, gold-covered yearbook to her (Go Panthers!). The second day, my last opportunity, I knew I must. I had to find the courage, given our recent exchanges, to have the most beautiful girl in the world sign my yearbook.

My unsteady and shaking legs somehow found their way down to a sitting Lisa. She smiled when I pushed my yearbook awkwardly towards her and found the courage to mumble, "Would you please sign?" All the time wanting to tell her she was the love of my life, followed up by a long-term marriage proposal. She let me off the hook and seemed at the same time honored and expectant that I was asking.

We exchanged yearbooks, and I wrote something not too revealing in her yearbook. This is what she wrote (her immortal words forever burned in my brain): "Dave, you're pretty strange, but lots of fun to be around! I hope to see you sometime over the summer and maybe we'll have some classes together! Have a great summer! See you next year! Keep smilin', Lisa Lette." And I read those words many times over the next few years. They were the words that sustained me, further inspired me, screamed out loud and clear that being inspired by a person to whom I could write to, for, and about gave my life its first real meaning.

I started writing a daily journal in ninth grade, almost exclusively because of the way Lisa was making me feel. I wanted to document every thought and feeling I had about her. Through this process, I discovered that I couldn't really feel my feelings until I wrote them down. It was the process of writing and feeling inspired that was finally bringing some meaningful meaning to my life. It was almost like whatever happened didn't really exist if I didn't write about it.

Summer came and was just about to go when I decided to take up Lisa's comment about seeing each other over the summer. I wrote her a strategically thought-out, very edited, very risky letter letting her know how I felt. I dropped that fateful letter in our family's mailbox, raised the flag on the red, white, and blue mailbox, letting our mail carrier know there was important correspondence that needed delivery. I remember watching our mailman pick up my letter to Lisa. This was the biggest moment of my life. I revealed my heart to another, and she had the power to crush me.

I didn't hear back but knew we'd see each other before our high school lives began with marching band practice. My anxiety was off the charts. Would Lisa scream, running away from me when she saw me?

It was worse than I anticipated. I arrived and saw her holding hands with an upperclassman. My heart didn't break. It didn't sink. It was shattered into a zillion pieces that not even my mom, the jigsaw puzzle expert, could ever put back together, although I never gave Mom the chance to try. Lisa was my most-secret secret.

I tried my best during our sophomore, junior, and senior high years to get over Lisa. I wasn't successful. As much as I tried to ignore her, hate her, get over her, she was always in my thoughts. But I miserably failed as I continued to publicly write to, for, and about her in our high school newspaper.

Our last semester of the last year I'd ever see her, it was like God was giving me an opportunity, or conversely torturing me, by making sure we were in the same class five out of the six hours of our school schedules. One of the classes was Mr. Cameron's creative writing class. Due to budget cuts, our school newspaper was cut between my junior and senior years, meaning I'd be the last ever editor of the *Charger Press*. Mr. Cameron let me create an underground newspaper distributed to as many of our classmates as possible. Being a fan of *Saturday Night Live's* "Weekend Update," I took this opportunity to create a parody of your typical high school newspaper.

Lisa was in the creative writing class, which blew my mind. She wanted to be a writer too?! Mr. Cameron began each class with a free-writing exercise, having us write whatever was on our mind during the first 15 minutes of class. I wrote about Lisa, sitting behind me a few tables away during this writing exercise. I will die wanting to know what Lisa wrote about.

Weeks before our senior prom, Mike Tichenor, another trumpeter, teased me that he heard from his girlfriend, a clarinetist, that Lisa wanted me to ask her to the prom. A cruel joke. There was no way Mike could have known the torture of my heartbreak of my hidden love. Of anyone he could have teased me about, why did he choose Lisa? I'll never know.

I spent most of my senior year of high school trying to avoid people. I was tired of the lack of connection, the lack of meaningful conversations, and all the meaningless drama of high school. I just wanted to get to the next stage of my life, believing it would be more meaningful. After lunch, I would head up to the band room to use one of the practice rooms to play the piano. I chose a college that none of my classmates were going to. I craved a fresh start.

There was one glorious moment in the spring of the year. Our concert band traveled up to northern Minnesota to play a joint concert with the Hibbing High School Band. Hibbing High School is listed on the National Register of Historic Places. The entire city was moved in the early 1900s after a mining company bought the previous city location, rich in iron ore. This led to the construction of the Taj Mahal of high schools, costing $3.9 million in the early 1920s.

Our concert was in the historic auditorium. We arrived early and had some time to kill waiting for our counterparts to join us. The auditorium had a stage and theater seating. I decided I would entertain my band mates, completely out of character at this point, by playing the piano at the corner of the stage. I banged out the opening chords of the Beatles' "Let it Be" and led a group singalong. On our way back home, a couple of my band mates said the singalong gave them chills. It's my fondest memory of high school.

YOUNG AMBITIONS

Growing up, I dreamed of being four things: a Major League Baseball player, the *Tonight Show* host, a meteorologist, and a school-bus cop. Only the latter was attainable. I also figured I was somehow destined for fame.

Bus cops were appointed by the administrative authorities in our grade school, with the most respected sixth graders getting the key gig. They wore a leather belt with a shoulder strap. The shoulder strap had a pouch to keep rolled-up paper and a pen, presumably to write down the names of anyone who misbehaved. The cool bus cops didn't buckle the belt, leaving the shoulder strap to hold things in place. The key responsibility was to keep order on the bus, primarily telling us to sit down when the bus was moving. The bus cop was the only one allowed to stand when the bus was moving.

The other key duty was to ensure an orderly exit of the bus when we got to school. The bus cop did this by walking back, row by row, to let students out four at a time (two from each side of the aisle). I thought this was the most impressive thing, having power over when my classmates were allowed to get off the bus. On a rare occasion, the bus cop would start in the back of the bus instead of the front.

It seemed like a major life accomplishment when I was chosen to be a bus cop before my sixth grade year. I officially was given my first authoritative power. I don't remember ever writing up a kid who violated the unwritten rules I was in charge of enforcing. Wanting to be a bus cop was less about wanting the power and more about looking cool to the other kids. There were two of us on duty on my bus. I came full circle going from being a troublemaker trying to impress Dee Dee Hasselburg to being the one tasked with enforcing the rules for safe bus riding. This later was somewhat mirrored with my ascent to becoming the state's election director.

My second obsession after music was baseball. And it seemingly hit me overnight. Mom loved baseball. She grew up in Wyoming and became a Chicago Cubs fan because she could hear their games on the radio. Her favorite player was Ernie Banks, who famously loved playing so much his saying on doubleheader days was, "Let's play two." Playing 18 innings in one day was no small feat, so obviously, the man loved playing the game.

I don't remember watching the Twins game on our living room TV. In 1973, we made the major decision to buy a portable 10-inch TV for Mom to watch while she was in the kitchen. This was the first time I remember watching baseball. Mom was watching the Twins play the Oakland Athletics on her new portable TV, and I sat on the high chair next to the microwave on which the TV sat on top. The Twins lost the game badly, something like 11-2. Charlie Finley's Athletics with their mustaches and colorful green and yellow uniforms became the World Champions later that fall. The next game I watched with Mom was the next weekend with the Twins playing the Yankees. Once again they lost badly, something like 14-1. Didn't seem to bother my mom much. I guess a Cubs fan learns to accept a losing baseball team.

Our family used to take car rides in our blue Plymouth station wagon around the many lakes of the Twin Cities. On one of the rides, I remember how excited Mom got when Harmon Killebrew hit his 500th home run. Dad later traded that blue Plymouth station wagon for an even larger one, a behemoth vehicle that was a paler blue with wood paneling. The car had three sections: the front seat where Dad and Mom sat, a middle section where my three sisters sat, and the back section where my brother and I sat.

My brother and I began playing our version of baseball in our backyard with a whiffle-ball bat and a tennis ball. Mom told me she loved watching how I mimicked the pitchers' motions, using Bert Blyleven's high arm stretch over his head and high leg kick with his tongue sticking out, in delivering the tennis ball to my brother waiting to hit my wayward pitch. We began to play every summer day from morning until it was too dark to see the ball. We played so much, we wore out the grass where our flat pitcher's mound and batter's box were.

Our diamond was the horizontal length of our backyard rather than vertical, mostly because we had a huge tree in the middle of our backyard that made a vertical diamond impossible. Thus, it didn't take much to hit a pitch over our tall hedge and backyard neighbors' chain-link fence, meaning the pitcher had to climb the fence into our neighbors' yard to retrieve the tennis ball. First base was next to our red-stained wood fence, the top section having a knot in the wood. Second base was one of two apple trees in our backyard. And third base was the large box elder tree in the middle of the yard, one that unfortunately attracted bees during the summer and thankfully was blown over in the tornado. We pitched against our garage's gray cement brick backstop so pitches not hit bounced back to the pitcher.

I was obsessed with my new love. Mom gave me the 1973 Twins yearbook that featured Manager Frank Quilici on the cover, arms outstretched arguing with an umpire. I consumed every word, every picture, every statistic in that yearbook. I read Twins players Tony Oliva's and Danny Thompson's autobiographies. Thompson's story was tragic, diagnosed with leukemia that ultimately took his life far too young. Oliva, a Twins legend, wrote about shooting tornadoes back in Cuba, his home country. I started collecting baseball cards. Baseball was all I talked about, forcing my sisters to take a crash course of learning the game so they could relate to me. One of my sisters later joked that if

I devoted my love and attention to something more important than baseball, I could have made something out of my life.

My desire to become the *Tonight Show*'s host came from Mom letting me stay up to watch Johnny Carson's monologue. I loved Johnny's jokes and the ultimate cool demeanor. I didn't know if I would ever be capable of having the casual conversations with guests that seemed so natural to Johnny, but I glommed onto his ability to always end things with a joke, making everyone smile even during troubling times.

Later, I became a huge David Letterman fan. Mom appreciated my love of Dave's jokes, agreeing that he was a great guest host when Johnny was on vacation and later sharing my love of his *Late Night* show's running bits like Stupid Pet Tricks and Stupid Human Tricks and Larry Bud Melman. Becoming a TV star also led to my desire to become a local weatherman.

In the mid-1970s, KSTP-TV (channel 5) hired our TV market's first meteorologist, Dr. Walt Lyons, to give the weather report. Prior to Dr. Walt, the weather forecast was delivered by self-proclaimed weathermen. Being a meteorologist gave Dr. Walt an air of expertise. Shortly afterward, KSTP bought the first weather radar in our media market and sparked an interest in a career as a weatherman within me.

I started an independent science project. Every day, I recorded the high and low temperatures in Duluth, Minnesota and Houston, Texas. I was hoping to learn how the weather in different parts of the country were both the same and different. I hoped to have a major revelation, but rather it became an exercise in discipline. I needed to look at the weather report in our daily newspaper that included the high and low temperatures of large cities throughout the country. I didn't want to miss a day. I think Mom was impressed that I stuck with this project for months.

For my birthday that year, I was given a weather kit that helped me record the temperature in our house. More impressively, I could measure the barometric pressure with a tube full of a red mercury-like substance. I bought some transparencies and erasable markers to recreate the weather maps Dr. Walt presented on his newscast. Becoming a meteorologist intrigued me, because it was all about predicting what would happen tomorrow based on some assumptions about what was happening yesterday and today. Weather usually moves across our country west to east, but it is still somewhat unpredictable. A storm can come from out of the blue.

My desire to become a Major League Baseball player, a *Tonight Show* host, and a meteorologist didn't come to fruition, but that desire in many ways led to my ultimate career. Baseball and weather taught me statistical analysis, the importance of numbers as an election administrator. Wanting to be a talk-show host taught me the value of listening, the value of conversation, and shaped my sense of humor, a personality trait that has always been valued by those who I work with.

PART SIX:
CROSSING THE RUBICON

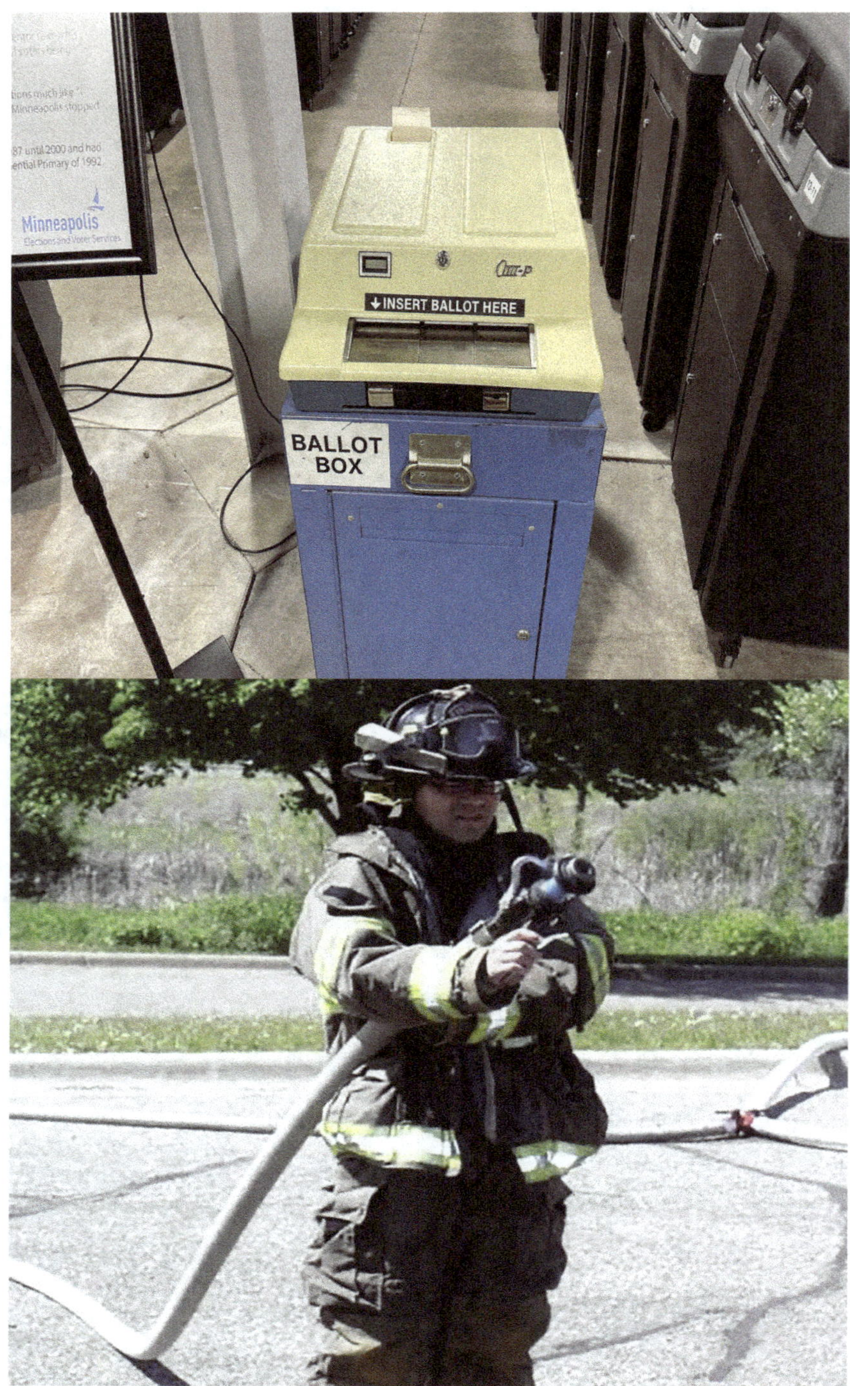
tions much like
Minneapolis stopped
87 until 2000 and had
ential Primary of 1992.
Minneapolis
Elections and Voter Services
INSERT BALLOT HERE
BALLOT BOX

*"There are two different types of people in the world, those who
want to know, and those who want to believe."*

—Friedrich Nietzsche

"Reality, what a concept."

—Robin Williams

So that's it? We're all just going to go on with our lives as if nothing
happened? The world shut down for a year and a half. Millions of
people died; tens of millions of others got seriously sick. Institutions
meant to hold society together splintered. Large numbers of us not only
fell down rabbit holes but are forever lost tumbling down bottomless
pits.

For me, it was like a slow descent into quicksand as everyday life
sucked the soul out of me almost without notice. Solitary confinement
has been declared a cruel and unusual punishment by those looking
to treat prisoners as humanely as possible. I can't fathom how those
with kids in school managed to adapt to teaching at home, telling
your kids they couldn't see their friends and classmates.

At the same time, I wonder if those who lived with others understand
how those of us living on our own suffered in a different way. Stir-
crazy and the lack of real human connection. I was left on my own
with two housemates of the feline species equally confused at what was
happening, equally wanting the routine to return to our once-upon-
a-time normal. When everything happens at once, nothing happens
at all. We lived through an alternate version of the TV show, *The
Leftovers*, where 2 percent of the earth's population vanishes overnight
and those left behind have to find a way forward without knowing

what happened, the meaning of it all. Was it the rapture, and those left behind were the corrupt sinners?

Since the apocalypse, I clearly am not on the same page as others. We are all deniers to our very cores, wanting to ignore flaming fires if only to move to a safer version of reality, or the reality we want to believe in order to take the next step forward.

Screw reflection; screw the past informing the present and future. Most seem willing to move beyond this craziness, and I'm not sure how to do so. I mourn a person of significance I knew who died from COVID. Many others mourn lost family and friends. COVID didn't kill me, but it did kill my softball career, my love of music, and is killing the passion I used to have for my career. There's a significant connection between the pandemic and the state of our elections.

The notion that this is it, we're all just going to move on with the rest of our lives, doesn't work for me. I can't ignore the elephant in the room, both the metaphorical elephant and the political elephant. We've suffered through the largest collective trauma of our lives, and many seem to just want to forget it, leave a gap in their memories, and get on with things like this trauma never occurred.

I didn't know anything about the concept of intergenerational trauma until I participated in a webinar about how the Japanese American generation after mine is still struggling with the World War 2 incarceration of 120,000 Japanese Americans. It occurred to me the concept of intergenerational trauma might have added to how much I struggled during the pandemic. My dad lost a couple of years of his life behind barbed wire in a concentration camp. I lost a couple years of my life watching society unravel at its seams.

It's like the Peggy Lee song, "Is That All There Is?" where the singer witnesses her dad's reaction when her childhood home burns down to the ground, and life just continues. She sings if that's all there is, we might as well all just continue dancing and break out the booze. Similarly, the singer rhapsodizes about watching the spectacle of a circus when she was a kid and falling in love as an adult only to be abandoned, left to wonder after both if that was all there is. She contemplates life's final act, all the while wondering why none of it matters, and that's all there is. Just keep dancing and break out the booze. Peggy Lee sings the truth as I don't know how to move on from the past couple of years without understanding what any of it meant.

We all tell ourselves our stories, day after day. We need to bring order to our lives. This is who we are. This is who others think we are. We develop daily routines mostly surrounded by the same people. Tomorrow may be different, but it usually isn't. Today is often like yesterday. Until it isn't and something shifts, something is lost, or sometimes something is gained that will change our way forward.

But often, our stories don't mesh. I'm under no delusion that anything I write is a universal truth. It's all my personal fiction coming from an unreliable narrator. I write about the events of my life, but it's all limited to my point of view.

A couple of years ago, I attended an elementary school reunion with nine of my other classmates at a local bar and restaurant. As we reminisced, it was clear we had different memories of the same events, just like Kurosawa's *Rashomon*. I trust my memory, especially since I began journaling in junior high and continue to write down significant moments of my life close to when they happened. But I have a singular point of view. My experienced reality is my reality alone.

There's a huge difference between dreams and fantasies, as large as the difference between a dinosaur and a dragon. Our dreams have basis in reality, things that happened in the past or present presented in juxtaposed situations, our mind working in tricky ways, pushing personal narratives through different lenses and perspectives. Fantasies have little to no basis in reality. They are us wishing for things that likely will never come true because they aren't rooted in reality.

Memories replace our dreams in our limited brain space. We stop believing things will be better in the future and start mooring ourselves in our actual experiences. Some of us cling on to fantasies to escape realities. We all want to believe what we currently believe, but that can be bleak or a punch to the gut. Better to believe in something that never happened, never will happen, than to let go of faith and all belief at all.

John Lennon told the story of a friend who went to Vegas to see fat Elvis perform and said that if you closed your eyes and pretended, it was the same as the young and vibrant Presley. Lennon said he wasn't interested in closing his eyes and pretending.

LOSING MY RELIGION

My family began attending St. Christopher's Episcopal Church in Roseville, Minnesota when I was in the fourth grade. My oldest sister Janet got married the summer before at St. Christopher's. It was one of the first times I had been in a church. Mom decided us kids should at the very least be exposed to religion. So instead of mid-Sunday breakfasts (rotating each week between pancakes, waffles, French toast, and eggs), we got dressed up and headed to church.

The service meant little to me. I liked singing the hymns, trying to follow the notes to figure out the melodies while reading the words. I ended up singing softly, slightly behind the rest of the congregation. The part of the service that confused me was when Father Henry Hoover read a list of names that we prayed for. Week after week, month after month, year after year, many of the names were the same. At first, I thought we were praying for the recent dead. It dawned on me slowly over time that these were people suffering from long-term illnesses, another world I had yet to be exposed to.

The stressful part of attending church was being dismissed into Sunday school. I joined a class where everyone knew each other. I was the new kid on the block. It didn't help my insecurity that I knew none of the Bible stories being discussed. I was a fish out of water, a piece of bread in a class full of toast. Our teachers were Mr. and Mrs. Miel. Mrs. Miel later told me at my mom's funeral that she used to babysit Bob Dylan. Part of the family eulogy was my brother reading something I wrote that quoted Bob Dylan. Mrs. Miel said Bob rarely said a word and that his younger brother David was the talker of the two.

A couple of years into my churchgoing experience, I became an acolyte. I got to help in the mechanics of the service, wearing a black and white robe, lighting the two candles that were placed on the left and right-side edges of the altar. There was an order to be lit and the opposite order to be extinguished. I helped Father Hoover prepare the Eucharist, pouring some wine over his fingers into a gold chalice. Father Hoover would drink the wine from the chalice.

Going to church instilled the fear of God within me. My ignorance of Christianity doomed me to hell. I needed to learn fast to save my soul. I began praying every night, although I was quite aware no one was listening to my prayers. I didn't know what I was doing, didn't know how to get through. Was it important to kneel when praying? Hold my hands together facing toward heaven?

Faith was something you couldn't see or touch, only something you could feel, and at my core, I knew I wasn't feeling it. At the same time, I firmly believed the world in front of me wasn't all that there was. There was something beyond, an afterlife, but I wasn't sure the rote services I attended from fourth grade until I graduated high school helped me unlock any clues, got me any further in my understanding, and ensured I'd end up in heaven. I wanted to be a believer but ended up adopting the 'spiritual but not religious' cliché when talking about my religious beliefs with others.

During my infamous blue period, after I got out of the hospital for my depression, I decided to visit a few churches to talk with the clergy, thinking I was suffering from a spiritual crisis. I wrote something that I shared with my family about getting lost after the Book of Deuteronomy, the second book of the Bible. My brother said it was a confusing book and encouraged me not to give up faith. The visits didn't help at all. We all agreed I was lost and depressed, but there were no words of wisdom that offered any comfort at all. It was exactly the same with the medical professionals I turned my life over to help me figure out how to feel just a little bit better.

The night my mom died, she spent much of the evening staring at a corner of the ceiling in her bedroom. She was seeing something, and I craved to know what it was. As Dad was dying years later, he questioned what dying meant. He didn't believe in an afterlife, but I got the feeling he wanted confirmation he lived a life worth living. I tried my best to tell him he did.

Religions seem to divide more than they connect. If my beliefs are different from yours, where is the middle ground we can agree on? Fanatics use their religious beliefs as absolute truths. And I truly wonder if there are any absolute truths.

A METAPHORIC LIFE

I never felt as sick in my life as I felt in late October 2018. My lungs were congested, and I was exhausted with my body trying to fight off whatever was making me sick. I felt like I'd been hit by a tornado the size of Niagara Falls, knocked down by a Muhammad Ali uppercut. But we were only a few days away from the election, so I dragged myself into work at the city of Minnetonka, even though my WebMD self-diagnosis indicated I very well might have pneumonia.

The Minnetonka community development director told me her mom was recovering from being hospitalized from pneumonia, and it was not something to take lightly. My boss told me to go home, but I couldn't. It's not like we could delay the election. The show would go on with or without me, but messing up the election wasn't an option either.

The smallest mistake can lead to a national front-page story or a lawsuit. I needed to push my way through no matter the personal cost. The Monday before Election Day, we had a long line of early voters that snaked down the hallway from the city council chambers down the community center hallways to City Hall. My boss checked in on how I was doing. I was walking wounded, struggling to stay upright. He convinced me to go take a nap in the fire department. I agreed.

The fire chief was more than happy to let me sleep in one of the station's beds but warned me if there was a call, the alarms would blare, and all hell would break loose. The bedroom was small, enough room for a single bed and a desk. When I closed the door and shut off the lights, it was the darkest room I've ever been in. No windows and a flap at the bottom of the door blocking light from entering, I couldn't see my hand in front of my face. I crawled underneath the blankets and quickly fell into a deep, dreamless sleep. My mind and body were exhausted and completely shut down. I wasn't sawing logs—I was obliterating the entire forest, all consciousness naturally anesthetized.

Suddenly, the fire station alarms blared, and there was the sound of scurrying in the hallway outside the bedroom door. I swear my head came within inches of hitting the ceiling. I was completely disoriented, with no idea where I was or why I was there. I regained my bearings, got up, and went back to doing my job. The short nap was helpful; I hadn't realized how exhausted I really was.

In the following years, I wondered if I didn't actually die in that fire station bed, and everything since is about being sentenced to some type of hell. It was an odd foretelling of what was to come in 2020: suffering from a respiratory illness while trying to get through another election. I was a pioneer of suffering, the simpering, vote-counting sage, at the forefront of what my colleagues throughout the country would eventually have to deal with a couple of years later.

I was appointed the Director of Elections for the Secretary of State in January 2019. It seemed like the perfect culmination of all the work that was my career. The poetic arc wasn't lost on me. I started with the same office years back at the lowest entry-level position, literally the easiest person in the office to replace, playfully throwing voter registration applications into a mailing bin.

Now I was the vicar of voters, the veteran of voter registration, the guy in charge of the statewide voter registration system. My team, and our local county, city, township, and school district election administrators were looking to me to lead our state's election processes. It was the cherry on the top of my career and one of the times I wished Mom and Dad were around to see it.

The *Star Tribune*, the largest daily newspaper in the state, ran a long story at the top of its metro section about my appointment. Getting a job that made the news was not something I envisioned. I hoped I was up to the task. I was to learn, however, I was less the leader of elections in the state than I was a firefighter, constantly putting out the latest blaze.

Late that fall, I was in bed in a downtown Denver hotel room. The lights from nearby buildings poured through the room's partially closed curtains, casting a mesmerizing cloud-like pattern on the ceiling. I was awoken around 4 a.m., and given my history with a chronic lifelong battle with insomnia, I knew it was a long shot being able to fall back asleep. I felt extremely exhausted with the accompanying feeling of doom and defeat, knowing that in a few hours, I would have to sleepily head down to a hotel conference room to attend an elections meeting.

Suddenly, my bed began to violently shake. I was paralyzed with fear. I noticed my cat Diego-san with his long black silky smooth fur lying in his familiar position between my right arm and my body, his head nestled on my shoulder. He seemed unfazed. It dawned on me I must be dreaming because Diego-san couldn't be in this strange bed in Denver with me. But it also dawned on me this must be a lucid dream with me aware that I was dreaming. I woke up, and the bed was still shaking, but Diego-san was gone. Was this an earthquake? What exactly was shaking? Was I having a seizure? After a few terrifying moments, I truly woke up. There was no going back to sleep. I was soaked in sweat not knowing if what I had just experienced was real or not. I didn't know what any of it meant, but I now wonder if it was a foreboding warning about what was about to come in 2020. A year Diego-san wouldn't survive.

In February 2020, I was returning home from another meeting in Denver. My Lyft driver told me he watched a documentary about the 1918 pandemic that killed over 500 million people. Pandemics were now the newest noise in the background of the 24-hour news cycle.

We heard there was a coronavirus shutting down China, but it didn't seem remotely possible it would disrupt our lives all that much. I was surprised I never heard of the 1918 pandemic, given how many people it killed. I made a note to myself to try and find that documentary.

Surely with our advances in science and medicine, there was no way things could be that bad again. A few weeks later, I learned the National Basketball Association was ending its season and that March Madness, men's and women's college basketball's hugely popular tournaments, were also being canceled. This was the first time I understood the seriousness of the virus.

Our office began making plans for our employees to work from home. We didn't get too far into the planning as society quickly shut down. We all grabbed the computer equipment we needed to work from home and then tried to adapt to online meetings talking to each other through our computers, slowly learning the rhythm of unmuting ourselves, not talking over others, trying to read the room when the room was virtual.

There were some incidents during 2020 and early 2021 that, in retrospect, seem like I somehow luckily escaped danger mostly unscathed. One morning, I was making toast in my toaster oven, the 40-year-old toaster oven that my parents gave me to bring to my college dorm. Diego-san napped in his familiar spot, next to my computer's mouse. Some cheese from previous cooking dripped onto the burner, and when I looked over at the toaster oven from my spot at the kitchen table, I saw flames shooting through the toaster oven's glass door. I quickly got up and unplugged it, and the flames subsided. There was a bit of an adrenaline rush, but for the most part, it just felt like another 2020 threat.

I noticed one morning that the bottom wood board on my garage became detached, thus creating a space for the rabbits, squirrels, and chipmunks living in my yard to get into an enclosed space. I didn't know how to make the necessary repair.

One day, my worst fear came true. I found a dead baby rabbit who got into my garage and couldn't get out. It was in the middle of summer, and as I tried to dig a grave, I found the dry ground too hard to dig deep, so I buried the dead baby rabbit in a shallow grave. I watched in horror as the man from the company I hired to mow my lawn, riding his riding mower, drove over the grave as the bunny's body flew into the air. There wasn't much left of the body, probably a predator finding it first. In the midst of so many COVID deaths, I hated all things about how symbolically this random rabbit's death devastated me.

One evening, I was participating in a fantasy baseball draft for a league I'd played in for a number of years. This was our first online draft. Usually, we met in a coffee store basement owned by one of the other players and spent hours drafting our teams. The online draft went much quicker. It's an auction league, meaning each of us took turns nominating the next player. Everyone had a chance to bid on the player, limited by our overall $260 budget. If a player was nominated that I wasn't interested in, or the bidding was higher than I wanted to go, there were a couple of minutes before the next nomination.

I joined the fantasy baseball league in 2005. The league was called the Grey Duck League, a poke at a Minnesotan oddity where we call the children's game "Duck Duck Goose" "Duck Duck Grey Duck," for unknown reasons. I was asked to join by a former coworker, and I discovered the commissioner of the league was a junior high classmate of mine. The league was National League players only plus the Minnesota Twins. It was a points league with points for batters for batting average, home runs, runs batted in, and stolen bases; for pitchers we got points for wins, saves, earned run average, and walks/hits per inning. Teams could retain players from the previous season, with the retained players' salary determined by what the winning bid was the previous year plus $4 or 25 percent increase, whichever was greater.

There was a $20 entry fee, and during the season, we could pick up free agents for 25 cents and make trades for 50 cents. The league champion, two division winners, and the team with the third-best record split the pot of money based on a formula. I came to love that it was a National League players only league (plus the Twins) because it forced me to pay more attention to the National League. Growing up, I mostly read the box scores in the newspaper for the American League because those teams impacted the Twins. I also learned in subsequent seasons my draft strategy differed from most of the other owners. I preferred players who weren't necessarily great in any of the scoring categories, but were good in all of them. I learned to not overpay for starting pitchers because the great ones cost too much, and the good ones were a roll of the dice since with any single pitch, the pitcher could injure their arm. I usually did well, winning the league three times in my 17 years and usually finishing in the money or close to it.

Fantasy sports are a weird concept. Money often is involved, but it's another way to pay attention to sports on a game-to-game basis. There are times I root for the Twins not to do well if it means my fantasy team benefits. I don't want the Twins to lose, but I do want my fantasy players playing against them to do well. Fantasy results are based on real players, real games, real statistics from those games. It's an odd mixture of fantasy and reality. How you succeed is based on actual games and performances. But the real emotion and importance of players playing games to earn a living has no place in fantasy.

I was recording a movie on my upstairs DVD recorder and drafting from my laptop in the kitchen. So I used those free couple of minutes to race upstairs, check the progress of the recording, and then race back downstairs to rejoin the draft. Theo and Diego-san sat by the stairs looking at me like I had finally lost my mind. On one of my trips downstairs, I missed the top stair and slid on my back down the dozen carpeted stairs. I grabbed the railing to stop my slide. I got up seemingly none the worse for the wear. Later, it dawned on me that if I had hurt myself and needed to go into the emergency room or hospital, I would have been out of luck. The beds were filled with COVID patients. It was no time to fool around.

My car's battery light illuminated one late winter afternoon in 2021. Since I hadn't ever changed my 2013 Mini Cooper's battery, this wasn't unexpected. My car repair knowledge basically was putting duct tape over the warning light, hoping things worked themselves out. I knew I couldn't do that with the battery, that I needed to get it replaced. I drove the car to a battery store, and an employee came out. I opened the hood, and we both looked for the battery. It was nowhere in sight. The employee went back into the store and grabbed a book to look up where a Mini Cooper's battery is located. The book informed him I needed to bring the car into my dealer. I didn't have time to drive to my dealer for a couple of days, so I tried to avoid driving my car during the night, not wanting to get stuck somewhere late in the dark.

I finally was able to set up an early-morning appointment. It was a foggy, warmer winter morning. When I started the car up, the battery light was no longer illuminated; instead, there was an odd hieroglyphic symbol that was lit by a yellow light. When I pulled out of my driveway onto the street, the yellow light and symbol changed to a red light and a symbol of a car up on a car lift. This couldn't be good. I drove a few miles and merged onto Highway 280. The highway merged onto I-94, one of our busiest interstates. The merge lane was on the left, and just as I was accelerating to merge onto I-94, my car died. There were cars speeding up from behind, and I knew I somehow had to merge three lanes over to get onto the side of the road. I turned on my emergency blinkers, and somehow, as my car was quickly de-accelerating, I made it over to the side. Cars buzzed by me, going 70 miles per hour.

Since I was situated just past a curve in the freeway and it was still slightly foggy, I was worried someone wouldn't be paying attention and would ram into the back of my car. I decided the safest thing to do was to get out of my car and sit on the hill by the side of the road. I recalled somewhere in time being taught that getting out of a broken-down car wasn't advised. I called 911, and they asked for my location.

I unfortunately was on the border of St. Paul and Minneapolis, so the dispatch wasn't sure which police department to call. We settled on Minneapolis, and they put me through. The police department put me through to a towing company. It took around 11 minutes for the truck to arrive. I sat shivering on the hill, knowing all this was terribly dangerous, and all the while not feeling anything.

The driver somehow managed to get my car up on the back of the truck, and we were on our way to the dealer. He told me I was really lucky. Had it happened an hour earlier, the fog was so bad it was almost certain I would have been rear-ended. I was numb throughout the entire ordeal, but once safely home, I started to shake, realizing how dangerous the situation was. I decided I needed to take warning lights more seriously from that point on, not only with mechanical things like cars but with all things in my life.

These are examples of major mind-numbing moments that cut through the pain of being more on my own than ever before. Things could've been a lot worse and turned out OK, but there was no one around to share the day-to-day, hour-to-hour, moment-to-moment events with, had I been going to a place where I'd be around others. Life's dangers were experienced in complete isolation. There was no reassurance, confirmation, that the latest danger would mean something, given the significance of our collective dangers.

OBJECTS OF MY AFFECTION

In the fall of 2013, my siblings and I were cleaning out Dad's house, the house I grew up in for the first 23 years of my life, after moving him into an assisted living facility. The five of us 'kids' were placing Post-It notes on the possessions we were interested in taking home with us, trying to not appear too vulture-like or selfish. Thankfully, there wasn't a lot of disagreement or more than one of us wanting any particular item.

The most important items I claimed were the wood coffee table with a glass top that we gave our parents for one of their milestone marriage anniversaries and the metronome many of us used during the years we took piano lessons to keep time during our practicing. When my oldest sister saw me claiming the metronome, she informed me it no longer kept time, so it was worthless.

I wasn't claiming it because I needed a device that kept a steady beat. I was claiming it because it reminded me of the eight years of piano lessons I took from Mrs. Good, and the many hours of practice and playing on the piano in our living room. While the metronome could no longer accurately keep time, it was still a time machine for me transporting me back, and how playing the piano was an outlet for my creative energy. Playing piano was the first antidepressant I consumed.

When my dad died a few years later, we again went through the items he had left when he moved from the assisted living facility into a group home, a residential house located less than half a mile from our family's longtime home. This time, the most important item I wanted was his gold watch.

Again, it wasn't to help me keep time since it had been a long time since I'd worn a watch. Rather, it was an important memento, a sentimental item from a past time. Dad wore his watch until the end, as he had done every day I knew him. He hated to be late to anything, perhaps because he hated when others made him wait, a value that became core to me as well. Being on time was a core value of his. I have a Buddha statue on top of a bookcase in my house, and Dad's gold watch is wrapped around Buddha's head as a fancy headband. The metronome sits on the shelf underneath.

Do I look at or think about either item frequently? Not at all. But I remain convinced I grabbed two vital items from my past. The items were purely sentimental to me. And one of the things I didn't understand about my dad when he was alive, especially after Mom died, was his clinging to the things in the past that had more meaning to him than things in the present or going forward.

But I finally began to get this need during the pandemic. The familiar is more comforting in dire circumstances than the unpredictable, the new. There are contrasting ways to move forward into the unknown. Hang on to the past, comforting us slowly to take the next baby step forward, or let go and jump into the deep end of the pool, even if it's a suspected cesspool, knowing the importance of getting to the next chapter of our lives.

This was when my lifelong love of music died. I just couldn't take listening to new music, not knowing what feelings the music would drudge up within me, especially when I lost Diego-san. I stopped watching new TV shows or movies I hadn't seen, sticking with reruns where I knew what was coming. I needed familiarity. More and more, younger employees at work conversed about pop culture references I had not heard of. I grew old seemingly overnight, and I now have a deeper understanding of my dad.

During the apocalypse of 2020, I forced myself out of the house during the summer by taking a ride on my 125cc ruby-red Genuine Buddy scooter. Many years before, Mom made my brother and I promise we would never buy motorcycles because they were too dangerous. My sister escaped serious injury with her boyfriend when they were involved in a motorcycle accident. That freaked Mom out.

One day when I was working in downtown Minneapolis, Amanda, the daughter of Dory, one of the staff I supervised who worked in another county office, came up from her job a floor below and said the three of us had to buy scooters because we could park them in the bike racks for free as long as they were below 50ccs. Anything above 49cc were considered motorcycles. So one weekend, the three of us went out to Scooterville located in Dinkytown, the area by the University of Minnesota campus. I didn't really think I would buy one, but upon taking the scooter for a test ride, my mind was quickly changed. The three of us spent the rest of the summer riding our scooters to work.

By removing the restrictors, we increased the maximum speed from 30 mph to 45 mph. Snelling Avenue, one of the major streets near my house, had a speed limit of 45 mph. But riding my scooter on Snelling felt unsafe since cars were zipping by me doing 55 to 60 mph. So I upgraded to a 125cc scooter. This required me to get a motorcycle license and violated my promise to my mom.

The day I drove my scooter out to the obstacle course to get my license, I was joined by others who rode their Harleys out. I justified my applying for a motorcycle license by continuing to call my bike a scooter. I zipped through the obstacle course, knowing I'd fail if my feet hit the ground maneuvering my way through orange traffic cones. Most of those on the much larger Harleys failed their attempts. And during the following years, whenever I'd ride by a motorcyclist riding on a Harley giving me a mocking thumbs up for me, a little Asian guy on a scooter, I remembered how I was at least smart enough to figure out the test beforehand.

For a dozen years, I rode the scooter from my home in St. Paul to my office in Minnetonka, 23 miles away. The route was all on city streets, but I had to be constantly alert, as several times a week, a driver would not see me and swerved their vehicle into my lane. When the Minnetonka police chief found out the new city clerk was riding his scooter from St. Paul, he joked that the city would be getting a new city clerk soon, a reference to the danger of motorcycle riding. I found a true ally, a cynical soul whose job was all about living on the edges of danger while acknowledging life's best moments might be about walking the razor edge between taking a risk to add to the meaning of life and taking a risk that would cut life short.

My route took me past a building on Lake Street that housed both an optical shop and a psychological clinic. One-stop shopping for those like me, with vision problems both long- and short-term, and near- and farsighted. The route was pretty much the same as the part of Minneapolis that was burned down during the riots following George Floyd's murder.

The first get out-of-the-house ride the summer of 2020, I wasn't sure where to go, so I decided to see what my childhood home, a five-mile scooter ride away, looked like. I had driven past it a couple of times since we sold it years back and noted slight changes like a new fence around the backyard, but mostly, it looked the same. The streets around that house became my go-to scooter ride. After a while, it dawned on me why. Those were the streets I used to ride my bicycle around when I was a kid. My scooter transported me back to the days when everything was in front of me, where, although at the time, nothing seemed easy, everything was rather simple.

In the fall of 2022, my scooter that had just shy of 30,000 miles on it was stolen. I was sadder than anything about losing my scooter.

It wasn't worth much monetarily, but it held loads of nostalgic value for all the roads we traveled together. My therapist told me it was OK to be angry at whoever stole it. Indeed, she encouraged me to be angry because anger is a higher level of emotion than depression. But I couldn't. It was a faceless person who stole my scooter. This was my fourth scooter, and our life together started off somewhat comically.

My previous scooter also had just shy of 30,000 miles on it. When one of its battery wires got severed, I brought it into Scooterville, where I bought all my scooters and had all my scooters serviced. Bob, the owner, said he'd never seen as many miles on this particular brand of scooter and said it was probably time to get a new one. Turns out they had just got another scooter, same year, make, and model, with "only" 15,000 miles on it. I decided to buy it, although I had driven my car to Scooterville, so I had to figure out how to get the scooter and my car home. I drove the scooter to the light rail stop nearest my house, about five miles away. I hopped on the light rail back to the stop near Scooterville. I drove my car back to the light rail stop where my scooter was parked. From there, I drove my scooter about a mile toward my house. I walked back to my car and drove it a mile from where I parked my scooter. I walked back to my scooter and drove it a mile past where I parked my car and continued this process until I was home with my scooter and my car. During this process, I passed a teenage kid walking in the opposite direction. He probably thought I was messing with him as I passed going the opposite direction multiple times.

During 2022, I also lost a living object of my affection. There was a tall ash tree in my front yard, too close to my house, at most maybe 20 feet away. The tree was likely planted when the house was built in 1950, so it grew to tower over almost every other tree in the neighborhood. It weathered many a storm, many a harsh Minnesota winter, to remain standing tall, true, and firm. During every bad thunderstorm or windy night, I worried about the tree falling on my house or my neighbor's house. When the emerald ash borer was confirmed in our city, I began having the tree treated with chemicals to ward off the insidious bug. Many ash trees came down throughout the city, including the one that stood on the boulevard in front of my house, not that far away from its sibling in my front yard.

The tree stood right outside the picture window in my living room, and it was an entertainment magnet for all the cats past and present to watch squirrels run up the trunk and hear birds chirp from the branches. Branches began falling from the tree with more frequency. By 2020, the foliage was noticeably thin and less hearty than before, an elderly aged man with a receding hairline. Worst-case scenario was a windstorm would knock the tree over, and I was more afraid of it landing on my neighbor's house than my own. I've learned to suffer on my own; I don't need to cause pain to others. So I decided it was time to take it down.

The 70-year-old tree had seen lots during its life. The neighborhood grew; families came and went. Society changed, but the tree remained until the day a crew with a truck with a rising bucket, extended up by a mechanical metal arm, and a man armed with a chainsaw took it down in a matter of hours.

The removal process was quite remarkable actually. Modern-day Paul Bunyans. The kitchen-sink-sized stump was all that remained. The cats hid under the bed, only to come out to find their view of the world was different, forever changed. The things we rely on and falsely believe will always be there all have an expiration date.

My worrying about the tree falling during a bad storm was gone. However, it was replaced by the worry that since the tree towered above my house, close lightning strikes would no longer hit the tree but my house instead. One night during a bad thunderstorm, I accidentally sat on my glasses, breaking off one of the bows. My previous glasses were too scratched-up to wear, and I lost the pair before that. So I was forced to wear glasses that were 20 years old and three prescriptions ago. Part of me hoped they would help me see things the same way I did 20 years prior when my outlook was more positive, a hopeful future still seemingly within my grasp.

VIRTUAL REALITY

In 2007, I read the news that Apple was going to release a $600 mobile phone, an outrageous price in the era of pagers, flip phones, and Blackberry devices. The obvious *Star Trek* comparison was having a communicator, but having the internet in your pocket, available wherever you were, it dawned on me the better comparison was the tricorder, the device the Enterprise crew used to get information about the latest planet, the latest society they were interacting with.

The evening the first iPhone came out, I drove to the closest Apple Store to take a look. There were lines and lines of people waiting to get their hands on the demonstration devices. I noted there was no one back at the store's registers actually buying the device. I knew if I got my hands on the iPhone, I'd buy it, already having committed to paying the price. So I walked back to the back of the store and asked to buy one sight unseen. The staff neatly placed a pristinely shaped rectangular box in a simple white Apple Store bag with gray handles. I couldn't wait to get home and check out my life-changing purchase.

It felt neatly comfortable in my hand as I booted up the device. As advertised, this was a life-changing technological step forward. Not only having the internet in my pocket, but also having a camera with me at all times. And this was before the explosion of social media applications that would propel the iPhone to the top of the list of world-changing inventions: Alexander Graham Bell's telephone;

Thomas Edison's light bulbs and radios; movies and television taking us into the Information Age.

Despite its promise, the iPhone turned out to be the beginning of the end. It's depressing enough to see two people out for dinner not talking with each other, but occupied by things on their phones; or parents walking with their kids, focused on text messages; people walking their dogs, not paying attention to the experience, but rather all attention focused on their phones. It's equally bad watching almost everyone riding on a light rail car ignoring the world outside the car instead of focusing on life existing somewhere else. Sure, the light rail route is unchanging, but it's taking us through the actual world, not a virtual one. People are doing things on their phones at concerts and sporting events. People need to take pictures to post on social media, rather than live in the moment and form true memories. I know more and more people that would be lost if their mobile devices were taken away from them. Silent contemplation is becoming a lost skill.

There's virtual reality applications and games that take people into another space to avoid the actual reality. I don't know for sure, but there must be virtual kites that fly high and far with no worrying about running out of string. Worse, there are social media applications on our phones that enhance communication and allow us to share our lives with others in order to get likes and shares and validation that our lives mean something more than our friends and connections. TikTok? No thanks, I'll stick with Tic Tacs, the tasty, breath-freshening treats.

When I first joined Facebook, the concept appealed to me. It was fun to see posts and pictures from friends. It also meant we didn't actually have to get together to catch up. Fine with me as well. And it was strangely intriguing to be 'friends' with the girl I was too shy to speak to when we were in fifth grade.

Virtual reality is a long way from the real thing. And the algorithms that place items in our feeds reinforce what we already believe in; we aren't challenged to look for different points of view or in any way encouraged to do so. They say we aren't too far away from artificial intelligence advancing to the point where computers will gain consciousness. I pray I'm unconscious when that happens.

Technology allows people to stop living in the moment, to stay constantly distracted. This countered what both my therapist and hypnotherapist independently suggested since 2020. They suggested I needed to focus on living in the moment; the past was gone, and the future was whatever happened next. All I could truly control was the very moment I was in. I found the most effective way to do this was to pay attention to whatever cat was on my lap or my chest, coordinate our breathing together, and enjoy the company that was with me in the moment.

The pandemic only accelerated our dependence on an alternate reality. During the lockdown, most personal connections were made over various social media platforms. My world had shrunk down to a device that fit inside my pocket. The internet, with its lack of regulation, allowed disinformation to spread like wildfire.

THE KUNG FLU

The 2020 presidential election gave birth to a new term, "election denialism." It's a frustratingly imprecise term. A better way to describe this insidious attack against our democratic foundation is "politically motivated reality denialism."

The idea that somehow the 2020 election was stolen and fraudulent had no basis in reality. It's a fantasy. The big lie. A lot of the root of the lie began with our reaction to COVID-19. That we didn't come together as a country to figure out a united way to deal with the pandemic was depressing. That our response quickly turned political was a sign of things to follow.

Wearing a mask in public settings to prevent the spread of a deadly airborne virus? Some saw it as a way for a worldwide government cabal to take away individual freedom. Social distancing? More liberal government overreach. The economic damage being done by the shutdown was a concern, but was it more of a concern than preventable deaths and overwhelmed emergency rooms and hospitals? How did we get to the point where a sizable number of Americans believed taking a malaria drug was a legitimate treatment for a new deadly virus and, even worse, that a horse dewormer was a better option than a scientifically proven, safe, and effective vaccine?

There was an opportunity to pull together with compassion and love to fight this once-in-a-lifetime global pandemic. To do so required strong leadership, starting at the top. Instead of trying to unite the country, the president seemingly decided COVID was a threat to his reelection and took the approach to politicize our response, dividing us at the time where the only meaningful way forward was to be united.

For whatever reason, there were elected officials, including the president, who decided the name of the virus that we all understood, COVID-19, wasn't sufficient. So the virus was the latest vehicle for a racial attack. "The Chinese or Wuhan Virus," "Kung Flu," these elected officials blamed China, and, because many people don't know the diversity of Asians is as diverse as any race, it led to increased hate crimes against Asian Americans. And all of it was avoidable, seemingly filling in a human need to blame things on somebody, best if it's someone different, someone foreign.

There were those who decried this attack against Asians, saying Americans were better than this, that "this isn't who we are." But it was clear that wasn't true. Race has never been something most of us can effectively discuss or even begin to figure out why it has always divided us and continues to do so on such an existential level.

Weeks after the pandemic shut down our country, there was disgusting video of a Minneapolis police officer murdering George Floyd by unnecessarily kneeling on his neck for an extended amount of time. "I can't breathe," Floyd exclaimed as his life drained out of him. COVID-19 suffocated its victims in a silently deadly way. A police officer's knee to the neck wasn't as silent. And riots erupted. I, like many Minnesotans, watched in horror as major parts of our cities burned down. And somehow it became a choice about supporting law enforcement versus decrying how black lives were being unnecessarily snuffed out in the name of peace and justice.

This is certainly who we are, whether we accept it or not. Diversity and inclusion efforts say we all have our own biases. Race is the deadly reminder. Those decrying teaching 'critical race theory' in K-12 classes were conveniently ignoring the fact that critical race theory was a law-school class level and not being taught in public schools. Those wishing to ban racism from being taught as part of our country's history pushed ignoring the factual, painful part of the backbone of things to be buried under a rug. We want to ignore our ugly parts in order to pass on our best parts to the next generation. But how can we collectively grow under this delusional way of learning to coexist with those who are different?

I've heard from several elected officials they don't view through the lens of different races; they view all people as individual people. That's a great idealistic view, but it ignores the struggles people of color have faced. It's nice to think that people see us as people, no matter our racial difference, but that ignores our actual individual stories. As a member of the Council of Asian Pacific Minnesotans, a state agency tasked with advising lawmakers and the governor, the most memorable experience was a listening session with members of our state's Karen community refugees who came from Myanmar. It broke my heart to hear people coming from countries torn apart by war and younger than me stating they had given up their own personal happiness knowing they'd likely never find their way in a foreign country, but they did so because their only wish was to give their children a chance at a better life.

In 2017 when a group of white supremacists marched in Charlottesville, Virginia carrying tiki torches and chanting, "Jews will not replace us," it led to the death of a protestor. The president declared there were 'good people on both sides.' Soon afterward, the mayor of Minnetonka showed me an email he received from a Korean American resident who lived in the city for over 20 years. This person said it was the first time he and his family felt unsafe.

It was like people were being given permission to say racist things that previously would have been kept hidden. The mayor wondered if in a strange way, this wasn't a step forward; no more hiding racism in the shadows, it was now out in the open in a growing way. The Council of Asian Pacific Minnesotans decided we needed to issue a statement to our community members condemning the events in

Charlottesville. We wanted our bipartisan legislative members to issue a joint statement but couldn't get the two Republican board members to agree to the language of the statement. So instead, we decided the statement would come from me, as the chair of the council.

My statement, issued as a press release from the Council, read as follows:

> Racism and anti-Semitism have no place in a pluralistic America. Our communities are a proud collection of the many communities that make the American one. For America to return to a time when people felt comfortable, even proud, to make vile and offensive comments in public, is disheartening, threatening, and unacceptable.
>
> I am heartened by the statements condemning the actions that led to the tragedy and the statements of support for the victims, across the political spectrum and most recently, corporate, military, labor, and academic communities. I join in this chorus.
>
> As chair of the Council, I speak from a unique perspective. The Council is a nonpartisan state agency charged with the responsibility of working within government for the implementation of economic, social, legal, and political equality for Minnesotans descended from Asia and the Pacific Islands. When the rhetoric of white supremacy is advocated so brazenly, we must take a stand.
>
> At the Council, we believe in an America of opportunity. We believe in a pluralistic, peaceful, moral, and welcoming America. We believe in an America where all people have the opportunity to make a better life for themselves and their families. We also believe that all of us have a responsibility to America and to each other...

I was a little uncomfortable stepping out of my career-long nonpartisan work, speaking out where there was unfortunately political divide. I talked to the Minnetonka city council about this, and if any of the council members thought I was being too political, I would pull the statement. On the contrary, the council members supported me speaking out. "It's never wrong to do the right thing," one of the council members said.

The major lessons I learned during my time on the council was that the best tool in the toolbox for fighting against racism was to authentically tell our life stories. If people view us as individuals with relatable life stories rather than a monolithic, race-based, foreign-looking group, then there was a chance for being accepted. That's the backbone behind why I've written this memoir.

Our election system allows a losing candidate avenues to contest an election through the courts. But in order to successfully do so, one has to produce actual factual evidence that the results of the election were wrongly decided. None of that was done following the 2020 election. Instead, over 60 lawsuits disputing the election were lost. When presenting a dispute in court, there has to be factual evidence.

As Rudy Giuliani told the Congressional January 6th Committee, the Trump campaign had theories, not evidence. There was no credible evidence to legally dispute the legitimacy of the 2020 election. Similar to the completely unnecessary political response to our pandemic response, those falling down the rabbit holes didn't want to believe "us" election experts who knew the processes worked and the results were true and confirmable.

Instead of listening to those of us who knew the safeguards in place for verifying accurate election results, significant numbers of Americans decided instead to listen to wild conspiracy theories about voting systems being hacked by foreign countries like Venezuela through Italian satellites and China. It all was completely and provably false. Mules stuffing ballot dropboxes ignored the fact of how mail ballots are verified before being accepted. The allegations of fraud transformed from unproved voter fraud to election administrator fraud. Trump lost because election administrators and poll workers, who are our neighbors and friends doing their best contributing to their communities, were all in on the fix to deny a highly divisive politician another term in office. It was complete and utter nonsense.

The real story of the 2020 election was the heroic efforts of election workers throughout our country in running a safe and secure election during a global pandemic. It's disgusting that the story was co-opted into Martians interfering with our elections in order to elect the wrong president. That so many Americans fell down that rabbit hole seriously calls into question how long our democracy can survive. We have become adept at becoming not mules, but ostriches, burying our heads in the sand because reality has flown off the rails.

During a December 2020 hearing of the Minnesota State Senate Election's Committee hearing, Ginny Gelms, the Hennepin County Elections Manager, our state's largest county, stated the county's absentee ballot board, those who accept or reject absentee ballots, were temporary employees trained to be nonpartisan. A Republican member of the committee skeptically asked Ms. Gelms how someone could be trained to be nonpartisan. I don't remember Ginny's exact response, but it was politely appropriate. If I'd been asked the same thing, I would have been a bit more pointed.

"Easy, Senator… we train our employees to follow the law. And our election laws are written to be nonpartisan." The basis of the question was election officials were biased, unable to distinguish between our own political beliefs and the ability to do our jobs in a fair and impartial manner. Again, total nonsense. I haven't known anyone in this profession willing to break laws in order to favor a particular candidate. I fear this may not be true going forward, given the focus on the importance of who's responsible for running our elections.

It drove me crazy when helping a voter vote absentee, when someone would ask, "This only gets counted if the election is close?" No, actually, all legally cast votes are counted. And how would we know if an election was close unless we counted all legally cast ballots? And how would an election administrator know which of the 35-40 races on a ballot were close enough to continue counting votes? President? Governor? County Commissioner? School board member? District Court Judge?

There are multiple processes and procedures in place to verify and certify election results. Those pushing crazy conspiracy theories about the 2020 election did so, at best without taking the time to learn about all the protections, but at worst were told of the protections but decided to destroy faith in free and fair elections to further a narrative that a candidate who clearly lost an election did so without any legal evidence proving otherwise. I wonder what the end goal is? Undermining confidence in our elections puts our country in perilous danger. Those of us working in elections do so to the best of our ability and integrity. Those that question the 2020 election seem to be willing to throw a communal belief in democracy under a steamroller in order to install candidates of similar political beliefs.

Former U.S. Attorney General Bill Barr, who served under President Donald Trump, called the allegations that the 2020 election was stolen or full of fraud "nonsense" and "bullshit." Once the nation's top law enforcement official, his department had investigated allegations of fraud and found nothing that would have changed the outcome of the presidential election. And as the nation's top law enforcement official, he knew there needed to be factual evidence provable in a court of law, not wild conspiracy theories, to contest an election.

And yet Barr's assessment was totally discounted by Trump and his avid followers. They believed Barr when he said the Mueller Report exonerated Trump and his 'collusion' with Russia (FYI, it didn't), but his assessment of the 2020 election was a betrayal and to be discounted. These people instead chose to believe a pillow salesman whose presentations of election fraud were spreadsheets and graphics that allegedly showed proof of hacks of election equipment but rather showed cartoons, something that could be cooked up by what Trump once said about Russian collusion—a fat guy in his basement in New Jersey.

And that is a difficult distinction to make by groups in Minnesota pushing out false information to elected boards and in public presentations to people questioning the validity of the 2020 Presidential Election. The false information almost always is based on a kernel of factual basis, but the factual basis is being used in an out-of-context, perhaps deliberately mistaken manner. The data is accurate at a moment in time, but it is being used in a way that distorts what it is meant for. Alternative facts.

A specific example of this in Minnesota was an individual who attended multiple county board meetings across the state showing that the voter history data he got from our office didn't match the number of votes certified in the 2020 election. After every election, the counties give history to voter records within the statewide voter registration database. One might assume that adding up the number of voters who voted in the election based on the voter history data would match the total number of voters reported statewide when we certified the election results. But one needs to understand the purpose of capturing voter history data and why it is not used to certify election results.

Voter history is captured for two purposes. The first is related to voter list maintenance. If a voter doesn't vote once every four years, their voter registration is inactivated. Posting voter history helps keep the voter data in the voter registration system up to date. The second purpose is candidates and others like to have data about who actually votes in particular elections. If I'm a city council candidate and I see you don't vote in city council races, I may choose to not try to get your vote, or I might do the opposite and target voters who don't vote in city elections as a campaign strategy.

Counties are required to get the posting of voter history done six weeks after the election but can get that deadline extended. Counties certify their results before the voter history deadline. Voter history data was never meant to be part of the certification process; it's not the purpose of the data. Any registered voter in the state can purchase a public information list that contains the voter history data.

The person going before county boards purchased a list at the end of November 2020, before many counties were finished getting the voter history data posted. For that very reason, it did not match the certified voter totals. And the voter history data in the public information list is only as good as the day it's produced. It's not static data. Voter records get updated on a daily basis. If I voted in St. Paul but moved to Minneapolis, my voter record would show I voted in the 2020 election but it would not be clear what jurisdiction I cast my vote in. Voters who died after the election might have voter history, but would not be part of the public information list. Voters who had their absentee ballot rejected because it was received too late to count still get voter history because it keeps their voter registration active another four years. Again, it's data that was weaponized to make it appear something was askew with the 2020 election.

One of the many threatening emails I received following the 2020 election was from someone who said that since our largest county, Hennepin, was a sanctuary county (untrue), all the votes in the county should be thrown out since it was clear noncitizens voted for Joe Biden. It was indicative of someone not understanding our legal system.

To suggest hundreds of thousands votes should not be counted requires legal proof of illegal votes. To assume that any alleged illegal votes obviously voted for one candidate over another also requires documented proof. This should be common sense. Should be. I had no response for this person. Technology allows people to anonymously vent without being obligated to put a face behind the nonsense (I hate when I allow myself to read the reader comments to news articles... mostly pure toxic filth).

Elections are precise. Certifying results is done at the minute level, from the election judges at the polling place, through levels of canvassing boards (school districts, townships, cities, counties, state) who are making sure the number of people who voted matches the ballots counted and the official result summary statements verifiably matches what was reported on election night.

In November 2020, following the election, someone else sent me a YouTube video showing what was allegedly the *New York Times* website on election night and into the next morning changing write-in votes in Minnesota for president over time, to Biden mostly but Trump much less. This was proof that the results were fraudulent, and whoever was changing the results were giving Trump votes in an effort to hide the hack. Algorithms changing results on servers located in foreign countries.

Again, I couldn't respond because, as Barr later said, it was nonsense. Taking the allegation on its face value, our office can't possibly control what a second-party website was reporting. More importantly, the results that show up on our website are clearly stated as unofficial. There's a whole process the counties go through the days and weeks after the election to certify the official results. This includes looking at the official results certified by the election judges on election night.

My office has an online tool available in many states that allows a person to check to see if they are an active registered voter. The intent is to inform the person what, if anything, needs to be done to vote in the next election. We got an email from a person claiming the online tool is meant to mine personal data so we can create illegitimate voter registrations used to cast illegal votes.

This is the crap election administrators are facing all across the country. No, our tool isn't being used to do that. And the easiest pushback is our voter registration system already has inactive records from voters who have moved or who haven't voted for four years or who have died. Why would we need to mine data from people visiting our website to create phony voter registrations? I'm not sure where this particular accuser came up with this scenario. Are those believing this disinformation so far gone that they will never believe in our elections? Sadly, yes.

The conspiracy theories caused threats against election officials, so much so that the Departments of Justice and Homeland Security created a task force to report the threats that crossed the line into something criminal. Although the emails I received in November and December of 2020 were angrier than any I ever got before, and it wasn't fun to be called a traitor or accused of committing treason, nothing crossed the line into something that made me feel unsafe. The same was not true for other election officials across the country who received death threats and had people showing up at their homes.

Ever since there's been elections, there's been allegations of voter fraud, some true, others sketchy, others based on urban legends. Think of dead people voting in Chicago. Think of Jim Crow laws that offered seemingly legitimate safeguards like literacy tests and poll taxes. Legitimate, in that the laws accomplished the goal of keeping African Americans from voting.

CONSPIRACY THEORIES

To live in the world in 2023 and beyond seemingly requires us to look for the truth while ignoring that may differ from actual reality. We live in social media bubbles. There are algorithms that track what we click on to match up posts that are similar.

I grew up a David Letterman fan. Dave was the master of sarcasm, so my humor was always about that. But it was a crutch. It hid who I really was, what I was really thinking and feeling from others. It built a wall, both deliberate and destructive, trying to use my humor as a bridge, even as it was at the same time a necessary wall.

Most who read horoscopes on a daily basis realize they aren't based on true science. Instead, they rely on a pseudoscience, predicting the future based on how the stars and planets align. Yet, when I read my own horoscope, I do so wanting to believe this pseudoscience will lead me to better times. It's quite simple to delude yourself into a better future.

Here is a list of theories I've come up with to explain the world we've lived in since the apocalypse:

Turtles have telepathic abilities to subliminally brainwash us. John Wilkes Booth was made to believe President Lincoln was anti-turtle because of his affection for turtle soup.

Cats are alien creatures from Venus sent here to spy on humans. They communicate back home through purring. Their tails are actually antennas.

The 1919 Black Sox scandal never happened. It was all fake news perpetuated by the National Football League to discredit baseball as our national pastime.

Elvis Presley was a Ukrainian spy. He communicated top-secret messages to the Ukrainian government through his hip gyrations.

Football is a communist plot meant to get Americans to wear brain-altering makeup on their faces and shout demeaning phrases like 'Dee-fence.'

Concrete doesn't exist. It was fabricated by a corrupt industry hoping to sell the fake notion that sidewalks and driveways are actual things.

President John Quincy Adams was our first Asian American president. He was Filipino, but the press covered this up because it was thought the American public would not accept him as a true American.

Velcro causes infertility and is the reason our birth rates have declined every year since 1973.

Glasses don't actually correct our vision. Blurred vision is our preferred state of being.

There is no such thing as a human spleen. Doctors invented it in order to perform profitable surgery.

The grapefruit-juice industry has falsely pushed a narrative that their product is healthier than whiskey for the human body. Whiskey kills other toxins, while grapefruit juice shrinks the human head.

For most of its existence (barring year one), *Wheel of Fortune* has been a sham created by the Canadian Secret Service. The players were all actors. Pat Sajak and Vanna White were holograms. It was all a plot to prevent Americans from having actual discussions during the dinner hour. The word puzzles contained subliminal messages meant to undermine Americans' confidence in capitalism.

Typewriters were built to illegally contain the letter 'B' that was banned by the American government in 1936 because it caused insanity.

Fish meat doesn't exist. What we've been fed is a lie from the American Chemical Consortium, a molecular combination of fluoride and false dreams.

Marilyn Monroe is still alive; her death was staged by the FBI. She currently is living a life as a 29-year-old woman in Golden Valley, Minnesota.

Paper towels are full of acid. Both the burning kind and the mind-altering kind. Anyone who has ever touched a paper towel will eventually have their mind altered in unknown ways.

Economic inflation and the price of corn is decided in a CPA firm in West Virginia. They run computers that supersede the stock market and crop market calculations. There's a Swedish college professor who alters America's economy based on a dice game between him and his former lover, Anita Ekberg.

White racism was originally created by pygmies working in a marshmallow factory in Kingman, Arizona. They realized early on that the fight against communism was based on the belief that Christopher Columbus was a pirate, a political piranha controlled by the Men from Uncle, a proprietary organization dedicated to the message of global discord and new musical notes sung by Julie London.

Cotton Q-tips are infected with a manmade organism that worms its way into an orifice and causes its users to believe the post office delivers actual physical mail rather than their true mission: creating kindergartners to believe paste is an edible delicacy that must be tried and consumed.

Chef Gordon Ramsey is an Antifa agent, and his cooking shows and berating of chefs are all an act to hide his secret love of postal stamps. Postal stamps control a global economy, with their pointed opponent being sea turtles, who communicated with Japanese submarines to build a high-profiting high-rise in Denmark that would generate profits for grocery-store owners long beyond the end of the world and members of our elected-official township communities.

Zachary Taylor was the winner of the 2020 presidential election. His 90 million votes were found in a wood hut on the shores of Costa Rica. This story was buried because the Fox News producer was a second cousin to the wife of Dr. Fauci.

COVID-19 isn't a virus. It's an outer-space bacteria that morphed into our ecosystem coming from the exterior of UFOs. The government has hidden this because it continues to deny the clear existence of visitors from outer space.

AUTHENTICITY

For me, January 6, 2021 was just as horrible as September 11, 2001. Not as many people died, but the perpetrator was the enemy within, people from our own communities, not a foreign foe bent on destroying our country. It's like the classic horror-movie cliché of the killer being in the house and not an existential outside foe who isn't a next-door neighbor.

Maria and I had a discussion as the riots were burning down our city following George Floyd's murder and her decision to buy an assault rifle to protect herself and her daughter. She didn't seem to be afraid at all about COVID, but seeing mobs of violent people in our cities scared her. I asked if that was because she could see the deadly threat versus COVID being an invisible killer. She agreed that might be a valid assessment.

I get that if you believe an election was stolen, and your beloved candidate wrongly deprived of the office they sought, you will do anything you can to protest. But assaulting police officers, hitting them with metal poles and weapons? Replacing American flags with Trump flags? Storming the Capitol to prevent the peaceful transfer of power? At county board meetings I've attended in 2022, I've heard these people described as 'political prisoners.' No, they are disillusioned and misguided, willing to put their hopeful political beliefs ahead of the good of our country. Violence is never the answer in a democracy.

If one questions the integrity of an election, the remedy is to prove it in our courts. You don't bash your way into a Congressional proceeding, injuring cops and endangering elected officials and staff with bear spray and flag poles. This was treasonous cowardly behavior by those who didn't know any better and were spurred on by ridiculous allegations, not even being allowed in a court of law. Fraudulent mail ballots? Dropbox mules delivering illegal votes? Voting equipment hacked from foreign adversaries flipping Presidential votes? Nope, none of that happened. NONE. There are processes in place to safeguard our elections.

The candidate in my lifetime I was most passionate about was John Anderson, who was a Republican, fiscally conservative, socially liberal, a white-haired wonk who ran against Ronald Reagan in 1980. I was too young to vote, but I did my best to voice my support. Anderson inspired me by being a maverick, sticking to his own political beliefs even if it meant challenging his own party's orthodoxy. That seemed courageous to me.

But as passionately and as much as I admired John Anderson, and wanted him to be president, I never would have considered becoming a part of an insurrection against our country. There isn't a soul on this earth that I'd fight so hard for. What is it about Donald Trump's believers that make them think the January 6th insurrection was somehow patriotic? I really don't get how people can let go of all reality in the belief some politician is worth dying for. Trump's appeal seems to be he's not a traditional politician; he's a populist who tapped into a real anger against the government establishment. His message seemed authentic, but it was phony, never about elevating his supporters, always about his thirst for power.

Fans of professional wrestling hopefully understand it isn't a 'real' sport. The end result is predetermined. The action scripted and staged. Yet professional wrestling fans are devoted and passionate about the 'sport' they love. One of the reasons sports appeal to us is that on any given day, any given game or match, a team or competitor can prevail against the odds. Anything can happen on the fields of play. The same applies to why we actually have elections. Past results and polls predict who probably will win, but it's the actual will of the voters on a particular day that matters.

Jesse Ventura was running behind in the polls when he won the election to become the Governor of Minnesota. While visiting polling places that election, I sensed Ventura would pull off the improbable and win the election. He was turning out voters who hadn't voted for a while. In 2016, I sensed Donald Trump would do the same thing in his run to be president. He was appealing to those who long ago gave up on government doing the right things to make their lives better. Populism is a powerful aphrodisiac.

The difference between Ventura and Trump, however, is stark and important. Ventura hired an impressive team of commissioners to run the state departments, pulling on people associated with both major political parties. He knew he didn't know what he needed to be an effective governor and relied on diverse political opinions. Trump never did the same. He never understood that to stay in power meant to actually make government work and to expand his base. Instead, he appointed far-right appointees to run the government and pushed division far above actually getting things done in a political divide. And ultimately, that's what cost him his reelection. If you are only polling favorably between 35-40 percent of the electorate, you're going to have a difficult time getting elected. Running firmly behind being divisive, your followers may follow you to the edge of hell, but you are also inspiring those who hate you to turn out to vote and those in the middle just wanting someone different.

I took the January 6th insurrection personally. These were terrorists attacking the very work I've spent most of my career dedicated to, not only working to do my best, but also trying to improve to make more secure, fair, and accessible. That they were so easily spurred to violence offended me as much as it depressed me.

I watched the Congressional January 6th Select Committee's hearings, wondering if they could make a difference in the political divide. Of course not. I was too young to comprehend what Watergate was, but I remember trying to learn as a 10-year-old what was forcing the president of the United States to resign in disgrace and what that would mean for our country. In the mid-1980s, I watched as much of the Iran-Contra hearings as I could, mesmerized by the exchanges between Oliver North and the attorney leading the proceedings, Arthur Liman. Liman's droll but steady questioning intrigued me to no end. I also watched the Clinton impeachment proceedings and the 9/11 commission hearings.

I've spent my career not being political, but being aware that politics drives our country out of necessity, but also in a divisive way. Much of the division is driven by what we believe about our government. And having spent most of my career in government, I see its weaknesses and strengths. The weakness is to believe government exists to solve all our problems. The strength is most of the people I've worked with were there trying to do the right thing, for the right reason, at the right time.

COVID KILLED
MORE THAN PEOPLE

Starting in junior high, Mom allowed us to watch the evening news during dinner. Previously, the television had to be shut off as we sat around the dining room table, a rare time for a family discussion. Our preferred choice was the *CBS Evening News* with Walter Cronkite. Cronkite would end his newscasts with the definitive statement, "And that's the way it was…" Uncle Walter, the baritone barometer, not only assured and comforted our nation that the news of the day was accurately reflected, but also, his newscast was meant to chronicle stories over time, so we all could better understand the world around us.

For my college journalism degree, I was required to get an internship at a media outlet. My internship was at the *Roseville Sun*, the weekly local newspaper of my hometown. I practiced writing news stories in the classroom, but covering my first city council meeting was a whole other ball of yarn. The meeting had a published agenda, but as the meeting concluded, I wasn't sure what I was to write about. Was it the agenda item the council spent the most time discussing? Was it the agenda item that got the most resident testimony? Was it the agenda item that interested me most?

It was then I saw how powerful a role the media played in our lives. The media ultimately determines what is news, what is worthy of reporting on, and what rises to the level of follow-up stories. I felt unequivocally unprepared and unqualified to make those decisions as a college junior working on an academic degree.

In 2017, Kellyanne Conway, an advisor to President Trump, coined the term 'alternative facts' when trying to explain why there were more people attending Trump's inauguration than the photographic evidence showed. The concept of the term only gained more currency during the entirety of Trump's presidency.

We all want to believe what we already believe; it gives us comfort and a way forward in the confusing world we live in. But if we can't agree to a set of facts, often scientifically arrived at, but sometimes as simple as what our eyes see, then our realities are impossibly splintered, and there's no communal way forward. When we begin to see our neighbors, those that have different political views, as the 'enemy,' then our country is staring at the edge of the abyss.

When a president calls the mainstream media "fake news" and the enemy of the people and gets his supporters to agree, then there will never be agreed-upon 'facts' that lead to productive political debates. This is made worse as people look for alternate social media sites that only confirm what they want to believe. Critical thinking becomes an illusion, with all of us believing we are being critical of the information we sought out but wanting to believe in it far too much because it reinforces our life views.

The mainstream media has always had its flaws and biases. But professional journalists are required to do fact-checking before publishing or broadcasting stories. You can argue a story is biased, but 99.999 percent of the time, it isn't fake from credible mainstream news organizations. Journalists found making up news are discredited, demoted (such as former NBC news anchor Brian Williams), and fired. There's bad journalism, but for a mainstream media outlet to continue to exist, there are standards to be met. Otherwise, the organization loses its credibility.

Oddly, I too joined those who no longer listened to the mainstream media. The news was too depressing. It wasn't the only thing that changed in my life.

I joined the Secretary of State's softball team in 1990 and continued to play on the team during its many variations the next 29 years. Mom and Dad used to come watch our games, Dad continuing to do so when Mom died. I became known for my speed, one of the fastest players in the state government league.

When I was appointed the State Election Director, an *Associated Press* reporter who was on an opposing team tweeted that I had years of elections experience and was a really fast runner. I was among our team leaders in home runs many seasons because we played on fields without fences, so if I hit a ball that got between outfielders and rolled until one of them could track the ball down, it was too late as I circled the bases.

Over the years, two of my teammates told me they loved watching me run. Free as the wind. I was a pretty good fielder too, with quick reflexes, meaning I played third base and sometimes shortstop. Softball was an outlet, a combination of my love for its sister game, baseball, and a way to use my athleticism to relieve stress. There was no league the summer of 2020, and I haven't played in a game since.

I found it increasingly difficult to listen to music in the summer of 2020, especially new music that I didn't know how it would end up making me feel. I didn't want to feel. So I relied on music from the past, mostly Barry Manilow and Frank Sinatra. Familiar, comforting music that wouldn't catch me by surprise.

Surprises were bombs detonating all around me; I didn't need any more. When Diego-san died, I stopped playing my guitar. Without him by my side, making music left me feeling empty, and I craved silence instead. And I couldn't watch political shows anymore either. It all was too depressing to endure.

I used to hate it when friends would tell me they weren't interested in politics because it was all too confusing and depressing. I looked down on them, believing we all needed to stay informed. When helping voters, it was always nails on a chalkboard when someone said since they had voted, they did their civic duty. I always wanted to reply but never did, "No, you did part of your civic duty. It's important to hold those we elect accountable for what they promised to do."

As society reopened, I began going to Twins' baseball games and Timberwolves' basketball games again. I have been a season-ticket holder to both sports franchises for many years. I forced myself to start attending games again, a reason to leave my house as I continue to work from home. But my love for sports has waned. I don't care who wins anymore. The Twins and Timberwolves continue to disappoint season after season. They've just been a distraction to me since 2020.

I've only gone to three music concerts since society resumed. I used to go to that many in a week most years. All three required proof of vaccination, and the first required wearing a mask. I just haven't figured out how to return to the life I was living before the pandemic.

THIS IS WHO I AM

In the summer of 2022, I attended my 35th college reunion. I had zero interest in going, but one of my classmates, Kori Kanayama, texted me asking if I planned on going. The way Macalester College reunions work, all past classes get together at the event that lasts for several days.

Kori and I actually met via Facebook. We didn't know each other when we were at Macalester. We ran in different circles of friends and never had classes together. She became friends in California with my sister and her husband and made the connection the two of us attended Macalester together. We occasionally messaged each other on Facebook. Now living in Michigan, she was attending the reunion but was concerned she wouldn't know anyone there. So I agreed to attend our reunion. It's an example of how social media can lead to true connection.

Returning to the campus was remarkably different from our days with the dorms and the buildings that housed our classes updated and upgraded. My alumni annual contribution of $25 was clearly well spent. There were a dozen or so of my graduating class in attendance. It was striking that, when I shared what I did for a living, there were some who didn't understand, thinking my job was helping out on candidate's campaigns. Many don't realize that there are people who make sure when Election Day comes, polling places are smoothly run. That ballots are accurately printed. That there are laws in place to ensure the integrity and accessibility of our elections. The long-running joke all of us in this profession hear is it must be nice to work in a job that only requires a couple of days a year of work every other year. The truth couldn't be light years away. I've heard some compare elections to weddings; there are many days needed to prepare for the big day. Many pieces have to fall into place to ensure a successful day.

I had avoided reunions, both high school and college, because they seemed to be about showing classmates you lived a more successful life than they did. Better job, high-achieving kids, bigger house, bigger bank account. I had a good career and lived a life that the college me might have been amazed with (particularly my relationship with Maria and my continued love of writing), and I didn't care at all how my life compared with my classmates. I was quite sure we all had ups and downs, moments of glory and moments of despair. But I was happy Kori asked me to be there. I had been back on campus but rarely inside the buildings. Kori was staying in the dorm I lived in my freshman and junior years. The building was completely renovated. The building, the music department where I spent many work-study hours in, was torn down and rebuilt.

Visiting the new music department conjured up a memory of a morning when a mutual friend told me our friend, Randy Wade, was sober, 'off everything but the hard stuff.' 35 years later I was taking doses of the hallucinogen, ketamine. I was no better (or worse) than those taking a horse dewormer to prevent COVID-19 since ketamine was originally a horse tranquilizer.

My latest ketamine treatment came the day after my birthday in 2022, two days after the 2022 elections. I feared I was using the treatment as a crutch, rather than an actual solution for my depression. But my depression had sunk to a level where I didn't want to live anymore, but what did that mean? Life goes on even if you don't, can't, or won't.

For this latest treatment, my therapist suggested I bring with me a meaningful physical object that I could hold onto as I took my trip. There was only one object that made sense, my most meaningful possession, the lucky, heart-shaped rock Stephanie had combed the shore of an Australian beach during her last day in the country for, just for me, that I held on tightly to 34 years after she gave it to me, a rock that helped me overcome my depression through its shared meaning. I once lost the rock when it fell out of my pocket. My mom found it months later in between sofa cushions. I stopped carrying it with me afterward, extremely thankful for its return.

My fourth ketamine trip was similar to the previous three. I fell into the same cosmic space, where there was a purplish flow and the three-dimensional world dissolved into a non-dimensional reality. The music I heard was the same, sounding reminiscent to either the theme song from my favorite childhood TV show, *Mannix*, or the opening chords to one of my all-time favorite songs, Beck's "Lost Cause." This safe, comforting, and welcoming place that I returned to again must be a part of my imagination, my DNA, but it felt like a real place each and every time.

As I was fading out of that space back into non-psychedelic reality, I felt my lucky rock in the palm of my right hand. It was wondrous to feel the rock's existence and its journey. For the first time, I truly understood and appreciated its journey almost as much as my own. Years of formation, washed upon the shores of Australia, picked for its near-perfect, palm-sized comfort; who knows how long this rock lay in its founding place? Displaced but passed with affection from one to another, it found its way to St. Paul, Minnesota. Broken knees to broken hearts, yet somehow, this heart of stone, mended but never fully recovered. Rock-solid heart of mine.

My lucky rock's journey inspired my own. My now 58-year journey was a lesson in survival, of persistence, of endurance. I never wanted to be someone who let my career define my life, my major accomplishment. And it hasn't. It is one of the things I can look back upon and feel a sense of pride. In the end, what's real or true isn't as important as living an authentic self, being courageous enough to share our souls with anyone willing to care enough to reciprocate and share the same. I don't know how I've survived and continued on, but I did. I'm proud I lived long enough to share my journey, my story.

BIOGRAPHY

David Maeda has spent most of his career in government as an election administrator. He was appointed the State Director of Elections for the Minnesota Office of the Secretary of State in January 2019. David also served on the Council on Asian Pacific Minnesotans for eight years, four of those as the Board Chair. Music has been his lifelong love, working over 20 years in a record store, and through scientific analysis, he definitely determined the five greatest songs of all time are: 1) Bob Dylan's "Abandoned Love," 2) Liz Phair's "Little Digger," 3) Lucinda Williams's "Am I Too Blue," 4) Sammy Davis Jr.'s "I've Gotta Be Me," 5) Barry Manilow's "Ready to Take a Chance Again." Ludwig Van Beethoven's *Symphony No. 3* just barely failed to make the cut. David currently lives in St. Paul with his two playful feline friends, Norma and Alias.

CREDITS

- Cover and Dalai Lama photographs (p. 36): Andrew VonBank

- Electoral college photographs(p. X): Julia Laden

- Cat paintings (p. 98): Jacque Bartosh

- Liz Phair, *Horror Stories* quote (p. V) used with permission from Random House

www.ingramcontent.com/pod-product-compliance
Lightning Source LLC
Chambersburg PA
CBHW051507150726
47997CB00001B/147